GCSE COMPUTER STUDIES

GUIDES.

LONGMAN REVISE GUIDES

Series editors: Geoff Black and Stuart Wall

TITLES AVAILABLE:
Art and Design
Biology
British and European History
Business Studies
C. D. T. – Design and Realisation
Chemistry
Computer Studies
Economics
English
English Literature
French
Geography
German
Mathematics
Mathematics: Higher Level and Extension
Physics
Religious Studies
Science
Social and Economic History
World History

FORTHCOMING:
C. D. T. – Technology
Commerce
Home Economics
Human Biology
Integrated Humanities
Music
Office Studies and Information Technology

GCSE
COMPUTER STUDIES

LONGMAN
REVISE
GUIDES

Roger Crawford

Longman

Longman Group UK Limited,
Longman House, Burnt Mill, Harlow,
Essex CM20 2JE, England
and Associated Companies throughout the world.

First published 1989

British Library Cataloguing in Publication Data

Crawford, Roger
 GCSE computer studies. – (Longman GCSE revise guides)
 1. England. Secondary schools. Curriculum subjects: Computer sciences.
 GCSE examinations.
 Techniques
 I. Title
 004′.076

 ISBN 0–582–03854–5

Produced by The Pen and Ink Book Company,
Huntingdon, Cambridgeshire

Set in 10/12pt Century Old Style

Printed and bound in Great Britain by
William Clowes Limited, Beccles and London

EDITORS' PREFACE

Longman Revise Guides are written by experienced examiners and teachers, and aim to give you the best possible foundation of success in examinations and other modes of assessment. Examiners are well aware that the performance of many candidates falls well short of their true potential, and this series of books aims to remedy this, by encouraging thorough study and a full understanding of the concepts involved. The Revise Guides should be seen as course companions and study aids to be used throughout the year, not just for last minute revision.

Examiners are in no doubt that a structured approach in preparing for examinations and in presenting coursework can, together with hard work and diligent application, substantially improve performance.

The largely self-contained nature of each chapter gives the book a useful degree of flexibility. After starting with the opening general chapters on the background to the GCSE, and the syllabus coverage, all other chapters can be read selectively, in any order appropriate to the stage you have reached in your course.

We believe that this book, and the series as a whole, will help you establish a solid platform of basic knowledge and examination techniques on which to build.

Geoff Black and Stuart Wall

AUTHOR'S PREFACE

Throughout this book the emphasis is on understanding how computers are used. The chapters are arranged in a fairly logical sequence but the order in which they are studied is not critical as each chapter is quite self-contained. There is a glossary of computer jargon in Chapter 4 that should help explain unfamiliar technical words.

In writing this book I have valued help given to me both directly and indirectly. I especially thank Stuart Wall and Geoff Black for their editorial advice. I would also like to thank Malcolm Brigg, Henry Meyer, Jo Williams, Trevor Gower and Mike Tomkinson for their help and assistance while I was Head of Information Technology at Rhodesway School and Keith Biggs, Theresa Battye, Martin Walker and Eddie Schack at Queensbury School where I am now TVEI Coordinator and Head of Maths, Computing and I.T.

My wife, Jennie, and sons Peter, Michael and Daniel and my mother and father have patiently tolerated the long hours I have spent at the wordprocessor. Thanks also to my brother Neil and my old friend Pete Walton who encouraged me to publish. Without the support of colleagues, friends and family this book would not have been written.

Roger Crawford

CONTENTS

ACKNOWLEDGEMENTS

I gratefully acknowledge the permission granted by the following examining boards to print some of their GCSE questions:

London and East Anglian Group (LEAG)
Midland Examining Group (MEG)
Northern Examining Association (NEA)
Northern Ireland Schools Examinations Council (NISEC)
Southern Examining Group (SEG)
Welsh Joint Education Committee (WJEC)

Answers to examination questions are my own and I accept full responsibility for them.

I am grateful to IBM(UK) Ltd for permission to reproduce photographs and certain other material.

THE EXAMINATIONS AND ASSESSED COURSEWORK

AIMS

ASSESSMENT OBJECTIVES

THE SYLLABUS
 LEAG

 MEG

 NEA

 NISEC

 SEG

 WJEC

GRADE DESCRIPTIONS

GETTING STARTED

There are six examination groups in England, Wales and Northern Ireland for the General Certificate of Secondary Education (GCSE). These are the:

 London and East Anglian Group (LEAG);
 Midland Examining Group (MEG);
 Northern Examining Association (NEA);
 Northern Ireland Schools Examination Council (NISEC)
 Southern Examining Group (SEG); and
 Welsh Joint Education Committee (WJEC).

These exam groups all publish syllabuses in GCSE Computer Studies. A **syllabus** states exactly which topics should be studied. Each syllabus is different but as they are all based on the same *aims* and *assessment objectives* they are very similar. The common assessment objectives or *core content* are defined in the National Criteria for Computer Studies.

Assessment is the process of finding out what a student can do and awarding a grade in recognition of the level of performance attained. This is done using a combination of *written exams* and *coursework*. The grades awarded range from A to G. In some cases a grade is not awarded.

Each exam group has its own system of assessment. All include some written exams. The written exams may be based on a case study. A *case study* is an in-depth look at a particular application of computers.

Every assessment scheme includes coursework. This consists of one or more *projects*. Students are expected to design, set up and document their own computer based solution to a problem which may be of their own choosing.

Grade definitions are provided to give an idea of what must be achieved to be awarded a particular grade.

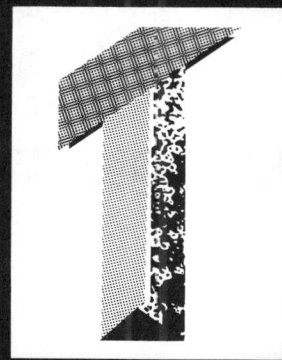

GCSE COMPUTER STUDIES

1 > AIMS

A course in Computer Studies leading to GCSE should be a worthwhile experience in itself. It should encourage you to develop your interest in computing and help you to become more confident and expert in using computers. It should put the use of computers in a broader context, so that you become aware of the many different ways in which computers are used to help people do their jobs. You should gain some knowledge of how computers work and be able to understand their capabilities and limitations.

The use of computers throughout society creates many ethical, social, economic and political problems for individuals, organisations and society as a whole. You should also be aware of how computers affect the people who use them as well as the people who have information about them stored on computers.

2 > ASSESSMENT OBJECTIVES

Assessment Objectives tell you what the examiners are looking for

There are five **assessment objectives**. These are as follows:

A   You should know and understand the techniques needed to solve problems related to practical applications.

B   You should use computers sensibly to solve a problem. This includes designing and setting up a simple system and documenting your solution.

C   You should have some knowledge and understanding of how the main hardware and software components of a computer system work and how programs and data are represented and stored.

D   You should be aware of the range and scope of possible computer applications.

E   You should have some knowledge and understanding of the social and economic effects of the use of computer based systems on individuals, organisations and society and be able to explain their potential advantages and disadvantages.

These five assessment objectives are common to *all* syllabuses and are the *core content* defined in the National Criteria for Computer Studies. Only those aspects of the aims and objectives which are *measurable* can be *assessed*. This will need to be taken into account when doing coursework and preparing for exams. Measurement of assessment objective B is based on *coursework*, whereas objectives A, C, D and E are assessed by *written exams*.

3 > THE SYLLABUS

Make sure you know what is in *your* syllabus

Each examination group has a **syllabus** in computer studies. While all the groups have the same assessment objectives, each board has a different syllabus. The syllabus shows in detail the topics that have to be studied. The different syllabuses will be similar, because they are all based on the same assessment objectives, but they will not be the same. Any actual assessment is always based on a *particular* syllabus. You can find out how to obtain a copy of *your* syllabus on page 9.

THE ASSESSMENT

The **assessment** is based on *written papers* and *coursework*. The emphasis of assessment is always on what you can do. You will be given marks for what you *can* do rather than having marks deducted for what you *cannot* do.

Most syllabuses require students to study a 'case study' which is referred to in the written exams. A 'case study' is an in-depth look at a particular application. Some boards devote a complete written paper to the 'case study'.

Coursework consists of one or more projects. A *project* involves the design, setting up and documentation of a computer based system to solve a practical problem. This may be done using a programming language or software packages.

LEAG

Students take either papers 1 & 2   (grades D–G)
                      or papers 3 & 4   (grades C–F)
                      or papers 3, 4 & 5 (grades A–F)
Papers 1, 2, 3 & 4 are worth 35% of the final mark.

Coursework is 30% of the final mark. A project must be completed using a programming language or software packages.

Papers 2 & 4 refer to the case study.

MEG

Students take one or two papers from 1, 2 and 3.
    Paper 1 (grades G–F)
    Paper 2 (grades E–C)
    Paper 3 (grades B–A)
The highest level of success determines the grade awarded. Papers 1, 2 and 3 contribute, in total, 50% of the final mark.

Paper 4 is taken by all students. It contributes 16.7% of the final mark. Paper 4 is on the case study.

Coursework is 33.3% of the final mark. It consists of between one and five projects.

NEA

Students take both papers 1 and 2. Each paper is worth 30% of the final mark. All grades are available on both papers.

Coursework is 40% of the final mark. It consists of one project.

The case study may be referred to in either paper.

NISEC

Students take either papers 1 & 2 (grades E–G)
                      or papers 2 & 3 (grades C–F)
                      or papers 3 & 4 (grades A–D)
For each combination of papers, the paper with the lower number is 35% of the total marks and the other paper is 40%. Coursework (up to 4 projects) makes up the remaining 25%.

SEG

Students take papers 1, 2 and 3. All grades are available.
Papers 1 and 3 are each 20% of the final mark.
Paper 2 is 30% of the final mark.

Coursework is 30% of the final mark. It consists of one project.

The case study is referred to in paper 3.

WJEC

Students take either papers 2 & 3 (grades A–E)
                      or papers 1 & 2 (grades C–G).
Papers 1 & 3 are worth 40% of the final mark.
Paper 2 is 30% of the final mark.

Coursework is 30% of the final mark. Two projects must be completed.

The case study may be referred to in paper 3.

4 ▷ GRADE DESCRIPTIONS

Grade descriptions give some idea of what you have to do to achieve a particular grade. What follows is a typical grade description for a grade C.

GRADE C

On the *coursework* you have attempted a worthwhile problem and have tackled it reasonably well. The testing includes all the important aspects of the system but it may not be fully working. You know the limitations of your system and are able to suggest improvements. You may not have chosen the most efficient way to solve the problem, but you can explain *what* you have done and *why* you have done it.

On the *written exam papers* you have a good grasp of terms and definitions. You can discuss the advantages and disadvantages of different hardware, software, etc. You can apply the general principles of information processing to particular examples and vice versa. You can design and describe computer based systems which are generally correct but may have some minor deficiencies. Your explanations are clear and you use a range of applications to illustrate your answers. Your answers are usually applicable to the questions but you are not always able to explain why.

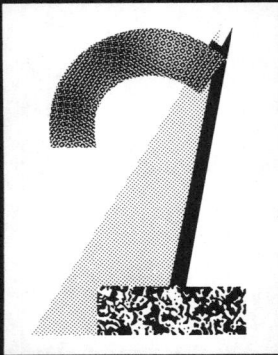

IMPROVING YOUR PERFORMANCE IN EXAMS AND COURSEWORK

KNOWLEDGE AND UNDERSTANDING

REVISION

PRACTICE

PLANNING

ALERTNESS

EXAM TECHNIQUES

USEFUL ADDRESSES

GETTING STARTED

Your eventual grade in GCSE Computer Studies is based on the assessed *coursework* and the written *examinations*. This could be an underestimate of your real ability. Your performance can be improved by better preparation, planning and presentation.

The coursework should be started as soon as possible. Work steadily and plan ahead to meet deadlines. Present your coursework in an attractive manner, illustrating it with pictures, flowcharts or diagrams.

Preparation for the examinations starts on the first day of the course. Do all the work you are asked to and improve your background knowledge by visits to computer exhibitions, etc. Before the exams, revise all your work, condense and learn it. Make sure you are alert on the day of the exams. Take with you all the equipment you will need. Arrive for the exam on time. During the exam, use your time effectively, write neatly and express yourself clearly. If you finish early, check your work. Never leave before the end of the exam.

Why is GCSE Computer Studies important to you? If you know you need a good grade at GCSE you will work harder and may do better. Many students study Computer Studies because they believe it will be a useful preparation for work. Some students particularly want to work with computers. If money is of interest to you, look at the adverts for jobs in computing. You will find they are well paid! Convince yourself it is important to succeed. Always do your best work. If you have a clear idea of why you are studying Computer Studies you may find it easier to put in the effort required to do well in the coursework and exams. If you are well motivated you are already on the road to success.

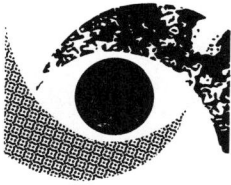

COURSEWORK

Coursework is an important part of GCSE assessment. It accounts for between 25% and 40% of the total marks available. Coursework usually takes the form of a project in some practical aspect of computing. You will be asked to use computers sensibly to solve a problem. This includes designing and setting up a simple system and documenting your solution. This may involve learning to use a programming language or, more often, a wordprocessor, a database, a spreadsheet or some other software package.

Coursework is an excellent opportunity to show what you *can do* if you have plenty of time. You will have to meet deadlines in handing in coursework, but you should still have enough time to work carefully and produce your best work. Don't leave things to the last minute. Start your coursework as soon as you know what is required of you. However, there is no need to do everything in the first week! Find out when the deadline is and plan ahead. It is possible that your teacher is planning lessons that will help you with your coursework. At some stage you will study systems analysis and design, data files and documentation. All these topics and others may be helpful to you. Don't rush your project. Don't leave it too late. Plan ahead and work steadily.

For your coursework assessment you will have to prepare one or more project reports describing the practical work you have done. The *evidence* that you have done what you describe in your project will be written work, drawings, printed material and possibly photographs. The assessment of your project will be based on the documentation you prepare and hand in. To improve your marks it is important to communicate clearly what you have done. Write neatly or use a wordprocessor. Express yourself clearly. Too much detail is much better than too little. Use diagrams, flowcharts, pictures, printed output, etc. to illustrate your work. A cheerful, topical front cover will make your project look more attractive. Show the examiner clearly what you have done and emphasise your achievements.

While you are doing your coursework you will have access to a wide range of resources. You can refer to any material you need to help you. You can ask other people for advice and discuss your progress with them. However, you must make sure that *you* do your project. You will be asked to sign a form by the examination board certifying that your coursework is all your own work.

If you find exams difficult and they make you nervous then coursework may be your best chance to demonstrate your skills. You must not neglect your coursework and expect to pass only on the results of the examinations. Every candidate who wishes to succeed must take coursework very seriously indeed.

> ❝ Coursework is an opportunity to show what you *can do* without the time pressure of the exam ❞

EXAMINATIONS

To do well in an exam you need to pay careful attention to preparing yourself for it. You will need knowledge of the subject. You will do better if you are alert and in good health. If you follow some simple techniques in the exam you may improve your marks.

1 ▷ KNOWLEDGE AND UNDERSTANDING

> ❝ Good, clear notes are an important part of developing understanding ❞

The purpose of exams is to test your *knowledge and understanding* of a subject. If you do not know your subject well then you cannot expect to do well in an exam.

A constant effort throughout the course is important. Try not to miss lessons. If you do, catch up with the work quickly. Keep all the notes you write and the work you do. Do all your homework to your best standard. Learn your work as you progress. If you have any spare time, go back over the course and revise the work. Make sure you understand *all* the work you do. Use the library to look up topics you are unsure of. Reading another book about the same topic can often make things clearer. Improve your notes in the light of any new insights. If you have problems, ask your teacher.

You can extend your background knowledge by a variety of other activities.

- Talk to a friend who is also doing Computer Studies and see if you can improve your knowledge of the subject by discussing topics which interest you.
- Read computer magazines.
- Go into local shops that sell computers and ask the sales staff about the computers they are selling.
- Go on trips to computer exhibitions.
- Get to know someone who works in computers and talk to them about their job.
- Try and arrange a visit to an office or factory where computers are used.
- If you have access to a microcomputer this can be helpful.

2 > REVISION

Summaries are helpful in revising

When you are preparing for the exams, this is the time to make sure you have learnt all that is required. A useful technique for learning a large volume of material is to repeatedly *revise, condense and learn*. Read through your notes and all the work you have done. As you revise your knowledge, make a *brief note* or *summary* of all the topics studied. These brief notes should cover all the important points in enough detail to refresh your memory of them at a later date. Try and learn these brief notes. If there is still too much material to learn, then condense these brief notes yet again. Your objective is to end up with condensed notes covering two or three A4 sheets which summarise the course. These can be learnt and revised frequently. You can carry them with you and revise on the bus, in the queue for the cinema, waiting for a friend or taking the dog for a walk!

3 > PRACTICE

There is no substitute for practice

Practise for the exam by doing questions from previous GCSE Computer Studies exam papers. Work through these carefully, making sure that you understand the answers to *all* the questions. It is possible that similar questions will appear on the written papers that you will take. Try to complete a paper under exam conditions in the time that was allowed for it. This will give you some idea of what you need to do to improve your performance.

4 > PLANNING

When you take your GCSE Computer Studies exam you will probably be taking other subjects which are also important to you. You will find that you are short of time. You will need to plan ahead and use your time effectively. Turn to the Revision Planner at the end of this book for help in the run-up to the examination.

5 > ALERTNESS

Try to be fresh for the exams

However much you know about Computer Studies, if you are not alert you will not do your best work. You will perform better if you are wide awake, healthy and relaxed. Make sure you get plenty of sleep in the days before the exam. You may think it is necessary to stay up late revising, but if you make yourself too tired you will not learn very much. If you need to do a lot of revision start it a long time before the exam. Go to bed reasonably early and you will be more alert and cope with the exam much better. This is particularly important the night before the exam. Don't go to a disco, party or any activity that might involve staying up late. You will regret it the following day when you are too tired to cope with the exam.

You are also likely to perform better if you are fit and healthy. A bad cold, hayfever, headaches, broken bones, sprained ankles and other illnesses can distract you from your work in the exam. The best remedy is to avoid situations that could make you ill. Perhaps the days before you exam are not the time to go horse riding, skiing, sky diving, etc. Avoid accidents. If you have unavoidable medical problems, your doctor may be able to help.

Lastly, make sure you go to the toilet just before the exam. You could waste five or ten minutes of valuable exam time if you have to go to the toilet during the exam!

Everyone else is nervous too!

Many people find that exams make them nervous. They get so nervous they make silly mistakes and are unable to do their best. Most people are affected by exam nerves to some extent. Being too nervous will probably have a bad effect on your work. On the other hand, some people are so relaxed they do sloppy, careless work. Being *too* relaxed is as inappropriate as being too nervous!

6 > EXAM TECHNIQUES

Exam techniques are not magic! Using them will not make up for ignorance or lack of thorough preparation. In an exam you try to communicate your knowledge to the examiner who will mark your work. Exam techniques are common sense methods to help you communicate what you know effectively.

- Before you arrive at the exam, make sure you have any *equipment* you will need in the exam. You will require a least a pencil, a pencil sharpener, a rubber, a ruler and at least two pens. A calculator might be useful. This equipment is essential for accurate, written communication. If you have to borrow a pen, for example, it may not suit you or it may not work properly and consequently you may work at a slower pace. It is possible that equipment may not be available to borrow and you will have to manage without it. Make sure you are well prepared so that you can get down to work quickly and not be interrupted.

- Always arrive on time for an exam.

- Find out *which questions you are expected to answer*. Doing extra questions will not earn extra marks but if you leave questions out you will *lose* marks.

- Work out how much time you can spend on each question. It is often useful to work out how many minutes you can devote to each mark. You can then work out how long to spend on questions that may not be worth the same amount of marks. For example, in a two hour paper you have 120 minutes to earn perhaps 100 marks. This is 1.2 minutes per mark. You can spend 2.4 minutes on a question worth 2 marks and 6 minutes on a question worth 5 marks. Having worked out the time you can spend on a question, stick to it. *This is very important.* The first part of each question is usually the easiest to answer and the first few marks on any question are the easiest to obtain. After the first half of a question, marks become increasingly difficult to obtain.

- Make sure you read the question thoroughly. Many candidates lose marks because they read the question in a hurry and do not fully grasp what it means. They then answer the question they *think* they have read. This means their answer may be inappropriate to the actual question. You will only be awarded marks for a correct answer to the actual question set. Read questions *slowly* and *carefully*.

- Try to answer all the questions. You cannot be given marks for questions you haven't answered. Higher marks will almost certainly be given for correct answers to part of all the required questions than for complete answers to a few questions.

- Never leave an exam before the end. Use all the time allowed to you in answering questions or checking your answers. Make sure that what you *can do* is done correctly and make sure that you have made a determined attempt at the more difficult questions. Marks are given for correct answers, but you will not have marks deducted if you are wrong.

- Write neatly and set out your work clearly. The examiner who marks your written paper will be looking for opportunities to give you marks. If it is impossible to read your answers because your writing is illegible you will probably lose marks.

- Give examples and draw diagrams to illustrate your answers. Communicate clearly and in full.

7 > USEFUL ADDRESSES

MAGAZINES

An occasional look at the following magazines might be useful.

Computer Weekly
from IPC Press Ltd
Dorset House
Stamford Street
London SE1

Computing
from The British Computer
Society
13 Mansfield Street
London W1M 0BP

Working in Computers
from Careers and Occupational
Information Service
Manpower Services Commission
Moorfoot
Sheffield S1 4PQ

EXAM GROUPS

See page 9.

3

THE IMPORTANCE OF THE TOPIC AREAS

ADDRESSES OF EXAM GROUPS

TOPIC AREAS

GETTING STARTED

Syllabuses are important because they outline in detail what is to be studied. The syllabus can be used as a checklist to make sure you have studied or revised all those topics you will be asked questions about in the written exams. You can buy a syllabus by writing to one of the addresses given in this chapter.

This chapter includes a table summarising the topics required by each examination group. This will be a useful guide. For a more detailed breakdown you should consult the syllabus you are studying. All the syllabuses are similar, but they are not *identical*.

EXAMINING GROUPS AND GCSE SYLLABUSES

If you want to be sure that you have covered all the topics for the GCSE exam you should buy a syllabus. Syllabuses can be useful when studying and revising as you can be certain you are learning the right topics. You can buy a syllabus from any of the addresses given below. Syllabuses cost around £2 each. Since each exam group has a different syllabus it is important to get the correct one. Find out which syllabus you are studying, then write to the *Publications Department* at the exam group, at the address given below.

London and East Anglian Group (LEAG)
The Lindens
Lexden Road
Colchester CO3 3RL
(Tel: 0206 549595)

Midland Examining Group (MEG)
Syndicate Buildings
1 Hills Road
Cambridge CB1 2EU
(Tel: 0223 611111)

Northern Examining Association (NEA)
12 Harter Street
Manchester M1 6HL
(Tel: 061 228 0084)

Northern Ireland Schools Examinations Council (NISEC)
42 Beechill Road
Belfast BT8 4RS
(Tel: 0232 704666)

Southern Examining Group (SEG)
Stag Hill House
Guildford GU2 5XJ
(Tel: 0483 506506)

Welsh Joint Education Committee (WJEC)
245 Western Avenue
Cardiff CF5 2YX
(Tel: 0222 561231)

THE TOPIC AREAS

All the syllabuses are based on the National Criteria for GCSE Computer Studies, which states what topics should be included. Consequently there is not a great deal of difference between the different syllabuses. Below is a table summarising the topics required by each of the GCSE examination groups. You will need to consult your particular syllabus for a more detailed breakdown.

	LEAG	MEG	NEA	NISEC	SEG	WJEC
4 An Introduction to Computing: Information Technology and Data Processing						
The data processing cycle	X	X	X	X	X	X
The Central Processing Unit	X	X	X	X	X	X
Mainframes and micros	X	X	X	X	X	X
Peripherals	X	X	X	X	X	X
Digital and analogue	X	X	X	X	X	X
Hardware and software	X	X	X	X	X	X
Glossary of Terms	X	X	X	X	X	X
5 Data Capture and Input						
Data capture	X	X	X	X	X	X
Verification	X	X	X	X	X	X
Mark sensing and OCR	X	X	X	X	X	X
Bar codes, laser scanners and light pens	X	X	X	X	X	X
Kimball tags	X	X	X	X	X	X
Magnetic Ink Character Recognition	X	X	X	X	X	X
Other input peripherals	X	X	X	X	X	X
Validation	X	X	X	X	X	X
6 Data Representation and Manipulation						
Data	X	X	X	X	X	X
The binary number system	X	X	X	X	X	X
Converting binary to denary and vice versa			X	X	X	X
Positive and negative integers	X	X	X	X	X	X
Binary fractions			X		X	
Octal and Hexadecimal				X	X	
Characters	X	X	X	X	X	X
7 Programming Languages						
Machine code and assembly language	X	X	X	X	X	X
Registers	X		X	X		
Typical instruction set	X	X				
Typical instruction format	X	X	X	X	X	X
Simple program		X	X	X	X	X
High level languages	X	X	X	X	X	X
Interpreters	X	X	X	X	X	X
Compilers	X	X	X	X		
Syntax, logic and execution errors	X		X	X	X	X
8 Operating Systems and Networks						
Operating systems	X	X	X	X	X	X
Standalone mode	X	X	X	X	X	X
Interactive processing	X	X	X	X	X	X
Multiprogramming	X	X	X	X	X	X
Networks	X	X	X	X	X	X
Terminals	X	X	X	X	X	X
Modems	X	X	X	X	X	X
9 Microelectronics: Logic and Control Systems						
Truth tables			X	X	X	
NOT, AND and OR logic			X	X	X	
Process control	X		X	X	X	X
Feedback			X	X		X

	LEAG	MEG	NEA	NISEC	SEG	WJEC
10 Output						
Monitors	X	X	X	X	X	X
Printer stationery	X	X	X	X	X	X
Printers	X	X	X	X	X	X
Graph plotters	X	X	X	X	X	X
Other output methods	X	X	X	X	X	X
11 The Memory, Files, Backing Storage and Security						
The memory	X	X	X	X	X	X
Files, records and fields	X	X	X	X	X	X
Serial and sequential access	X	X	X	X	X	X
Random or direct access	X	X	X	X	X	X
File operations	X	X	X		X	X
Backing storage	X	X	X	X	X	X
Magnetic tapes and magnetic discs	X	X	X	X	X	X
Security	X	X	X	X	X	X
12 The Computer System's Life Cycle and Jobs in Computing						
The system's life cycle	X	X	X	X	X	X
Documentation	X	X	X	X	X	X
The job of a systems analyst	X	X	X	X	X	X
The job of a computer programmer	X	X	X	X	X	X
The job of a data preparation clerk	X	X	X	X	X	X
The job of a data control clerk	X	X	X	X	X	
The job of a computer operator	X	X	X	X	X	X
Other jobs in computing	X	X	X	X	X	X
13 Computers at Work: Information Technology						
Wordprocessing	X	X	X	X	X	X
Electronic mail	X	X	X	X	X	X
Graphic design	X	X	X	X	X	X
Spreadsheets		X	X			
Databases	X	X	X	X	X	X
Expert systems	X	X	X			
Videotext, teletext and viewdata	X	X	X	X	X	X
14 Computers at Work: Data Processing						
Applications packages	X	X	X	X	X	X
Batch processing	X	X	X	X	X	X
Payroll	X	X	X	X	X	X
Master and transaction files	X	X	X	X	X	X
Real time processing	X	X	X	X	X	X
Airline booking system	X	X		X	X	X
On-line interactive processing	X	X	X	X	X	X
Stock control	X	X	X	X	X	X
15 Social Implications						
Computers at work	X	X	X	X	X	X
Privacy	X	X	X	X	X	X
Lifestyle and leisure	X	X	X			X

AN INTRODUCTION TO COMPUTING: INFORMATION TECHNOLOGY AND DATA PROCESSING

WHAT IS A COMPUTER?

MAINFRAMES AND MICROS

PERIPHERALS

HARDWARE

SOFTWARE

GETTING STARTED

In order to make any sense of Computer Studies it is important to know the meaning of the *jargon* being used. Throughout this book a lot of space will be devoted to explaining what is meant by a number of terms and ideas frequently used in computing. It is worth learning this jargon and becoming familiar with its use.

What exactly are computers and what do we use them for? The use of computers is often referred to as **data processing** or **information technology**. This is because computers process *data*, which is meaningless to them; but we use them as part of the technology available for processing *information*. Information is data that we understand. The computer is not intelligent and does *not* understand. In using a computer we become involved in a **cycle** involving the **input, processing** and **output** of data.

This data processing cycle is controlled by a **program** stored in the **memory** of the computer. The program requests the input of data to be processed. When data is *input*, and is being *processed*, it is **stored** in the memory of the computer. When processing has been done, the program will *output* data. In response to this output, more data may be input.

When the computer is switched off, the programs and data in its memory will be lost, i.e. the memory is **volatile**. If these data are needed later they can be saved on **backing storage**, and loaded into the memory of the computer whenever they are needed.

The programs that control the computer are known as **software**. **Applications packages** are software bought to do *specific* tasks, whereas **content free software** packages are used for wordprocessing, databases, etc.

The machinery of a computer system is known as **hardware**. This consists of the computer itself and various **peripherals**. Peripherals are devices that are connected to the computer to give it the use of some facility, such as printing.

A comprehensive *Glossary of Terms* is provided at the end of this chapter and can be referred to when reading other chapters in the book.

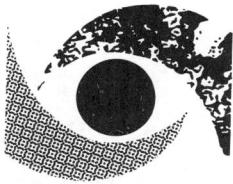

ESSENTIAL PRINCIPLES

1 › WHAT IS A COMPUTER?

A **computer** is an automatic, information processing machine which inputs, processes and outputs data under the control of a stored program.

INFORMATION AND DATA

■ **information = data + meaning**

Computers process data. Data is words or numbers. The data is not understood by the computer. Computers cannot tell the difference between sensible data or nonsense, unless we tell them how to. The use of computers is often referred to as **data processing**. However, because we are only interested in doing *useful* tasks with computers, we actually use them to process information, that is, data that has some meaning to us. For this reason we often call computers **information technology**.

"Information is data that has some meaning"

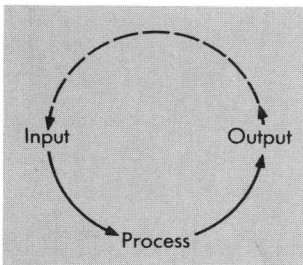

e.g.   230575 is *data*.
If we add *meaning* it could be any of the following:
a date; a telephone number; a serial number; £230,575; etc.
It then becomes *information*.

THE BASIC DATA PROCESSING CYCLE

Fig. 4.1 Data processing cycle

Data processing is a **cycle** of data input, processing and output (see Fig.4.1). We input the data we have collected, then process it. When the data has been processed, or while it is being processed, some data is output. In response to the data output we may wish to respond by inputting further data in reply. This is in turn processed and the cycle continues until we have no further data to input.

The data processing cycle may be based on a computer (see Fig. 4.2). The **Central Processing Unit (CPU)** of the computer does the actual processing of the data. Within the CPU are the **Immediate Access Store (IAS)**, the **Control Unit (CU)** and the **Arithmetic and Logic Unit (ALU)**.

■ The **IAS** is the memory of the computer. Programs and data are stored in the IAS while the programs are run and the data is processed. There are two types of memory:

  • **Random Access Memory (RAM)** is the *volatile* or temporary memory in which programs and data are stored.

  • **Read Only Memory (ROM)** can only be read and is not volatile. It is used to permanently store programs such as the Operating System.

■ A **program** is a set of instructions that tell the computer what to do. Programs are stored in the memory of the computer and *executed* or *run* in order to process the input data. The input data is also stored in the memory of the computer while it is processed. The processed data is then output. When the computer is switched off the programs and data in the RAM memory of the computer are 'wiped out'. To avoid losing the programs and data when we switch off, the programs and data can be saved on **backing storage**. Another name for backing storage is **secondary storage**.

■ The **CU** controls the hardware so that it carries out the instructions given in the program being run. It controls the input and output of data and the transfer of data between different parts of the CPU.

■ The **ALU** is a specialised unit within the CPU that does all the arithmetic and logic.

EXAMPLE: CALCULATING A GAS BILL

Suppose we want to use a computer to calculate a gas bill. We will have to do the following:

1   *Switch on* the computer.
2   *Load the program* which will do the calculation into the memory of the computer.
3   *Run* (or *execute*) the program.
4   *Input* the old and the new meter readings in response to requests from the computer.

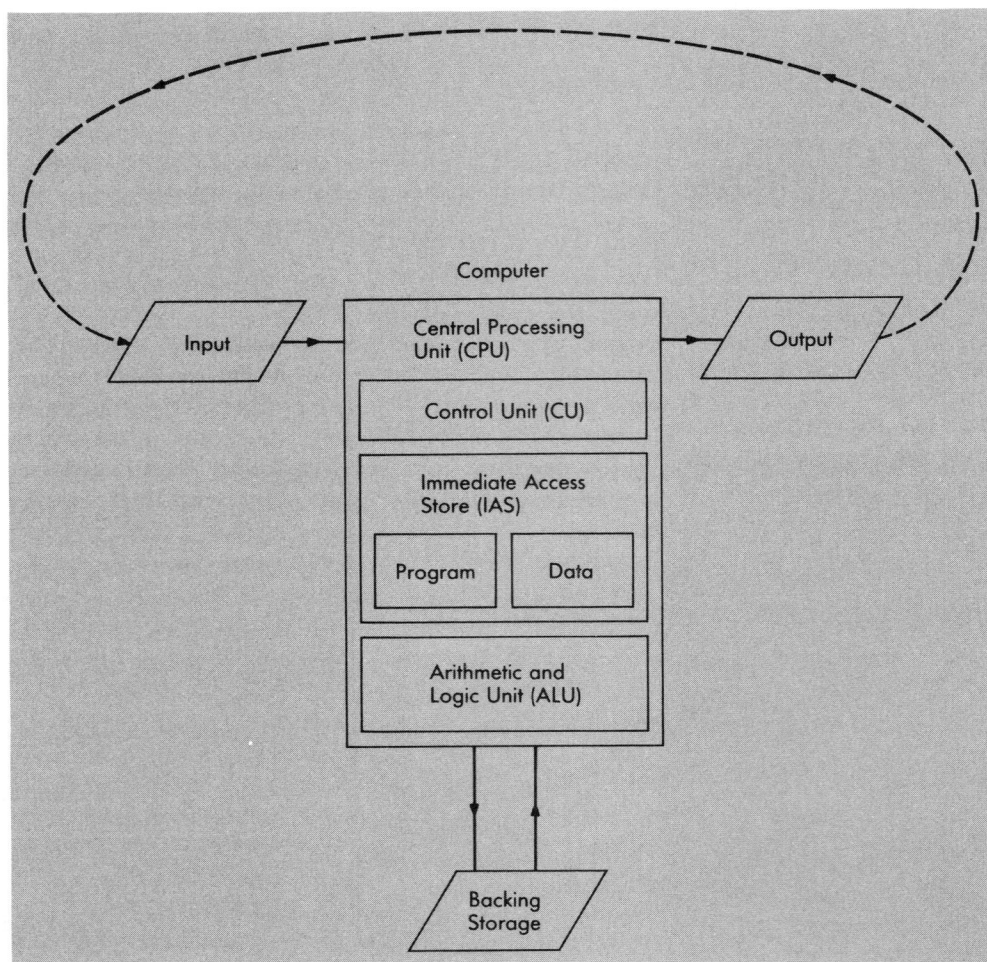

Fig. 4.2 The basic data processing cycle based on a computer

The computer can now:

5   *Process* the meter readings to calculate the gas used and the cost.
6   *Output* the gas used and the cost.
7   *Save* the results of any calculations on backing storage.
8   *Ask for further input* and, if this is not required, bring this run of the program to an *end*.

2 > MAINFRAMES AND MICROS

Computers come in different sizes. Essentially, microcomputers are small computers whilst mainframes are large computers.

A typical **microcomputer** is small enough to fit on an average-sized desk. Microcomputers are found in homes, offices, schools, etc. They may be 'personal computers', 'desk top', 'portable' or 'lap top' computers, in *descending* order of size and power. In industry the standard microcomputer is the IBM Personal Computer. The latest version is the IBM PS/2 (see Fig. 4.3).

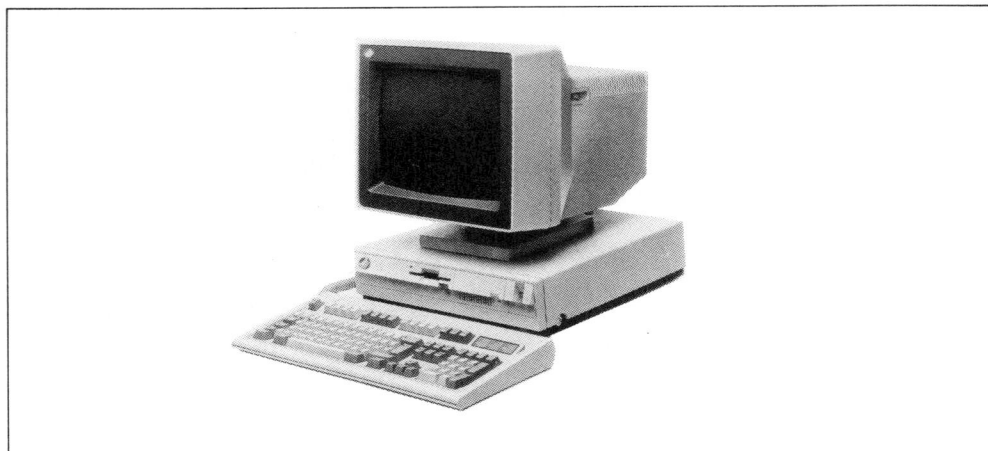

Fig. 4.3 The IBM PS/2 Personal Computer System. This is the latest update of the industry standard IBM PC. It is a typical example of a powerful desk top computer.

"Note the differences between *mainframe computers* **and** *microcomputers* **"**

Mainframe computers are many and varied. They offer a wide range of facilities and can vary dramatically in size and power. Most of them are very big in size, extremely fast in operation, have very large memories and offer access to a wide range of complex software and hardware. Mainframes are used in large companies and similar organisations, such as major banks, Local Authorities, etc. Typically they are housed in a room measuring 15m × 50m, or more.

Mainframe computers need *special environments*:

- in particular they need *air conditioning* to dissipate the heat generated when they are in use.

- *False floors and ceilings* may be used to hide the miles of cable connecting the computer to the various peripherals.

- The electricity supply is often 'smoothed' to prevent power surges or 'spikes' which may damage the expensive equipment.

- The computer may have its own *electricity generator* for emergency use in case of a power failure.

- *Filters* are used to keep the air free from dust particles.

- *Smoke detectors* are used to help prevent the outbreak of a serious fire.

The IBM Model 3090 is a typical mainframe computer (see Fig. 4.4).

Fig. 4.4 The IBM Model 3090 Mainframe Computer System. (Reproduction courtesy of IBM UK Ltd.)

3 ⟩ PERIPHERALS

Peripherals are machines attached to the computer. They are often essential to the successful operation of the computer but they are not part of the computer. They usually have a special purpose.

The following are examples of peripherals:

Input peripherals

keyboard, mouse, joystick
graphics pad, scanner, video digitiser
mark sense reader, OCR reader
light pen, laser scanner for bar codes
Kimball tag reader
MICR reader

Backing Storage peripherals

magnetic tape drive; using reel to reel and cassette tape
magnetic disc drive; using floppy discs and hard discs

Output peripherals

VDU or monitor, printer
COM recorder

4 > HARDWARE

66 Another important distinction is between hardware and software 99

Hardware is the physical machinery that is part of a computer system. Peripherals are hardware. Hardware is hard! You can touch it and even bump into it and hurt yourself!

Computer hardware is usually **digital**. In practice, this means that most computers and peripherals use *binary codes* to represent numbers and characters. Where this is *not* the case it is necessary to *convert* the data to digital form. For example, a heat sensor produces a small voltage in response to temperature changes. This is known as an **analogue** signal. Before the computer can process the analogue data it must be converted to digital form. This is done using a 'Analogue to Digital Converter' or **ADC**.

5 > SOFTWARE

Software refers to the *programs* that control the running of the computer. Programs are present whenever a computer is used. Software can be held in the memory of the computer. It can also be recorded on floppy discs, cassette tapes or any other computer readable medium. Software is NOT floppy discs or cassette tape. It is the *programs recorded on* the floppy discs, etc.

Software can be obtained in many ways. You can write your own, using a computer language such as BASIC, PASCAL or COBOL. You can buy software. Bought software is referred to as a **package**. Most packages have a specific purpose or application. You might buy an **applications package** to do the stock keeping in a shop, to calculate the wages for a factory or to do your budgeting at home.

The use of **content free packages** has recently become more important. These are packages which are useful in a *variety* of ways, but in practice are often used to do *similar* data processing tasks. These packages cover application *areas* rather than specific applications. For example, content free packages are used for Wordprocessing, Databases, Spreadsheets and Graphics Design.

One of the most important programs that a computer runs is the **operating system**. The operating system is always present when a computer is being used. The operating system makes the hardware available to other software. Applications packages and other user software run on the operating system which, in turn, runs or controls the hardware. The operating system also helps the user do a variety of tasks associated with the day-to-day operation of the computer, such as copying or formatting discs, loading and saving programs, and transmitting data to or from backing storage, etc.

GLOSSARY OF TERMS USED

Algorithm	A set of rules to solve a problem.
Amend	To change.
Analogue to Digital Converter (ADC)	A hardware device to convert analogue voltage to binary digital numbers.
Ancestral system	The ancestral system for file backups consists of the *son* (the latest version), the *father* (the previous version) and the *grandfather* (the version before the previous version).
Applications software	Software designed to do a specific job, e.g. payroll.
Arithmetic and Logic Unit (ALU)	The part of the CPU where arithmetic and logical operations are done.
ASCII	The **A**merican **S**tandard **C**ode for **I**nformation **I**nterchange. This is used to uniquely represent characters in binary code.
Assembler	A program that converts a program written in *assembly language* (the source code) into *machine code* (the object code).
Assembly language	A low level computer language close to machine code. Each instruction is one machine code instruction.
Backing storage	A means of storing programs and data outside the IAS, e.g. magnetic disc or tape.
Backup	A *backup* of a file is another copy of it. The ancestral system is often used for backups.

Bar code	A code represented by a series of vertical black and white lines, often used to encode an identity number.
Bar code reader	A hardware device used to read a bar code. This could be a light pen or a laser scanner.
Batch processing	A method of processing data where the data is collected into batches before being processed.
Binary	The base 2 number system. Allowable digits are 0 and 1.
BIT	A **BI**nary Digi**T**. This takes the value 1 or 0.
Block	A block is a group of records on magnetic tape or disc that is read or written together.
Buffer	A printer buffer is extra memory, usually in the printer itself, which is used to hold output while it is waiting to be printed.
Byte	A byte is a set of bits used to represent one character. There are normally eight bits to the byte.
Catalogue	A list of all the files on a disc.
Ceefax	The teletext service broadcast by the BBC.
Central Processing Unit (CPU)	The main part of the computer, where all the processing takes place. It consists of the CU, the IAS and the ALU.
Character	One of the symbols that can be represented by a computer. Characters include A to Z and 0 to 9.
Character code	A code used to represent characters, e.g. ASCII.
Character printer	A printer that prints one character at a time, e.g. a dot matrix printer.
Character set	All the characters that can be represented by a computer.
Character string	A list of characters.
Check digit	An extra digit calculated from the original digits in a number, using a predetermined formula, and attached to the number. It can be re-calculated to check that none of the digits in the number have been altered.
Compiler	A program used to convert another program written in a high level language (source code) to machine code (object code). The whole of the *source code* is converted at the same time to produce the *object code* which can be saved on disc. The program is run from the object code. The compiler will report syntax errors in the source code.
Computer	A computer is an automatic information processing machine which inputs, processes and outputs data under the control of a stored program.
Computer Output on Microfilm (COM)	Output from a computer written directly onto microfilm. Output in this form is compact and does not deteriorate in storage as rapidly as printout.
Content free software	Software designed to do a range of similar jobs, e.g. a spreadsheet.
Control switch	A switch built of logic gates that is used to switch data lines on and off.
Control total	A meaningful total calculated from a batch of source documents that is used to check that the batch is complete.
Control Unit (CU)	The part of the CPU that controls the running of programs and the input and output of data.
Corrupt data	Corrupt data is data that has been altered so that it is no longer meaningful.
Cursor	Usually a rectangular block one character in size that appears on a monitor screen at the point at which the next character entered through the keyboard will be displayed. The cursor often flashes on and off to attract attention.
Daisy-wheel printer	A printer that has a daisy-wheel print mechanism. Daisy-wheel printers give high quality printout.
Data	Numbers or character strings.
Data capture	Data capture is the collection of data prior to input. Data capture can be on-line, e.g. POS terminals for stock keeping, or off-line, e.g. questionnaires.

Data control clerks	The job of a data control clerk is to monitor the flow of data through a computer system.
Data preparation	This is the transfer of data from a source document to a computer readable medium, e.g. disc.
Data preparation clerks	Data preparation clerks work in the data preparation department.
Data processing	Computers input, process and output data. In commerce this is known as data processing.
Database	A database is a collection of data structured to allow the data to be accessed easily.
DataBase Management System (DBMS)	The software needed to organise and access a database.
Delete	Remove. A file is deleted from a disc when it is removed from it.
Denary	The base 10 number system. Available digits are 0 to 9.
Desk Top Publishing (DTP)	Combines graphics and wordprocessing in a format typical of a newspaper with text in columns, varying character sizes, photographs and other illustrations.
Direct access	A method of accessing a file where it is possible to store or retrieve data records without the need to read other data records first. Direct access is used with magnetic discs.
Direct data entry	Data entry to the program that processes the data while it is running.
Directory	See Catalogue.
Disc	Magnetic discs are a backing storage medium. Microcomputers use floppy discs (5¼″ or 3½″) or hard discs. Mainframes use disc packs that may be exchangeable or fixed.
Documentation	A written description of what a program does and how it is run. Often containing details of program design, coding and testing.
Dot matrix printer	A printer that has a print head consisting of a matrix of steel pins. Character shapes are made up from a pattern of dots.
Electronic funds transfer (EFT)	A paperless method of transferring money between bank accounts using a communications network.
Electronic mail	A paperless method of sending mail, i.e. letters, etc., from one computer to another using a communications network.
Errors	*Logic* errors are mistakes in the logic of a program. *Syntax* errors are mistakes in the format of a programming language, e.g. PRONT instead of PRINT. *Execution* errors occur when a program is run, e.g. division by zero.
Execute	To execute a program is to run it.
Expert system	Software that allows users to recognise particular situations and that gives them advice on the appropriate action to take.
Feedback	Feedback occurs when a sensor detects a situation that causes the computer to initiate action that alters the data collected by the sensor.
Fibre optics	The use of very thin fibre glass strands to transmit data encoded as light pulses.
Field	A field is an item of data within a record.
File	A file is an organised collection of related records.
File librarian	The person responsible for the library of discs and tapes kept by a computer department.
File server	A computer attached to a network whose main function is to enable network stations to access files on the network.
Flowchart	A graphical representation of the flow of data through a computer.
Font	A set of consistently shaped characters.
Front end processor	A small computer used to control communications between a larger mainframe computer and the terminals and other peripherals connected to it.
Full adder	A logic circuit that inputs three bits and adds them together. *Input* is the two bits of the numbers being added and a carry bit

	from the addition of the two bits to the right. *Output* is a carry bit and a sum bit.
Graphics pad	A peripheral which allows the user to transfer drawings to the computer by drawing on paper resting on the graphics pad.
Graph plotter	An output peripheral that produces detailed pictures and diagrams on paper using a pen.
Graphic design package	A software package that allows the user to draw on the screen, providing a range of design tools, different colours and patterns.
Hacker	An unauthorised user of a computer system who has broken into the system either by guessing a user identification (Id) and the associated password or by bypassing them.
Half adder	A logic circuit that inputs two bits and adds them together. Two half adders are used to build a full adder.
Hard copy	Printout.
Hardware	The physical components of a computer system.
Hash total	A total calculated from a batch of source documents that is used to check that the batch is complete. The total has no meaning in itself.
Hexadecimal	The base 16 number system. Allowable digits are 0 to 9 and A to F.
High level language	A problem orientated programming language, e.g. COBOL, BASIC, Pascal.
Information	Information is data that is meaningful to us.
Information technology (IT)	IT is the use of computers and other technology used to process information.
Immediate Access Store	The part of the CPU that is used to store programs while they are running and data while it is being processed.
Insert	To put into. 'To insert a record' means to put a new record into a file.
Integer	Positive and negative whole numbers, e.g. 1, -6, 0, 3, 7.
Inter block gap	A gap left between two data blocks on a magnetic tape.
Inter sector gap	A gap left between two sectors on a magnetic disc.
Interactive processing	Interactive processing takes place when the user and the computer are in two-way communication.
Interface	The interconnection between two different systems.
Interpreter	An interpreter is a program that converts another program written in a high level language to machine code. It converts one line at a time while the program is run. The program is run from the source code. Syntax errors are reported.
Key field	A field in a record used to identify the record. Used when searching for the record or when sorting the file.
Key-to-disc	A method of data preparation where data is entered at a keyboard and saved on disc.
Key-to-tape	A method of data preparation where data is entered at a keyboard and saved on tape.
Kilobyte (K)	1024 or 2^{10} bytes.
Kimball tag	A small punched card that identifies a garment and holds details of its size, colour, price, etc.
Laser printer	A page printer that works by etching a stencil of the page to be printed in an electrostatic drum.
Laser scanner	A hardware device that inputs bar codes by scanning the pattern of light reflected off a bar code by a laser beam.
Light pen	A hardware device that inputs bar codes by scanning the pattern of light reflected off a bar code. It is shaped like a pen.
Line printer	A printer that prints one line at a time.
Local Area Network (LAN)	A network with permanent links between all the hardware connected to the network. Probably located in one building.
Logic circuit	A circuit made up of individual logic gates.
Logic gate	A fundamental logic operation, e.g. AND, OR, NOT, etc.
Low level language	An assembly language.
Machine code	Program instructions in binary code that can be executed by a

	computer. All programming languages are converted to machine code before running.
Magnetic Ink Character Recognition (MICR)	A method of input where characters printed in magnetic ink are read directly into a computer.
Mainframe computer	A large, fast computer, probably having a variety of peripherals, including a high capacity backing store and many terminals.
Mark sensing	An input method where pencil marks on paper are detected. Their position on the paper determines their meaning.
Master file	A data file which is used to store most of the data for a particular application. It is updated by the transaction file.
Memory address	A number used to identify a storage location in memory.
Memory map	A plan of the computer's memory giving the addresses where programs and data are held.
Merge	To combine one or more files into a single file.
Microcomputer	A small computer based on a microprocessor. They are usually relatively cheap, slow and have limited backing storage.
Microfilm	An output medium similar to photographic film.
Microprocessor	A single microchip containing all the elements of the CPU, except the IAS.
Mnemonic	Assembly language operation codes are mnemonics, e.g. LDA represents 'load the accumulator'.
Modem	A MOdulator/DEModulator. Used to convert digital data output by a computer to analogue signals that can be transmitted along a telephone line and vice versa.
Monitor	A screen used to display the output from a computer.
Mouse	A hand-held input peripheral having buttons on top and a ball underneath. When the mouse is moved over a flat surface, a pointer on the screen moves in a corresponding direction.
Multiaccess	When many users are connected to a single computer using terminals, this is multiaccess computing.
Multiprogramming	When one computer is apparently running more than one program at the same time, this is multiprogramming.
Multitasking	When one user is apparently running more than one program at the same time, this is multitasking.
Network	A network is a system of connecting cables. For example, networks can be used to connect computers; the telephone network connects telephone users.
Network station	A terminal connected to a network.
Non-volatile memory	Non-volatile memory does not lose its contents when the power is switched off. ROM memory is *non-volatile*.
Object code	A machine code program generated by a compiler or an assembler.
Octal	The base 8 number system. Allowable digits are 0 to 7.
Off-line	Not connected to the computer or connected, but not in communication with it.
On-line	Connected to the computer and in communication with it.
Operating system	The operating system is a program that makes the computer hardware more easily accessible to other programs. An operating system is always present when a computer is used.
Operator	An operator looks after the computer while it is running, changing discs, tapes and printer paper as required.
Optical Character Recognition (OCR)	An input method that can read printed characters. Special fonts are often used.
Page printer	A printer that prints a page at a time, e.g. a laser printer.
Parity	An automatic hardware check that data that has been transferred or stored has not been corrupted. An extra bit is added to make the number of bits set to 1 odd (odd parity) or even (even parity).

Password	A code that restricts access to a computer system. Usually associated with the User Identification.
Peripheral	A peripheral is a hardware device that is connected to a computer system but is not the part of the computer itself, e.g. a printer.
Pixel	The smallest area of a screen that can be used in building up a picture.
Point Of Sale (POS) terminal	A terminal used to collect data at the point of sale. Often incorporates a laser scanner to read bar codes, and a dot matrix printer to print receipts. May be on-line to the supermarket's computer system.
Port	A connector used to link peripherals to a computer.
Portable	Portable programs can be run on a variety of different computers.
Prestel	The viewdata service run by British Telecom.
Printout	The output from a printer.
Program	A set of instructions used to control the operation of a computer.
Programmer	A computer programmer designs, codes, test and documents programs for a computer.
Pull-down menu	A feature of a WIMP user interface where a hidden menu can be revealed, i.e. pulled down, by pointing at it.
Random access	See direct access.
Random Access Memory (RAM)	Read/write memory within the IAS. RAM is *volatile*.
Range check	A check that a data value is within realistic limits.
Read Only Memory (ROM)	Memory within the IAS that can only be read. ROM is *non-volatile*.
Real time processing	The processing of input data that takes place so fast that when more data is input the results of the processing are already available. Real time processing occurs in real time, i.e. as it happens.
Record	A record is a collection of related fields.
Relocatable	A relocatable program can be stored in any part of the computer's memory.
Remote access	Access to a computer using a terminal located a long way from the computer.
Sensor	A device used to sense environmental conditions.
Sequential access	Similar to serial access but the data records are stored in some order.
Serial access	A method of accessing data records. In order to access a data record in a serial access file, it is necessary to start at the beginning of the file and read all the preceding records. The records are not stored in any particular order.
Software	Computer programs.
Software package	A complete set of programs and documentation to enable a particular computer program to be used.
Sort	To put into order. Records in a file are often stored in key field order.
Source code	A program written in a high or low level programming language.
Source document	A document or questionnaire used for data capture. It is the source of the data input to the computer.
Speech recognition	A method of input to a computer by speaking to it.
Speech synthesis	Sounds generated by a computer that synthesise human speech.
Spooling	A method of queueing output directed to a printer before printing it.
Spreadsheet	Spreadsheets are used to calculate and display financial and other numerical information in columns.
Standalone	A computer that is not connected to any other computer is being used in standalone mode.
Systems analysis and design	The in-depth analysis of the software and hardware requirements of a computer based system and its detailed design.

Systems analyst	A systems analyst is responsible for the progress of a computer based system throughout the system's life cycle.
System's life cycle	Computer systems go through the cycle of systems investigation; feasibility study; systems analysis and design; program design, coding, testing and documentation; implementation; systems documentation; maintenance; evaluation.
Syntax	The set of rules which define the way an instruction in a programming language can be written.
Tapes	Magnetic tapes are a backing storage medium. Microcomputers use cassette tapes, tape streamers use tape cartridges and mainframes use reel-to-reel tape.
Teletext	A form of videotext accessible using a specially adapted television set, e.g. Oracle broadcast by ITV, or Ceefax by the BBC.
Terminal	A hardware device used to communicate with a computer from a remote site.
Time sharing	A method of meeting the demands of a multiaccess system where many programs are required to be run apparently at the same time. Each program is given access to the CPU for a very short period of time (a *time slice*) in rotation.
Track	A track is the path on a magnetic tape or disc along which data is stored.
Transaction file	A file used to store recent data captured since the last master file update. The transaction file is used to update the master file.
Truth table	A table showing all the possible inputs to a logic circuit and the corresponding outputs.
Turnaround document	A printout which has data written on it and is then used as a source document.
Two's complement	A method of representing negative numbers in binary. The place value of the leftmost bit is negative.
Update	To bring a file up-to-date by amending, inserting or deleting data records.
User Id	The User Identification number that enables a computer system to recognise a user.
Utility	A program that is used to do a task that is useful only in relation to the organisation of a computer system, e.g. a screen dump.
Validation	A check that data is realistic.
Verification	A check that what is written on a source document is accurately transferred to a computer-readable medium.
Videotext	A page-based information retrieval system, i.e. Teletext and Viewdata.
Viewdata	A form of videotext that is accessed by using a microcomputer and a modem via the telephone network to connect to a computer that holds the information required, e.g. Prestel run by British Telecom.
Visual Display Unit (VDU)	A keyboard and screen used as a terminal.
Volatile memory	Volatile memory loses its contents when the power is switched off. *RAM memory is volatile.*
Wide Area Network (WAN)	A network spread over a wide area, possibly international, making use of both permanent cable connections and temporary connections using the telephone network.
Windows, Icons, Mouse, Pointers (WIMP)	A user interface that avoids the need to remember complex operating system commands by providing *icons* that represent the commands. To select a command the user points at it and clicks a button on the mouse.
Wordprocessing	The preparation of letters and other documents using a computer in a manner similar to a typewriter but with additional features.

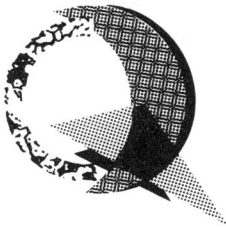

E X A M I N A T I O N   Q U E S T I O N S

1   Ring **two** of these units which are part of the Central Processing Unit.

arithmetic   input   control   output   processing   *(2)*

(MEG; 1988)

2

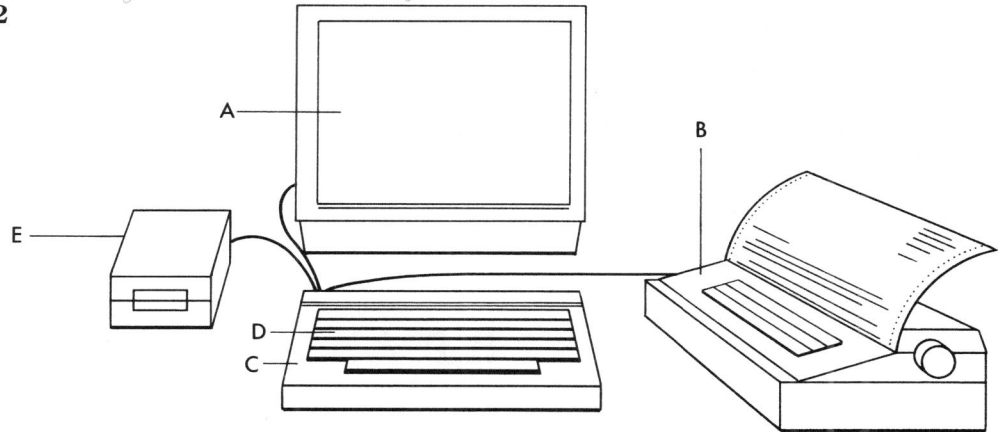

Fig. 1 The parts of a computer system.

Figure 1 shows a typical micro computer system. Using the words **secondary storage**, **input**, **cpu**, **output** complete the following table. *One of the words is used twice.* *(4)*

Label	Description
A	Output
B	Output
C	cpu
D	Input
E	secondary storage

(WJEC; 1988)

3   Which one of the following is essential for a computer system?

A   A keyboard   D   A backing store

B   An interface   E   A processor

C   A visual display unit

(NEA; 1988)

4   Which one of the following is a computer output peripheral?

A   joystick   D   monitor

B   disk drive   E   keyboard

C   mark sense document

For each of the questions 5 to 7 a common computing term is described. You are required to write down the term that has been described.

5   *Description:*   Programs and procedures, with their documentation, which can be implemented on a computer system.

Term: Software

6   *Description:*   The physical components of a computer system, including the peripherals.

Term: Hardware

7   *Description:*   A set of instructions written in a computer language that tells the computer what to do.

Term: Program

(NEA; 1988)

OUTLINE ANSWERS

MULTIPLE CHOICE QUESTIONS

1 (arithmetic) input (control) output processing
2 A, output; B, output; C, CPU; D, input; E, secondary storage.
3 E
4 D

SHORT STRUCTURED QUESTIONS

5 Software
6 Hardware
7 Program

A STUDENT'S ANSWER WITH EXAMINER'S COMMENTS

QUESTION

(A) _Keyboard_ → (D) Central Processing Unit → (B) _Screen_

(C) _disc_

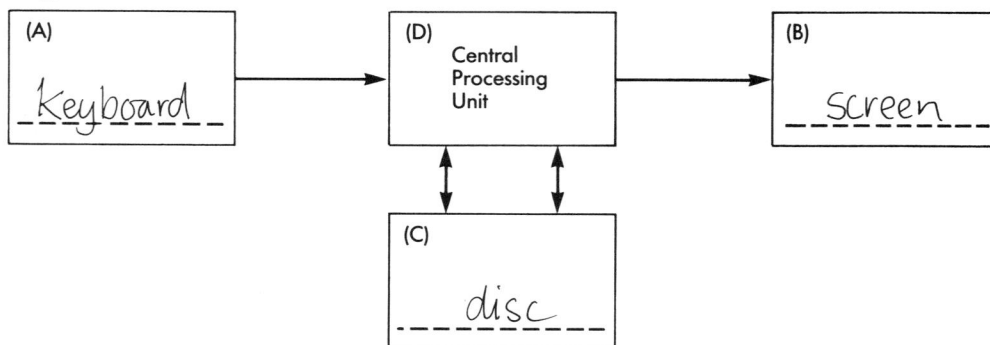

a) The diagram above shows the flow of data in a computer system. On the diagram give the name of the parts labelled A, B and C.

b) In which box on the diagram would you expect to find the Immediate Access Store?

D

c) Give one use of the Immediate Access Store.

stores programs and data

(LEAG; 1988)

Examiner's comment

a) The student has given examples of the peripherals used, instead of what they are used for, ie:
   A) INPUT
   B) OUTPUT
   C) BACKING STORAGE

b) and c) good answers.

CHAPTER 5

DATA CAPTURE AND INPUT

MAINFRAMES
MICROCOMPUTERS

GETTING STARTED

Data Capture is collecting data for input to a computer. We try to make sure that the data we collect is accurate and that it is input to the computer without mistakes. There are various methods of doing this. Different methods of data capture are largely due to the different *peripheral devices*, i.e. hardware, used to input the data to the computer.

There are *two* very important concepts that should be thoroughly learnt in connection with the careful monitoring of data capture and input. These are verification and validation.

Verification ensures that data is recorded accurately.

Validation is a check that the data is realistic.

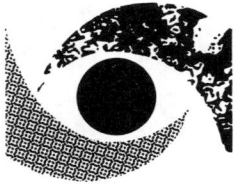

ESSENTIAL PRINCIPLES

The types of input peripheral in use are generally different depending on whether we are using a *mainframe* computer or a *microcomputer*. Mainframes are owned and used by large companies, whereas microcomputers are used in offices and homes for a wide variety of tasks.

1 ⟩ MAINFRAMES

QUESTIONNAIRES AND OTHER FORMS

Getting people to fill in a *questionnaire* or *form* is one way of collecting data. An example of a form that might be filled in when reading an electricity meter is shown in Fig. 5.1.

ELECTRICITY BOARD

Account Number   B 025741X

Customer   MR J.B. Priestley

Address   5 Mill Bank Drive

Hexham

HX2 4PD

Previous Meter Reading   5 7 2 1 4

New Meter Reading

Instructions
1. Fill in the New Meter Reading.
2. Check that it is BIGGER than the previous Meter Reading.
3. If any details have changed, fill in the new details in the boxes on the right hand side.

Fig. 5.1 A data capture form used to read an electricity meter

❝❝Useful steps in constructing a questionnaire❞❞

When designing a form we:
a) Use simple language so people can easily understand;
b) Say clearly and unambiguously what is needed;
c) Give examples if necessary;
d) Provide enough space for the answer;
e) Provide help in answering if possible;
f) Collect all the information that is needed, but no more;
g) Avoid asking questions that may not be answered truthfully;
h) Record information in a way which will help computer input.

A questionnaire or form used for data capture is known as a **source document**. The data on a source document must be transferred to a computer-readable medium *before* it can be input to a computer. This can be done in several ways, all involving the use of a **keyboard**, for example:

a) Using 'key-to-disc' – the data is transferred to a magnetic disc.
b) Using 'key-to-tape' – the data is transferred to a magnetic tape.

VERIFICATION

In order to be sure that the data has been accurately transferred from the source document to the computer-readable medium, the data is '**verified**'.

To verify data we use the 'double entry' method:

❝❝the double entry method❞❞

a) Transfer the data to the computer-readable medium.
b) Transfer the data to the computer-readable medium again.

c) Compare the results of a) and b). If these are the same then we have transferred the data accurately. If they are *not* the same then we have made a mistake and must correct it.

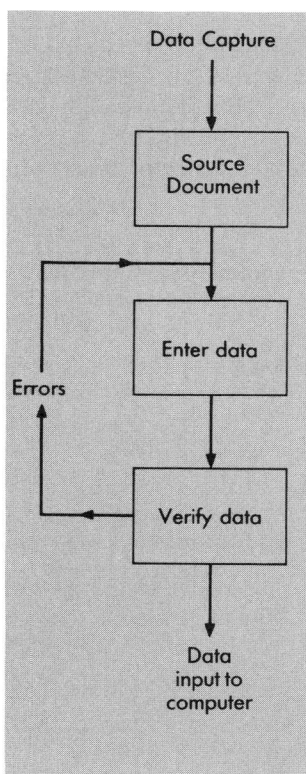

This process is illustrated in Fig. 5.2.

The purpose of verification is to make sure that what is written on the source document is accurately transferred to the computer-readable medium.

The data can now be input to the computer.

The process of transferring the data from the source document to a computer-readable medium is expensive. It is necessary to employ many people and to buy expensive equipment. For this reason, methods of data capture and input have been developed that *avoid* the need to key-in and verify data. These are described below.

MARK SENSING AND OPTICAL CHARACTER RECOGNITION (OCR)

In **Mark Sensing**, marks are made on a specially designed form or questionnaire using a pencil (see Fig. 5.3). The position of the mark on the form or questionnaire gives it meaning. By shining a light onto the paper and recording the intensity of the reflected light returned to it, a *mark sense reader* attached to the computer reads the data directly into the memory of the computer. This avoids the need to key-in the data. There is no verification of the input data. Mark Sensing is often used for multiple choice exam papers and to make it easier for Sales and Delivery employees to record the sale or delivery of goods.

Fig. 5.2 Verification

Fig. 5.3 A Mark Sensing form

Mark Sensing and OCR *avoid* the need to key-in and verify data

For **Optical Character Recognition (OCR)** written or printed text is read using a special reader, or scanner, that works in a similar way to a mark sense reader. In OCR it is not the position of the marks on the paper that gives them meaning but the *shape* of the different characters and numbers. There are many different shapes of printed characters, i.e. **fonts**, and a greater variety of writing styles. For this reason the highly sophisticated software needed is still being developed. It is possible to use OCR with some very limited fonts, but widespread use of OCR is not yet practical. OCR will be most useful when it is possible to read the pages of a book or a typed A4 sheet directly into the computer and immediately wordprocess the input text. This will then enable libraries to transfer their books to the computer and offices to store letters on a magnetic disc.

Magnetic Ink Character Recognition (MICR) has been used more successfully than OCR, and is described later in this chapter.

BAR CODES AND LIGHT PENS OR LASER SCANNERS

Bar Codes and **Light Pens** or **Laser Scanners** are most often found in use in supermarkets. The light pen or laser scanner is used to *read* the bar code. The bar code is used to *identify* a specific item, e.g. an 850 gram can of baked beans. For an example of a typical bar code see Fig. 5.4. When shopping is taken to the checkout the cashier passes the items over a scanner which will read the bar code. The bar code is printed on most of the items stocked. If the bar code is *not* on the item then the price is entered on a cash register in the usual way. The cash register and scanner used are connected to a central computer and are known as a Point of Sale terminal (**POS terminal**).

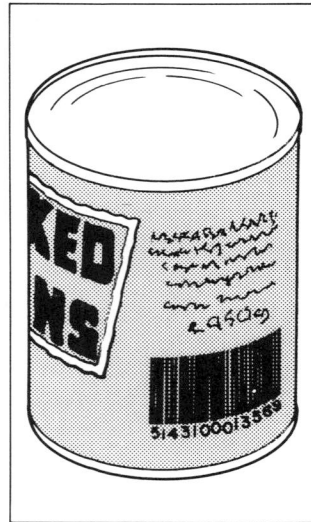

Fig. 5.4 A bar code on a can of baked beans

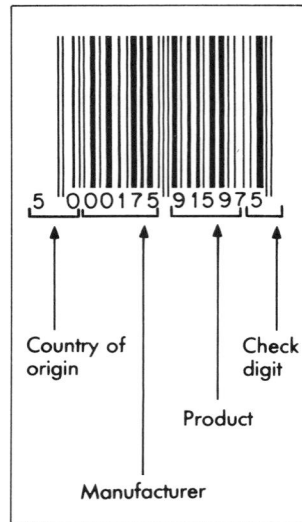

Fig. 5.5 The information contained in a bar code

SPONGE PUDD	0.54
CASSEROLE	4.75
400 STFGRAIN	0.40
BAKED BEANS	0.29
AMERCN GNGR	0.43
DOLMIO SAUCE	0.89
PEAR HALVES	0.37
MUSHROOMS	
0.70lb	
@ 1.32/lb	0.92
TOTAL	31.23
45 ITEMS	
CHEQUE	31.23
CHANGE DUE	0.00

THANK YOU

16/12/88 17:30 011116
6022   2231

Fig. 5.6 Receipt printed at a POS terminal

The bar code contains codes which identify the *country of origin*, the *company* which manufactured the item, the *product* and a *check digit* (see Fig. 5.5). This information is read by the laser scanner at the POS terminal and sent to the computer. The description of the item and its price are stored in the computer and instantly sent back to the checkout where they are printed on the receipt (see Fig. 5.6).

Unfortunately, data input using this system is not verified. However, the likelihood of entering the occasional wrong or damaged bar code is very small, so this is not a problem. If an incorrect bar code is entered it is likely that a *validation check* (see below), using the check digit or matching the input bar codes against a list of valid bar codes, will highlight such errors.

This system also provides detailed information on what has been sold, which is useful to the supermarket for stock-keeping and re-ordering. Staff operating the checkout need less training, can work faster and can be paid less as the job is made easier. Fewer staff are also needed at the checkout. The customer is provided with more detailed information on purchases made. Unfortunately it is likely that goods will not have individual price labels; this will make shopping more difficult as price comparisons cannot be made in different parts of the store.

KIMBALL TAGS

Fig. 5.7 A Kimball tag

Kimball tags are small punched cards (see Fig. 5.7). They are most commonly found in clothes shops. They usually have printed on them information that identifies the garment they are attached to, e.g. description, size, colour, price and other details. This data is also recorded on the Kimball tag by means of punched holes in a special code. When a garment is sold, the Kimball tag is retained by the shop. The data on the Kimball tag can be input directly to the computer using a *Kimball Tag Reader* attached to the POS terminal. Otherwise, the tags can be collected and posted to the central computer installation for processing at a later date. Kimball tags carry essentially the same function as bar codes, but they can hold more data. As with bar codes, the data input cannot be verified. Since Kimball tags can be torn easily this could also be a problem. However, they are helpful in keeping accurate stock records.

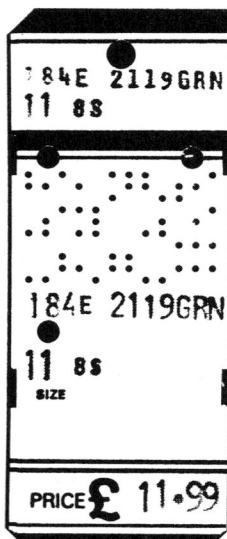

MAGNETIC INK CHARACTER RECOGNITION

Magnetic Ink Character Recognition (MICR) is most commonly used with bank cheques (see Fig. 5.8). MICR is only possible with a very restricted font. The font in use in the UK, has only 14 possible characters, including the digits 0 to 9. Numbers are printed in magnetic ink along the bottom of the cheque. These numbers are codes which identify the bank, the customer's account and the cheque. They can be read directly into the computer. When paying for goods in a shop, the customer fills in a cheque in payment for the goods bought. When the cheque is filled in the amount is written on the cheque by the customer. The customer gives the cheque to the shopkeeper who deposits the cheque at the bank. The MICR reader at the bank cannot read the amount written by the customer in normal ink. This must be typed onto the cheque in *magnetic ink* before it can be processed. The MICR reader will read the information on the cheque directly into the computer.

Cheques can be quite badly damaged before it is necessary to enter the data in some other way. There is no verification of input data. However, data input can be fast – up to 2000 cheques per minute are possible. When the cheque is processed, money will be transferred from the customer's account to the shopkeeper's account.

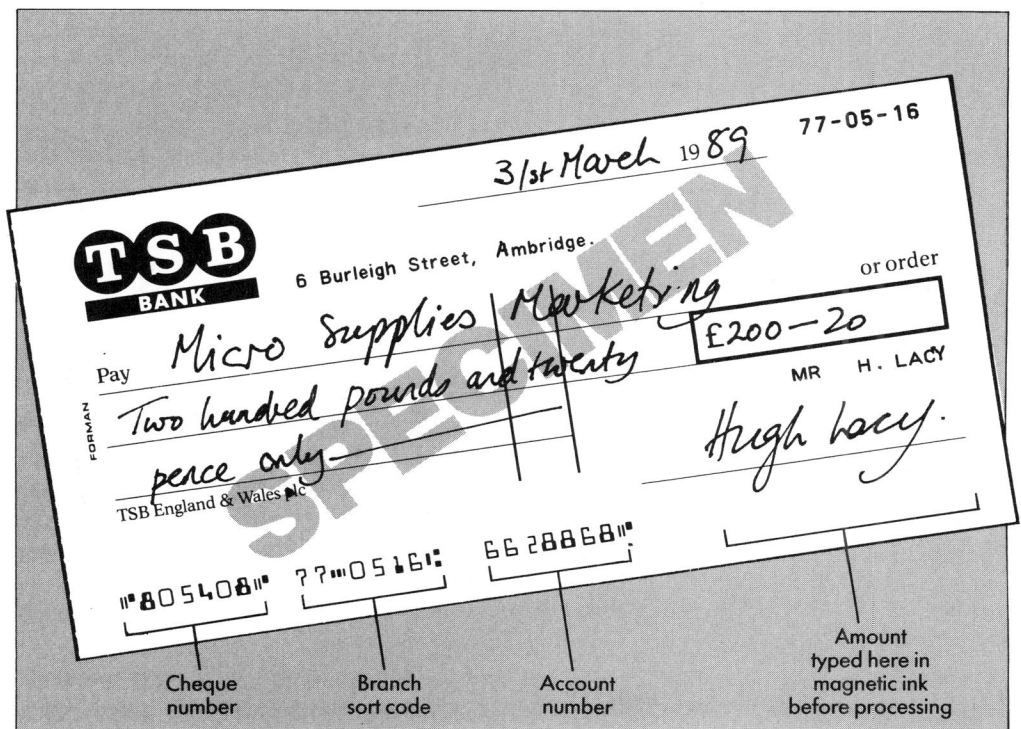

Fig. 5.8 MICR used on a bank cheque

Acknowledgements: TSB plc

MAGNETIC STRIPES

A **magnetic stripe** is a short length of magnetic tape sealed into the surface of a plastic card. Plastic cards containing magnetic stripes are used by banks and credit card companies to make sure that the owner is credit-worthy. These magnetic stripes carry enough information to allow a computer to identify the owner so that their credit limit can be checked.

Plastic cards are also used as phone cards. Some telephones accept phone cards instead of cash. The number of units unused is recorded on the card. When the user makes a telephone call the units used are deducted from those left on the card and the new total recorded on the card.

VOICE RECOGNITION

Using a microphone as an input device, computers can be programmed to recognise a limited range of spoken input. This is **voice recognition**. At present, the method is unreliable, although its long-term potential is promising. It would be a useful method of input for workers whose hands are occupied, or for disabled people with little hand movement.

2 > **MICRO-COMPUTERS**

When using a microcomputer it is usual to enter data while the program we are using is running. We expect to get a fast response from the micro. This is **interactive** processing. Although the most common method of input is through the keyboard, there are other methods. There is no reason why any of the following methods could not be used with a mainframe computer, but in practice this is not often done.

JOYSTICKS

66 Ways of inputting data 99

Joysticks are widely used for playing games with computers in the home (see Fig. 5.9). They can be made using two small potential dividers (*pots*). These provide voltages of between 0 and 5 volts which are input to the computer. The voltages are converted to numbers which the computer can process by an Analogue to Digital Converter (ADC). One pot provides an X coordinate, the other provides the Y coordinate. The position of a point on the screen is found using its (X,Y) coordinates. When the joystick handle is moved, the voltages input to the computer change, leading to different converted (X,Y) values. The software responds by moving the screen pointer. In this way the screen pointer can be moved to any part of the screen. Screen pointers often represent spaceships, etc., when playing a computer game.

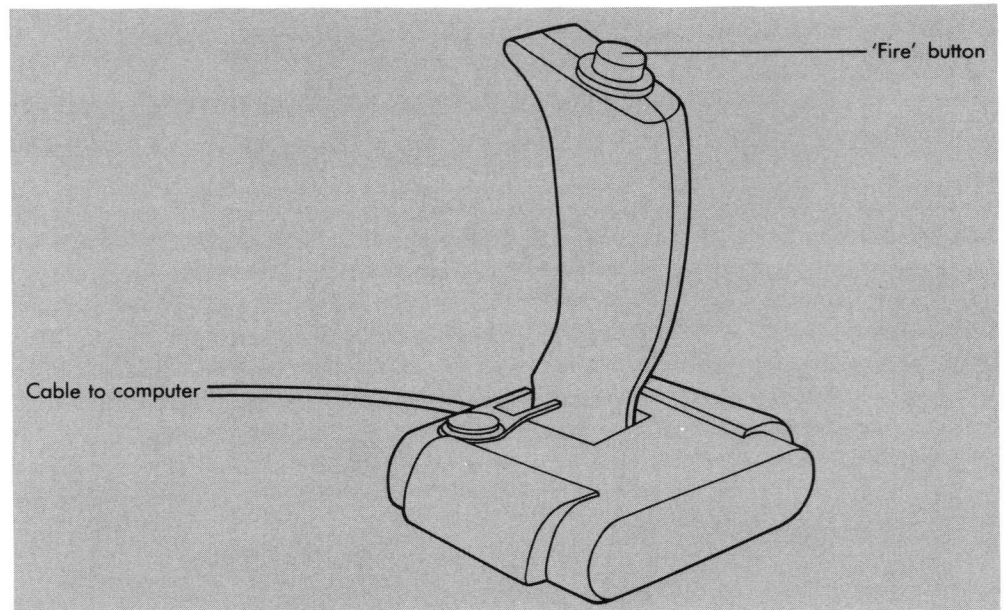

'Fire' button

Cable to computer

Fig. 5.9 A joystick

MOUSE

A **mouse** is now very common with microcomputers (see Fig. 5.10). It is possible to buy graphics software for most micros that will allow the user to draw pictures on the screen using a mouse.

A mouse is a small hand-held input device with a ball fitted underneath. When the mouse is moved, the signal created by the movement of the ball is transmitted to the computer. This controls a pointer on the screen which moves in a direction corresponding to the direction of the mouse.

There are usually 2 or 3 buttons on the mouse. If a button is pressed and held, and the mouse moved, then a line is drawn on the screen. Besides drawing on the screen most *graphics software* offers other facilities, such as:

- different colours;
- solid or dotted lines of different width;
- the ability to 'flood' areas of the screen with colours and patterns;
- text of varying height and in unusual fonts, e.g. medieval writing;
- the ability to define areas of the screen called 'blocks' which can be changed in shape and size and can be copied or moved anywhere on the screen;
- pictures that can be printed or saved on disc.

Some more recent graphics programs allow the user to scan images, which may be photographs or text, onto the screen where they can be changed or enhanced.

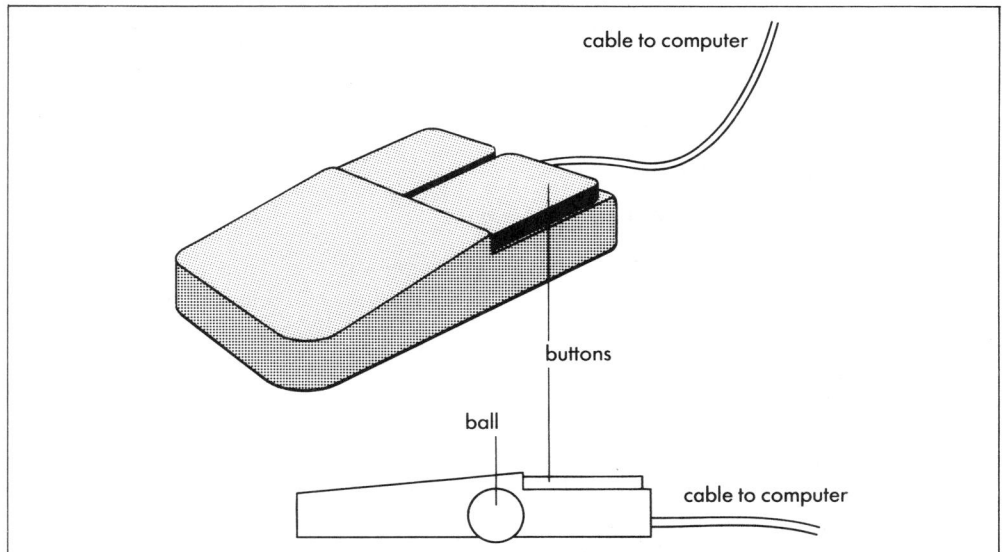

Fig. 5.10 A mouse

There may also be many other features available through pull-down menus and icons.

Pull-down menus are accessed by pointing at them with the mouse. They consist of lists of features which can be *selected* by *pointing* at them *and clicking* a button on the mouse.

Icons are pictures that suggest the feature they represent, e.g. a picture of a floppy disc may give the user the possibility of saving or loading pictures on disc. Icons are quite small and occupy the border of the screen. The user can select the icon by pointing at it and

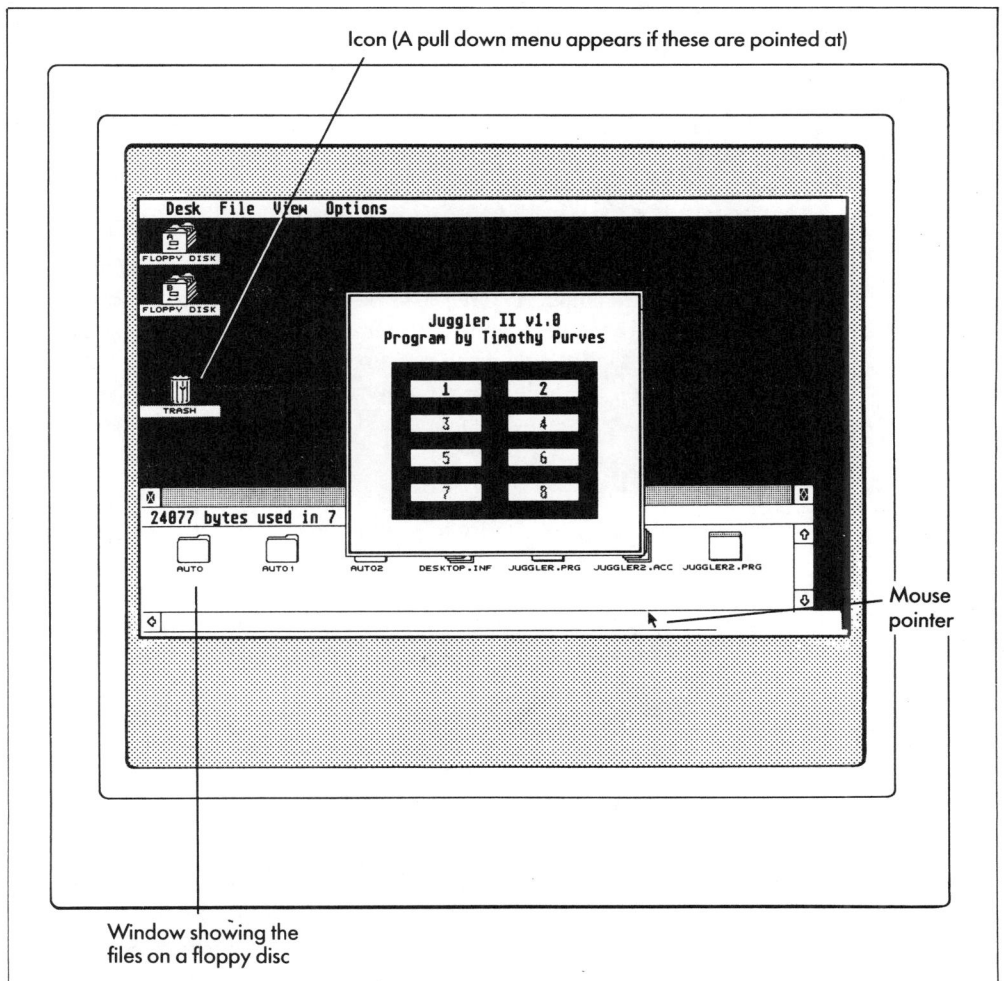

Fig. 5.11 A WIMP screen from the Atari ST

clicking a button on the mouse. Graphics programs can be used for artwork, textile design, CDT, etc.

The mouse has proved to be such a useful, easy-to-use and versatile input device that several computers are now sold with one. In these cases it is often difficult to use the computer *without* a mouse. Instead of entering commands to the computer using text command lines, there is a WIMP user screen (see Fig. 5.11) that allows the user easy access to the facilities of the computer using a mouse. **WIMP** stands for 'Windows, Icons, Mouse, Pointers'.

GRAPHICS PADS

Using a mouse and a graphics program, it is possible to draw on the screen. However, the technique of using a mouse is quite different from drawing with an ordinary pencil. In order to make drawing easier and more natural, a **graphics pad** can be used. This consists of a flat surface containing a touch-sensitive membrane (see Fig. 5.12). When the user presses on the surface using a rigid stylus, the membrane registers the pressure on the surface and a corresponding mark is displayed on the screen. If paper is placed on the surface of the graphics pad, a normal pen or pencil can be used in place of the stylus and the user can draw on the paper and on the screen at the same time. In this way maps can be traced and diagrams and pictures, etc., can be transferred to the graphics program for further enhancement.

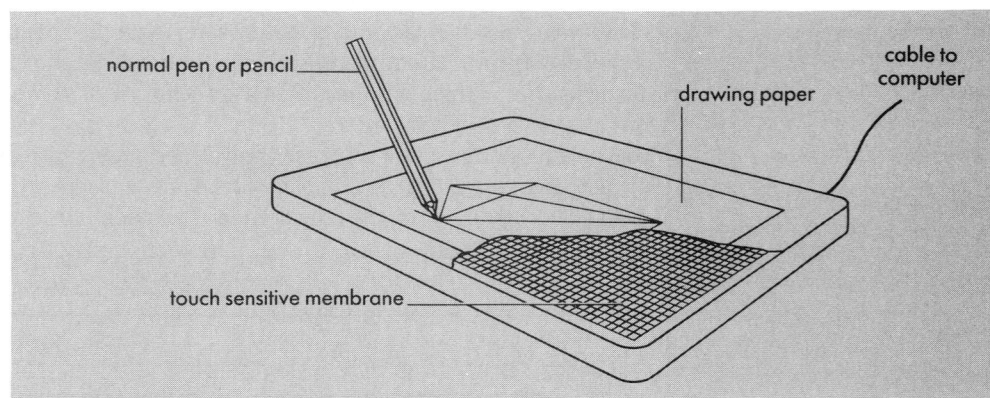

Fig. 5.12 A graphics pad

SCANNERS

Scanners are used to digitise printed text, diagrams and photographs into the memory of the computer. They can be hand-held but are more usually about the size of a desk-top photocopier. Some scanners will scan, print and act as a photocopier! Using the associated software, a digitised representation of the scanned image can be saved onto disc. This can then be loaded into a graphics program or Desk Top Publishing (DTP) program where it can be enhanced and printed as part of a magazine or booklet.

VIDEO DIGITISERS

Video digitisers convert a video signal into a digitised representation in the memory of the computer. They consist of hardware to intercept the video signal and specialised software. Each frame in the video signal is digitised. At the press of a button, or in response to a pre-programmed sequence, the digitised image is saved onto disc. This can be done for a single frame, or a series of frames. Using a video digitiser it is possible to capture a single frame from a video and print it as a picture in a magazine. A series of frames can have graphics or cartoons added using a graphics program. This technique is used to make TV adverts, Pop-video sequences, etc.

SENSORS

Sensors are often attached to micros. There are many types of sensors and they have a wide variety of uses. They can be used to record temperature, humidity, light intensity, etc. A combination of sensors could be used to control a greenhouse, keeping the conditions suitable for optimum plant growth. Sensors usually produce a voltage which must be converted to a digital signal using an Analogue to Digital Converter (ADC). The digital signal is interpreted as a binary number which can be used by the software to monitor or display a graph of the 'sensed' condition.

VALIDATION

All data entered into a computer for processing are validated if at all possible. **Validation** is a check to make sure that all the data to be processed are realistic. Some common validation checks are described below:

66 Common validation checks 99

Table lookup

The input data, for example a bar code, is checked against a table of *all* the bar codes that are used. If it is not in the table, then it is not acceptable.

Range Check

Numbers input are checked to see if they are either too big or too small. For example 021285 is a valid date, but 213488 is not, as 34 is not a valid month. Months must lie in the range 01 to 12.

Check digit

A check digit is an extra digit added to a number. The check digit is calculated in a prescribed way that is known to all users. Every time the number is transcribed, possibly read over the telephone, the check digit is re-calculated. If the correct check digit is *not* obtained from the calculation, then an error has been made and the data must be re-checked. The **International Standard Book Number (ISBN)** contains a check digit in the rightmost position.

ISBN number	0	6 3 1	9 0 0 5 7	8
Weight	10	9 8 7	6 5 4 3 2	1

The check digit has a value that makes the sum of the products of the digits and the weights exactly divisible by 11. This is known as a *'weighted modulus* 11' check digit. It can take the values 0 to 9 and 10 (which is represented by an X). You will find an ISBN number on every published book including this one – look at the back cover!

Totals

The use of totals is best explained using an example. Suppose we are doing the payroll for a company. We may have the following batch of data to process:

Employee number	Name	Hours worked
34532	Jones	34
55234	Patel	37
89686	Singh	29
45378	Hardcastle	27
76859	Stratton	40
301689		167

In the example the employee numbers and the hours worked have been totalled. The total hours worked is a meaningful total. It is the total length of time worked by all these workers. This is known as a **control total**. The total of the employee numbers is meaningless. This is called a **hash total**. However, provided the details for this group of workers is kept together in a batch, neither of these totals will change. If the totals are re-calculated and they are *not* the same, then the details for some of the workers are either missing or have been changed. This example uses only a few workers to illustrate the use of totals. In large companies with many workers, totals help keep track of all their details.

GARBAGE IN, GARBAGE OUT (GIGO)

It is most important to be certain that the data input for processing is correct. When data is captured on a source document, it must be verified to ensure that what is written on the source document is accurately transferred to a computer-readable medium. When data is input for processing, it should be carefully validated to make sure that it is realistic. If incorrect date is input, then the result of any data processing must be wrong . . . **GARBAGE IN, GARBAGE OUT.**

EXAMINATION QUESTIONS

1   Ring **two** of these items which are methods of data collection for input to a computer system

survey forms   bar codes   printers   televisions   **ROM**   *(2)*

(MEG: 1988)

2   Name **two** devices which can be used for input only, describing a suitable use for **each** device.   *(6)*

a) *Device:* Keyboard,
    Use: For typing in data.

b) *Device:* Scanner
    Use: To take information

(WJEC; 1988)

3   A keyboard operator is entering information into a computer system. Information is read from the data capture forms and typed in. Describe a method of verification which would help reduce errors. (5 lines available)

_____

_____

(LEAG; 1988)

4   A computer program is written to process marks out of 100. A validation routine will give an error message when a number is not in the range 0 to 100. After writing the routine the programmer will use **test data**.

a) What is meant by **test data**?

_____

_____

(MEG; 1988)

b) Give **three** different numbers which would be suitable test data.

i) _____   ii) _____   iii) _____

(MEG; 1988)

5   A bar code is shown in Figure 1. Bar codes are being used on an increasing range of items.

a) Where are bar codes often used?

b) Give **two** reasons why bar codes are used.

i) _____

ii) _____

(6)

(WJEC; 1988)

Fig. 1 The different parts of a bar code.

Lloyds Bank

12-4 19 89

6-23

AMBRIDGE BRANCH
13 SIDNEY STREET AMBRIDGE

30-91-56

Pay Andromeda Software Limited

or order

Eighty seven pounds

£87

D LINES

Deborah Lines

Lloyds Bank Plc

꠷58220꠷꠷ 30꠷꠷9꠷56꠷ 52꠷577꠷꠷

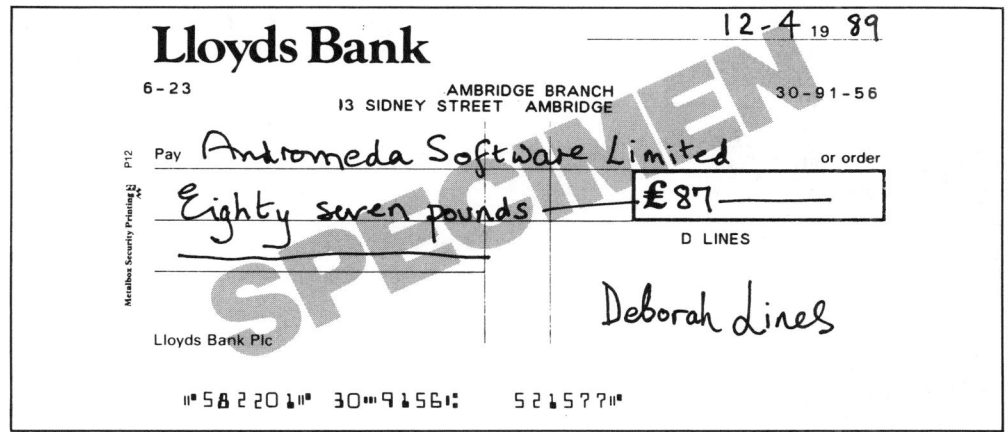

Fig. 2 Example of a cheque.
Acknowledgements: Lloyds Bank plc

6 The most common use of *Magnetic Ink Character Recognition* is in banks.
Give **two** reasons why *MICR* is used in banks. *(4)*

i) _____

ii) _____

(WJEC; 1988)

7 Many computer applications make use of optical methods such as mark sensing and OCR (optical character recognition) to input data.

a) Name an application that uses mark sensing. State what data is input using mark sensing.

Application: _____

Data input: _____

b) Name an application that uses OCR. State what data is input using optical character recognition.

Application: _____

Data input: _____

c) Both of these methods of input have advantages. Give **one** advantage of **each** method of input.

Mark sensing _____

OCR _____

(NEA; 1988)

8 A company records the worker's clocking in and out times on time sheets. There is no night shift. The format for each sheet is: A five digit works number, followed by 5 or 6 pairs of times in 24 hour clock notation (time of arrival followed by time of leaving), each field separated by a slash /. An example is shown below. It has three errors in it.

20023/0900/1703/1706/0859/0885/1659/0901/1702/0859/17084/0900/1330

a) Find the three errors and draw a ring around each.

b) For each error give a validation rule that might be used in the data entry program to detect it.

i) Validation rule for 1st error _____

_____

ii) Validation rule for 2nd error _____

_____

iii) Validation rule for 3rd error _____

_____

(LEAG; 1988)

OUTLINE ANSWERS

1 (Survey forms) (bar codes) printers televisions ROM

2 a) *Device:* Keyboard
    Use: used to enter commands to control the operation of a microcomputer
  b) *Device:* Joystick
    Use: used with computer games to control movement, etc.

3 A method of verification to reduce errors would be:
  a) Type in data.
  b) Type in the same data again.
  c) Compare the data entered at a) with that entered at b).
  d) If they are the same then the data has been entered correctly.
  e) If they are *not* the same the data has been entered incorrectly.

4 a) Test data is used to test if a program processes data as required.
  b) i)   111 ; out of range
     ii)   37   ; in range
     iii) 0   ; a limiting condition

5 a) Bar codes are often used in supermarkets. They are printed on all goods sold and read by laser scanners at the POS terminal.
  b) Bar codes are used because:
    i)   there is no need to price individual items as the prices are kept on the computer.
    ii)   stock control is improved as all sales of an item are known.

6 The branch sort code, account number and cheque number are printed in magnetic ink before giving the cheque to the customer. When the cheque is processed only the amount is typed in.

  The reasons MICR is used are:

  i)   the amount of data to be entered during data preparation is reduced.
  ii)   cheque processing is done much faster.

7 a) *Application:* Marking multiple choice exam papers.
    Data input: For each question, the answer chosen, i.e., one of A to E.
  b) *Application:* Transferring books onto a computer.
    Data input: A page is scanned and the text printed on it is input to the computer.

  c) *Mark sensing:* The candidates sitting the exam do the data preparation.
    OCR: It is faster than typing in the printed text at the keyboard.

8 a) 20023/0900/1703/(1706/0859/0885)/1659/0901/1702/0859/(17084)/0900/1330

  b) i)   Time of arrival should be less than time of leaving.
     ii)   Minutes should be less than 60.
     iii) Times should not be bigger than 23 59.

A STUDENT'S ANSWER WITH EXAMINER'S COMMENTS

QUESTION   The date 24th May 1988 is stored as 240588 on a computer data file.

a)   Give **two** reasons why a date should be coded rather than stored in full

Reason 1   _it takes up less space in memory or on backing storage_

Reason 2   _it is easier to check_

(4)

b)   When the date is entered it is both verified and validated. Explain the terms verification and validation.

Verification   _makes sure the data is correct when it is entered_

Validation   _makes sure the data is correct before it is processed_

(4)

(MEG; 1988)

Examiner's comment:

a)   *Reason 1*   a good answer
     Reason 2   'check' is too vague.
     What are we checking?

b)   'correct' is too vague:
     Verification makes sure the data is *accurately transferred* from the source document to a computer-readable medium, e.g. disc.
     Validation checks that the data is realistic.
     e.g. 241388 is invalid because there is no thirteenth month.

DATA REPRESENTATION AND MANIPULATION

GETTING STARTED

All data stored in memory is represented using **binary logic**. Each **binary digit** or **bit** can be set to 1 or 0. A **byte** is the number of bits used to represent one character. A **word** is the largest amount of memory that can be manipulated by a computer in a single operation and may consist of one or more bytes. The size of the memory is measured in **Kilobytes** or **K**. There are 1024 bytes in a K byte.

Data can be *numbers* or *characters*. We use the **denary** or **base 10** number system, whereas computers use the **binary** or **base 2** number system. **Integers** are whole numbers and can be represented using *8 bit binary numbers with negatives as 2's complements*. It is important to be able to convert binary to or from denary and to add and subtract binary numbers. **Real** numbers are represented as *fixed point* binary numbers or as *floating point* binary numbers.

Other number systems are sometimes used, because binary is difficult for us to remember. **Hexadecimal** or **base 16** is useful because binary is easily converted to or from hexadecimal. **Octal** or **base 8** is useful for the same reason.

Characters are represented using **codes**, e.g. A is 100 0001. Every character in a *character set* must have a different code. Most characters in a character set are meaningful to us, but some are *control characters*. These are used to represent peripheral operations, e.g. pressing the <RETURN> or <ENTER> key.

The most common character code in use is the **ASCII** code.

ESSENTIAL PRINCIPLES

The Immediate Access Store or 'memory' is used by the computer to store programs and data while the programs are edited or run and the data is processed. In this chapter we look particularly at the way data is represented, or coded, when it is stored in memory or on backing storage.

Most computers are digital, electronic machines. Their electronic circuitry is constructed using binary logic. **Binary logic** is two-state logic. This means that only two states are possible. These two states are voltage levels of 5V or 0V. 5V is used to represent the digit 1 and 0V is used to represent 0. The memory of the computer is simply a very large number of 1s and 0s that form patterns that are recognised as programs or data by the computer. The computer is described as being **digital** because everything in its memory is represented using 1s and 0s, i.e. binary digits.

1 MEMORY SIZE

Data is represented using patterns of 1s and 0s. A 1 or a 0 is a **binary digit** or **bit**. Bits are grouped together to form bytes. A **byte** is the number of bits used to represent one character. Bytes vary in size from computer to computer, but it is very common for microcomputers to have 8 bits in a byte. A **word** is the largest amount of memory that can be manipulated by the computer in a single operation. Most microcomputers have 1 byte to a word but larger mainframe computers may have 4 or more bytes to a word.

Memory size is usually measured in words. However, for microcomputers, because a word is one byte, memory size is measured in bytes.

The *units of memory size*, in bytes, are as follows:

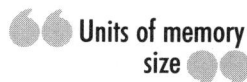

❝Units of memory size❞

- 1 **Kilobyte** or 1K byte   = 1024 bytes   = 2^{10} bytes
- 1 **Megabyte** or 1M byte   = 1024 K bytes = 2^{20} bytes
- 1 **Gigabyte** or 1G byte   = 1024 M bytes = 2^{30} bytes

2 DATA

Data can be *numbers* or *character strings*. Most high level languages for computers require the programmer to distinguish carefully between numbers and characters. For example in BASIC, a commonly used language with microcomputers, character strings must be enclosed in quotes, whereas numbers are not. For example, "34 High Road" is a **character string**; 45.6 is a **number**. Note that numbers can be characters as well as numbers (but not both at the same time!) For example, "23" is a character string, but 23 is a number. The bit patterns in memory can be interpreted only if we know whether they are meant to be numbers or characters, and if we know the codes and conventions being used.

3 DENARY OR BASE 10 NUMBERS

While computers use bit patterns to represent numbers, people use **denary**, ie. **base 10** numbers. Computer number systems are constructed using the same system we use for base 10, so it is useful to analyse our own number system before looking at how the computer represents numbers. By making use of a **place value number system** we can represent any number using only the digits 0, 1, 2, . . ., 9 and no others.
This works as follows:

10^3	10^2	10^1	10^0: base	Available digits are
1000	100	10	1 : place value	0,1,2,3,4,5,6,7,8,9
2	5	7	4 : denary number	

This number is read as two thousand, five hundred and seventy four. We can construct other number systems using this framework.

BINARY OR BASE 2 NUMBERS

We construct binary numbers as follows:

2^7	2^6	2^5	2^4	2^3	2^2	2^1	2^0	: base	available digits
128	64	32	16	8	4	2	1	: place value	0,1
0	1	0	1	1	1	0	1	: binary number	

Binary numbers are constructed using only two digits, 1 and 0, making this system very easy for computers to represent in an electronic two state system. Unfortunately, this system is not so easy for people to use! We must be able to convert binary to denary and vice versa before we can begin to use the same system as the computer.

The above is the basis of a binary number system for computers but it does not cover all the different types of numbers. Using the method above we can represent **positive integer** binary numbers. Integers are whole numbers, e.g. 1, 45, 23, 101, etc. **Positive** numbers are bigger than zero.

We will also need to store other types of numbers, for example, negative numbers and numbers with fractional parts.

CONVERTING BINARY TO DENARY

Look again at the binary number 0101 1101 used in the example above. Each bit has a place value depending on its position in the number. These values are expressed in denary. Where there is a 1 in the binary number we add in the place value; where there is a 0 we do not add in the place value. The calculation is as follows:

128	64	32	16	8	4	2	1	: place value
0	1	0	1	1	1	0	1	: binary number

denary number = 64 + 16 + 8 + 4 + 1
             = 93

CONVERTING DENARY TO BINARY

To convert 86 in denary to a binary number we use the following algorithm:

Write down the denary number;
REPEAT the following until the place value is 1
    IF the denary number is bigger than the place value
        THEN
                subtract the place value from the denary number
                put a 1 in the corresponding position
                write down the new denary number
        ELSE
                put a 0 in the corresponding position;
    IF END;
REPEAT END.

Let's do this for the denary number 86:

number	place value	binary digit
86	128	0
86	64	1
22	32	0
22	16	1
6	8	0
6	4	1
2	2	1
0	1	0

So, denary 86 = binary 0101 0110.

ADDING BINARY NUMBERS

Adding in binary follows the same principles as adding in denary. As an example we will do the following addition:

$$0101\ 1101\ \ +\ \ 0000\ 1110$$

set out like this: $\begin{array}{r} 0\ 1\ 0\ 1\ \ 1\ 1\ 0\ 1 \\ 0\ 0\ 0\ 0\ \ 1\ 1\ 1\ 0\ + \\ \hline 1\ 1\ \ 1 \qquad\qquad \\ \hline 0\ 1\ 1\ 0\ \ 1\ 0\ 1\ 1 \end{array}$ carry

Starting at the left hand side $1 + 0 = 1$, so write down 1.
and $0 + 1 = 1$, so write down 1.

Adding binary numbers

But $1 + 1 = 2$ in denary
and 2 in denary $= 10$ in binary.
In this case we write 0 down and carry 1.
Now adding in the carry, $1 + 1 + 1 = 3$ in denary
and 3 in denary $= 11$ in binary,
so write down 1 and carry 1.
We continue from left to right, as above, to get the answer shown.

It is always a good idea to check your addition in binary by converting the numbers to be added into denary, adding them together and then converting the sum back to binary. You should get the same answer using both methods.

CONVERTING A NEGATIVE DENARY NUMBER TO AN 8 BIT BINARY NUMBER WITH NEGATIVES IN 2'S COMPLEMENT FORM

So far, most of the binary numbers referred to have been 8 bit binary numbers. **8 bit binary representation** uses 8 bits to represent a binary number. It is especially important to note now that we are going to look at the way in which computers represent **negative binary numbers** using **2's complementation**.
2's complementation is best explained using an example:
Suppose we want to convert the denary number -45 into 8 bit binary 2's complement representation. We proceed as follows:

$$\begin{array}{lll} 45 \text{ in denary} = & 0010\ 1101 & \text{in binary} \\ \text{reverse bits} & 1101\ 0010 & \\ \text{add 1} & \qquad\quad 1\ + & \\ \hline -45 \text{ in binary} = & 1101\ 0011 & \end{array}$$

This seems a rather meaningless exercise at first but, as we shall see, it is a very effective way of expressing negative binary numbers.

CONVERTING AN 8 BIT BINARY NUMBER WITH NEGATIVES IN 2'S COMPLEMENT FORM TO A NEGATIVE DENARY NUMBER

As an example, we will convert 1101 0011 to denary, our answer to the above conversion from denary, to illustrate this process. The answer should, of course, be -45!

-128	64	32	16	8	4	2	1	:	place value
1	1	0	1	0	0	1	1	:	binary number

Notice the leftmost bit now has a place value of -128. Using this method, i.e. 8 bit binary representation with negatives in 2's complement form, we have:

$$\begin{aligned} 1101\ 0011 \text{ in binary} &= -128 + 64 + 16 + 2 + 1 \\ &= -45, \text{ as required.} \end{aligned}$$

SUBTRACTION USING ADDITION

Suppose we wish to do the subtraction $63 - 45$.
Now $63 - 45 = 63 + -45$ so we can do the subtraction by addition. This is useful for computers where extra circuitry costs money. It is possible to do all subtraction using the circuits that must be provided for addition.

Let's see how this works:

denary	:	8 bit binary with negatives in 2's complement form
63	:	0011 1111
−45 +	:	1101 0011 +
	:	1 0001 0010
18	:	0001 0010

Notice that the answer to the addition in binary has 9 bits. Since only 8 bits are available, the leftmost bit is 'lost'. This is fortunate as otherwise the answer would be wrong!

SOME INTERESTING POINTS ABOUT 8 BIT BINARY NUMBERS WITH NEGATIVES IN 2'S COMPLEMENT FORM

Positive numbers always have leading 0s at the left hand side, whereas negative numbers always have leading 1s. In particular the leftmost bit in a positive number is 0 and in a negative number is 1.

We can think of the leftmost bit as a **sign** bit; if it is 0 the number is positive, if it is 1 the number is negative. For example:

denary	8 bit binary with negatives in 2's complement form	comments
	sign bit	
23	0 001 0111	
−5	1 111 1011	
127	0 111 1111	largest positive number
1	0 000 0001	smallest positive number
−1	1 111 1111	largest negative number
−128	1 000 0000	smallest negative number

As we can see from the above table the range of numbers that can be represented in 8 bits with negatives as 2's complements is from −128 to 127.

5 > REAL NUMBERS

So far we have looked at ways of representing **integers**, that is, positive and negative whole numbers, e.g. 1, −45, 127, −5, etc. However, not *all* numbers are integers and we will need to develop some way of representing all the different possible numbers. We call all numbers **real numbers**. Integers are just one type of real number. Computers usually deal with integers and real numbers in different ways and it is not uncommon for programming languages, etc. to distinguish between them.

We will now look briefly at some ways of representing real numbers.

FIXED POINT BINARY FRACTIONS

With *fixed point binary fractions* we extend the binary number system to include a decimal point and numbers to the right of it, in the same way as we do with the denary system.

For example, a fixed point binary fraction with 8 bits for the integer part, to the left of the decimal point, and 4 bits for the fractional part, to the right of the decimal point, would look like this:

2^7	2^6	2^5	2^4	2^3	2^2	2^1	2^0	.	2^{-1}	2^{-2}	2^{-3}	2^{-4}	: base
−128	64	32	16	8	4	2	1	.	½	¼	⅛	1/16	: place value
0	1	0	1	1	1	0	1	.	1	0	1	0	: binary number

So 0101 1101. 1010 in binary = 93⅝
= 93.625 in denary

When fixed point numbers are represented in the computer, the decimal point is not stored. The computer remembers where the point is located and treats the number as if it were present. Using this notation, we can store numbers in the range:

1000 0000. 0000	to	0111 1111.1111 in binary
−128.0	to	127 15/16 = 127.9375 in denary

FLOATING POINT BINARY FRACTIONS

Floating point numbers are represented using a **mantissa** and an **exponent**. An example will illustrate this:

$$34 \text{ in denary} = 100\ 010 \text{ in binary}$$
$$= 0.100\ 0100 \times 0110 \text{ in floating point form}$$

> **The floating point form of a binary number**

0110 is the **exponent**.
0110 in binary = 6 in denary.
If the decimal point in the **mantissa**, i.e. 0.100 0100,
is moved 6 places to the right we get   0100 010.0
which is the original binary number, i.e.   100 010

As before, the computer does not store the decimal point, nor does it store the '×'. It simply remembers where they are and takes them into account in any calculations.

Using this notation, we can store numbers in the range:

1.000 0000 × 0111	to	0.111 1111 × 0111	in floating point form
−1000 0000.	to	0111 1111.	in binary
−128	to	127	in denary

Floating point notation is often used when a number is too large to realistically display all the digits in it. For example, 6,000,000,000,000,000 could be shown as 6 E15, where the 'E' stands for exponent. This more compact notation is useful for calculator displays where the number of possible digits is likely to be twelve or less. It is occasionally adopted by BASIC interpreters for screen displays involving very large numbers.

6 ▷ HEXADECIMAL OR BASE 16

Computers store numbers using the binary number system. Unfortunately, binary numbers are hard for us to remember and when we look at them we do not always get an impression of their relative size. When copying binary numbers it is easy to make mistakes!

For these reasons, other number systems are often used instead of binary. The choice of base number is determined by how easy it is to convert *to* and *from* binary. The most important of these other number bases is **hexadecimal** or **base 16**. This number system is constructed as follows:

> **The hexadecimal or base 16 number system**

16^3	16^2	16^1	16^0	: base	available digits:
4096	256	16	1	: place value	0,1,2,3,...9,A,B,C,D,E
2	8	A	3	: hexadecimal number	

In base 16 we should use the single digits 0,1,2,3,4,5,6,7,8,9,10,11,12,13,14,15. However, 10,11,12,13,14,15 expressed in decimal all contain two digits. To avoid this problem we use the digits A,B,C,D,E,F to represent the single digits 10,11,12,13,14,15 respectively.

CONVERTING HEXADECIMAL TO BINARY AND VICE VERSA

Any hexadecimal digit can be represented as four binary bits and four binary bits, are always equivalent to a hexadecimal digit. For example:

binary number	:	hexadecimal digit		binary number	:	hexadecimal digit
0000	:	0		1000	:	8
0001	:	1		1001	:	9
0010	:	2		1010	:	A
0011	:	3		1011	:	B
0100	:	4		1100	:	C
0101	:	5		1101	:	D
0110	:	6		1110	:	E
0111	:	7		1111	:	F

To convert *hexadecimal to binary* we change each hexadecimal digit to four binary bits, e.g. A43E = 1010 0100 0011 1110.

To convert *binary to hexadecimal* we divide the bits into groups of four, putting in leading 0s on the left hand side, where necessary, and convert each group to a hexadecimal digit, as follows:

10111 in binary = 0001 0111
= 17 in hexadecimal

If we have to convert *hexadecimal to denary* it is easiest to first convert the hexadecimal to binary and then convert the binary to denary as we did earlier in this chapter.

To convert *denary to hexadecimal*, first convert the denary to binary then convert the binary to hexadecimal.

7 ▷ OCTAL OR BASE 8

Another number system commonly used with computers is **octal** or **base 8**. Again, the choice of base number is determined by how easy it is to convert to and from binary. The octal number system is constructed as follows:

8^3	8^2	8^1	8^0	: base	available digits:
512	64	8	1	: place value	$0,1,2,3,\ldots,7$
5	7	3	2	: octal number	

Notice that in base 8 we only use the digits 0,1,2,3,4,5,6 and 7.

CONVERTING OCTAL TO BINARY AND VICE VERSA

Any octal digit can be represented as three binary bits, and three binary bits are always equivalent to an octal digit. For example:

binary number	:	octal digit
000	:	0
001	:	1
010	:	2
011	:	3
100	:	4
101	:	5
110	:	6
111	:	7

To convert *octal to binary* we change each octal digit to three binary bits, for example 463 = 100 110 011.

To convert *binary to octal* we divide the bits into groups of three, putting in leading 0s where necessary, and convert each group to an octal digit, as follows:

10111 in binary = 010 111
= 27 in octal

If we have to convert *octal to denary* it is easiest to first convert the octal to binary and then convert the binary to denary as we did earlier in this chapter.

To convert *denary to octal*, first convert the denary to binary then convert the binary to octal.

8 ▷ CHARACTER STRINGS

Character strings are lists of characters, e.g. 'Albert Greenhill' is a character string containing 16 characters include the space.

Characters are represented using codes. These codes are simply bit patterns that we agree to interpret as a particular character. They are arbitrary, although they may be quite well organised. There is no particular reason why a bit pattern should represent one character rather than another. For this reason there are several different codes used to represent characters. They have been developed by different manufacturers of computers and others for their own purposes.

9 > ASCII

Part of the ASCII Code

ASCII (American Standard Code for Information Interchange) is the most common code in use for representing characters. Part of this code is shown in the table below:

Character	:	Binary code	Character	:	Binary code
Space	:	010 0000	G	:	100 0111
0	:	011 0000	H	:	100 1000
1	:	011 0001	I	:	100 1001
2	:	011 0010	J	:	100 1010
3	:	011 0011	K	:	100 1011
4	:	011 0100	L	:	100 1100
5	:	011 0101	M	:	100 1101
6	:	011 0110	N	:	100 1110
7	:	011 0111	O	:	100 1111
8	:	011 1000	P	:	101 0000
9	:	011 1001	Q	:	101 0001
+	:	010 1011	R	:	101 0010
−	:	010 1101	S	:	101 0011
=	:	011 1101	T	:	101 0100
A	:	100 0001	U	:	101 0101
B	:	100 0010	V	:	101 0110
C	:	100 0011	W	:	101 0111
D	:	100 0100	X	:	101 1000
E	:	100 0101	Y	:	101 1001
F	:	100 0110	Z	:	101 1010

Notice that although ASCII code is in ascending binary number order, the code for the character 3 is not the binary number for three.

10 > CONTROL CHARACTERS

Control characters are not usually displayed or printed. They are not characters that are meaningful to most people as part of a routine communication. When entered at the keyboard or sent to a peripheral they are treated as a signal to begin or end some operation. For example, there is a control code associated with pressing the <ENTER> or <RETURN> key on the keyboard; there are others that tell the printer to turn on and off features such as bold printing and underlining. Control characters are part of the character set and must have different codes from other characters.

THE SIZE OF THE CHARACTER SET

Each different character must have a different binary code associated with it. Hence the number of bits used determines the number of characters it is possible to code. The **character set** is all the characters it is possible to represent using the code. The **size** of the character set is the number of different characters represented. This cannot be more than the maximum number of different codes. The relationship between the number of bits and the maximum size of the character set is shown in the table below:

The relation between the number of bits and the maximum size of the character set

Number of bits	different codes	maximum size of the character set
1	0 1	$2 = 2^1$
2	00 01 10 11	$4 = 2^2$
3	000 001 010 011 100 101 110 111	$8 = 2^3$
4	0000 0100 1000 1100 0001 0101 1001 1101 0010 0110 1010 1110 0011 0111 1011 1111	$16 = 2^4$
5	....	$32 = 2^5$
6	....	$64 = 2^6$
7	....	$128 = 2^7$
8	....	$256 = 2^8$
x	....	2^x

Since ASCII is a 7 bit code, the maximum number of possible characters is 128, more than enough for most purposes!

EXAMINATION QUESTIONS

MULTIPLE CHOICE QUESTION

1 For **each** of these items of data, ring its type.

DATA	TYPE OF DATA	
a town name, e.g. Banbury	numeric	string
the number of words in a sentence, e.g. 11	numeric	string
a car registration number, e.g. B353AXB	numeric	string

(3)

(MEG; 1988)

SHORT STRUCTURED QUESTIONS

2 Write the number 6 in binary.

_____ *(1)*

(MEG; 1988)

3 Using 8-bit two's complement notation, convert the numbers 35 and −35 into binary. Show all your working.

Working   Answers

35 = _____

(2)

−35 = _____

(2)

(SEG; 1988)

4 a) Two's complement notation has been used to represent an integer in binary. It is 01010011. What is this as a base 10 number? Show the method used to work out the answer. (*3 lines available*)

b) 73 is 01001001 in binary two's complement notation. What is −73 in this notation? (*5 lines available*)

c) 01001001 also represents the letter 'I' in the character set used by many microcomputers. What else could this bit pattern represent?

_____

_____

(LEAG; 1988)

5 What is a group of eight bits called?_____

(1)

(SEG; 1988)

6 Integer overflow can happen whilst the CPU is executing an arithmetic instruction. Show how by working through a sum. Label the point where the integer overflow would occur. (Your sum may be in binary or in ordinary base 10 numbers).

_____

_____

(LEAG; 1988)

7 A coding scheme for the numbers 0 to 9 and the characters A to Z has the following bit pattern:

		Bit pattern
0	——————————————	0 0 0 0 0 0 0 0
1	——————————————	0 0 0 0 0 0 0 1
2	——————————————	0 0 0 0 0 0 1 0
9	——————————————	0 0 0 0 1 0 0 1
A	——————————————	0 1 0 0 0 0 0 1
B	——————————————	0 1 0 0 0 0 1 0
Z	——————————————	0 1 0 1 1 0 1 0

a) Write down the bit pattern for
   i) the number 3 ————————————————————————
   ii) the character C ————————————————————————

b) Modern computer keyboards allow a wider range of characters than those shown above.
   Suggest **three** types of characters that are missing from the above coding scheme.
   i) ————————————————————————————————
   ii) ————————————————————————————————
   iii) ————————————————————————————————

(7)
(WJEC; 1988)

O U T L I N E   A N S W E R S

1 Banbury is a *string*;
11 is a number;
B353AXB is a string.

2 110

3

−128	64	32	16	8	4	2	1	place value
0	0	1	0	0	0	1	1	= 35 in denary
1	1	0	1	1	1	0	0	reverse bits
							1	add 1
1	1	0	1	1	1	0	1	= −35 in denary

4

a)

−128	64	32	16	8	4	2	1	place value
0	1	0	1	0	0	1	1	

64 + 16 + 2 + 1 = 83 in base 10

b)   73 (base 10) = 0100 1001 (base 2)
                      1011 0110   reverse bits
                             1   add 1
   −73 (base 10) = 1011 0111

c) Bit patterns can be one of:
   number
   character
   machine code instruction
   Since 0100 1001 could be 73 or 'I', only the possibility of a machine   code instruction   is left.

5 A byte.

6   Supposing integers are held using 8 bits and negatives are represented as two's complements, the maximum number that can be held is:

0111 1111 in binary = 127 in base 10

If the result of an addition is bigger than this maximum value we have integer overflow.

e.g.   127   = 0111 1111
e.g.   127 + (base 10) = 0111 1111 + (binary)
        254   1111 1110

    integer overflow has occurred here

1111 1110$_2$ is the number -2 in base 10 not 254 as it should be.

7   a)   i) 0000 0011
             ii) 0100 0011

    b)   i)   Control characters, e.g. <RETURN> or <ENTER>, <TAB>
             ii) Lower case letters, e.g. a, b, c
             iii) special characters, e.g. £, #, <, %.

A STUDENT'S ANSWER WITH EXAMINER'S COMMENTS

QUESTION   A computer uses 8 bits to represent integers in two's complement form.

a) Fill in the bit pattern for the highest positive number the computer can hold.

1	1	1	1	1	1	1	1

b) What is the denary value of this number?

    255

(2)
(MEG; 1988)

Examiner's comment

The answers to parts a) and b) are both wrong.
If 1111 1111 was a binary number in a system that did not have negatives, the answers would be correct.
But , using 'two's complement form' means negatives are represented, so the leftmost bit is the sign bit and has the value -128. The correct answers are:
a) 0111 1111
b) 127

PROGRAMMING LANGUAGES

GETTING STARTED

A **program** tells a computer what to do. It is written in a high level language, such as BASIC, or a low level language, such as assembly language. Programs must be converted to machine code before they are run, as this is the only language the computer will execute.

Machine code is not easy for writing programs. It consists of binary codes.

Assembly language is closer to English than machine code, but it is still a very inaccessible language. Assembly languages must be translated to machine code using an **assembler** before they can be run.

Assembly and machine code programs are **machine orientated**, i.e. they can only be run on the type of computer they were designed for. Consequently, they are not **portable**, that is, they cannot be run on several different computers.

Assembly language is a **low level language** because it is very close to the language of the computer. Programmers do not use machine code or assembly language unless there is no other choice.

High level languages are closer to English than to machine code. They are designed to be easy to understand and write. They are **problem orientated**, that is they provide a range of programming tools that are helpful in solving particular types of problem. Examples of high level languages are BASIC, PASCAL, COBOL, FORTRAN and LOGO.

High level language programs must be translated to machine code before they can be run. **Interpreters** convert one line at a time to machine code and execute it while the program is being run. **Compilers** translate the whole high level language program to machine code. When the program is executed it is the machine code version which is run. Programs written in interpreted languages are quickly developed and tested, but they run slowly. In contrast, programs in compiled languages are relatively slow to develop, but run much faster.

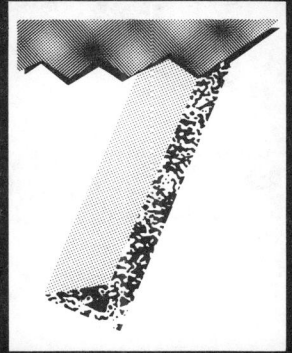

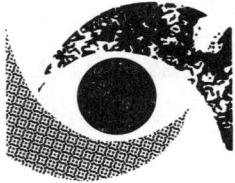

ESSENTIAL PRINCIPLES

1 WHAT IS A PROGRAM?

A **program** is a list of instructions to the computer. The program will be written in a computer language. The computer always starts at the beginning of the program and executes, or runs, the instructions one at a time. It begins at the top of the list and works down the list, one instruction at a time, unless told otherwise.

When a computer executes an instruction, it is always in machine code. Programs can, however, be written in other languages and *converted* into machine code before running on a computer. This chapter looks at machine code, assembly language and high level languages, such as BASIC and PASCAL.

2 MACHINE CODE AND ASSEMBLY LANGUAGE

Machine code is the language that computers use. Every different type of computer will have its own machine code. Machine code instructions are written as binary codes. This is a typical machine code instruction:

operation code	data or address
0000	0000 0101

NB. Another name for an operation code is an *operand*.

Unless we knew that 0000 0000 0101 was a machine code instruction, we might easily mistake it for a character code or a number in binary. Even so, it is not immediately obvious what is meant! Machine code instructions are understood by computers, but are very difficult for most people to remember and use. For this reason it is very unlikely that a programmer would write a computer program in machine code.

To make programming at this level easier, **low level languages**, or **assembly languages**, have been developed. Assembly language is slightly easier to understand than machine code. Every machine code instruction has a single corresponding assembly language instruction. The above machine code instruction could be written like this:

> *Changing machine code into assembler language*

mnemonic	data or address
add	5

This is easier to understand! However, it is not clear what we are to add, or what the 5 stands for.

In a typical machine code, or the corresponding assembly language, all arithmetic is done using an **accumulator** – a special register located in the Arithmetic and Logic Unit (ALU), within the Central Processing Unit (CPU). A **register** is a small memory located outside the Immediate Access Store (IAS) that can do more than simply store data. In the case of the accumulator, arithmetic and logic operations are possible. All addition, subtraction, etc. is done using the accumulator. Other registers are the Program Counter and the Current Instruction Register (see below).

However, the instruction 'add 5' is not telling us to add 5 into the accumulator, as might be expected. It is instructing the computer to add the data stored in memory address 5 into the accumulator.

Every memory location in the IAS has an address. The **memory address** directs the computer to the location of the stored data. The data can then be taken from the address and added into the accumulator. The layout of the memory of a computer can be shown in a **memory map**. This is a plan of the memory, giving the addresses where programs and data will be stored.

To help understand the idea of a memory address and the data stored at it, think of a memory address as the address of a house. The data stored in the memory address are the people who live in the house. A memory map is a street plan which has the addresses of the houses on it.

An example should help to make these ideas clearer. The machine code used is simplified to illustrate the principles of machine code programming, rather than to demonstrate an actual machine code. The equivalent assembly code is also shown. Again, this is not an actual assembly language.

EXAMPLE: MACHINE CODE AND ASSEMBLER PROGRAM

Some of the program instructions available in our example machine code and assembly language are as follows:

machine code	assembly language	
operation code	mnemonic	meaning
0000	add	add the data stored at the address given to the contents of the accumulator leaving the result in the accumulator
0001	sub	subtract the data stored at the address given from the contents of the accumulator leaving the result in the accumulator
0010	mult	multiply the data stored at the address given by the contents of the accumulator leaving the result in the accumulator
0011	div	divide the data stored at the address given into the contents of the accumulator leaving the result in the accumulator
0100	lda	load the data stored at the address given into the accumulator
0101	sta	store the data in the accumulator at the address given
0110	in	input data into the accumulator
0111	out	output data from the accumulator
1000	halt	halt program execution

Each instruction has the following format:

Machine code

operation code	address

e.g.   0010 0000 0111

Assembly language

mnemonic	address

e.g.   mult 7

Running a short program

We now look at how a short program runs. The program is given in both assembly and machine code. The machine code program is shown as it might appear in the memory of the computer and the address of each memory location is shown. Several locations are shown in memory after the program has been ended by a halt instruction. These addresses contain data.

memory address	data and instructions stored in memory				
	machine code			assembly language	
	operation code	address		mnemonic	address
0001	0100	0000	1000	lda	8
0010	0000	0000	0111	add	7
0011	0001	0000	0110	sub	6
0100	0101	0000	1000	sta	8
0101	1000	0000	0000	halt	
0110	0000	0000	0011		
0111	0000	0101	0101		
1000	0000	0001	0010		
1001	0000	0001	0010		

Executing the program instructions

The program instructions are executed, starting at the beginning with the first instruction.

The memory address of the first instruction is held in the **Program Counter (PC)**. This instruction is *fetched* from memory and stored in the **Current Instruction Register (CIR)**. One is added to the PC so that it points to the next instruction. The instruction in the CIR is now *executed* or run. When the current instruction has been executed the next instruction is fetched from the memory address contained in the PC, which is in turn executed, and so on. This is the *fetch/execute cycle*.

When the example program instructions are executed they have the following effect:

lda 8   This loads the data stored at address 8 (1000 in binary) into the accumulator. The accumulator now contains   0000 0001 0010

add 7   The data stored at address 7 (0111 in binary) is added to the data in the accumulator and the result is stored in the accumulator. This is shown below:

data in accumulator before 'add 7'	0000 0001 0010
data from address 7 (0111 in binary)	0000 0101 0101 +
data in accumulator after 'add 7'	0000 0110 0111

sub 6   The data stored at address 6 (0110) is subtracted from the accumulator and the result is stored in the accumulator. Subtraction is done by adding the corresponding negative number in two's complement form.

The equivalent base 10 calculation is $103 - 3$
$$= 103 + -3$$
$$= 100$$

This is done as follows;

data in address 6	0000 0000 0011
two's complement of data in address 6	1111 1111 1101
data in accumulator before 'sub 6'	0000 0110 0111 +
result of addition	1 0000 0110 0100

Notice that we have gained an extra bit on the left hand side. This is overflow which is lost.

data in accumulator after 'sub 6'	0000 0110 0100

sta 8   The contents of the accumulator are left untouched but they are stored in address 8 (1000), as follows:

data stored at address 8 before 'sta 8'	0000 0001 0010
data stored at address 8 after 'sta 8'	0000 0110 0100

halt   This instruction brings the program to an end.

The program instructions are stored in the memory starting at address 0001 and ending at address 0101 with the halt instruction. The numbers involved in the calculation are also stored in the memory, after the program, starting at address 0110. The halt instruction must be present to separate the program instructions and the data.

This is a short program to add two numbers together and subtract a third number from the result. The numbers are already stored in the memory and the result is returned to the memory. This is a rather lengthy and complex process just to do an addition and a subtraction.

A further difficulty is that the program is not **relocatable in memory**, i.e. it has to be placed in a *particular* location in the memory. If it was placed elsewhere, the address of all the program instructions and any data used in the program might change and consequently the program would have to be changed. This problem particularly affects 'jump' instructions.

Assembly programs can usually be made relocatable in memory by the use of labels. A **label** takes the place of an address. If a program contained the instruction 'jump 20', which means go to the instruction at address 20, then if the program was moved in memory, the address and the 'jump' instruction would be changed. This is avoided by using a label. For example:

```
    jump end
      "
      "
 end. halt
```

Assembly programs that use labels, rather than addresses, in 'jump' instructions are relocatable in memory, whereas machine code programs, which do not have this feature, are not relocatable in memory.

Programs written in assembly language must be translated into machine code before they can be executed. **Assemblers** convert assembly languages to machine code. They work in the same way as compilers (see below) except that the source code is written in an assembly language rather than a high level language.

Assembly language and machine code programs are **machine orientated**, that is, they will not run on any computer other than the particular make they are designed for. Every computer runs a machine code, but they do not all run the *same* machine code. This means that a machine code or assembly language program cannot be run on *all* computers. When programs can be run on any computer, we say that they are **portable** from one computer to another. Assembly language and machine code programs are not portable between different makes of computer.

Because machine code and assembly languages are difficult to understand, may not be relocatable in memory and are not portable, they will not be used unless there are good reasons to do so. Assembly language is always used in preference to machine code unless it is unavoidable. Programs in assembler language or machine code are usually small compared to other languages. They will be needed if a program is likely to be too big to fit into the amount of RAM memory available. Also, machine code runs *very quickly* and is therefore used if a program must be fast.

For these reasons, games programs for home microcomputers are often in machine code, as there is a need to write fast programs to run on computers with relatively small memories. Competition between software writers to produce more varied games encourages the introduction of more and better graphics (see Fig. 7.1) which use up more memory. Similarly, they attempt to cram programs with more and more facilities in the same amount of memory. Machine code programs give software writers a competitive edge in these circumstances.

F16 Combat Pilot, by Digital Integration

Fig. 7.1 A graphics screen from a computer game

Some industrial machine tools, robots and modern domestic appliances, such as washing machines, are microprocessor-controlled devices. A **microprocessor** is a 'computer on a chip' (see Fig. 7.2), i.e. a computer consisting of a CPU and very small amounts of RAM and ROM memory built onto a single silicon chip. A machine code program, either stored in ROM or loaded into RAM, controls the device when it is used.

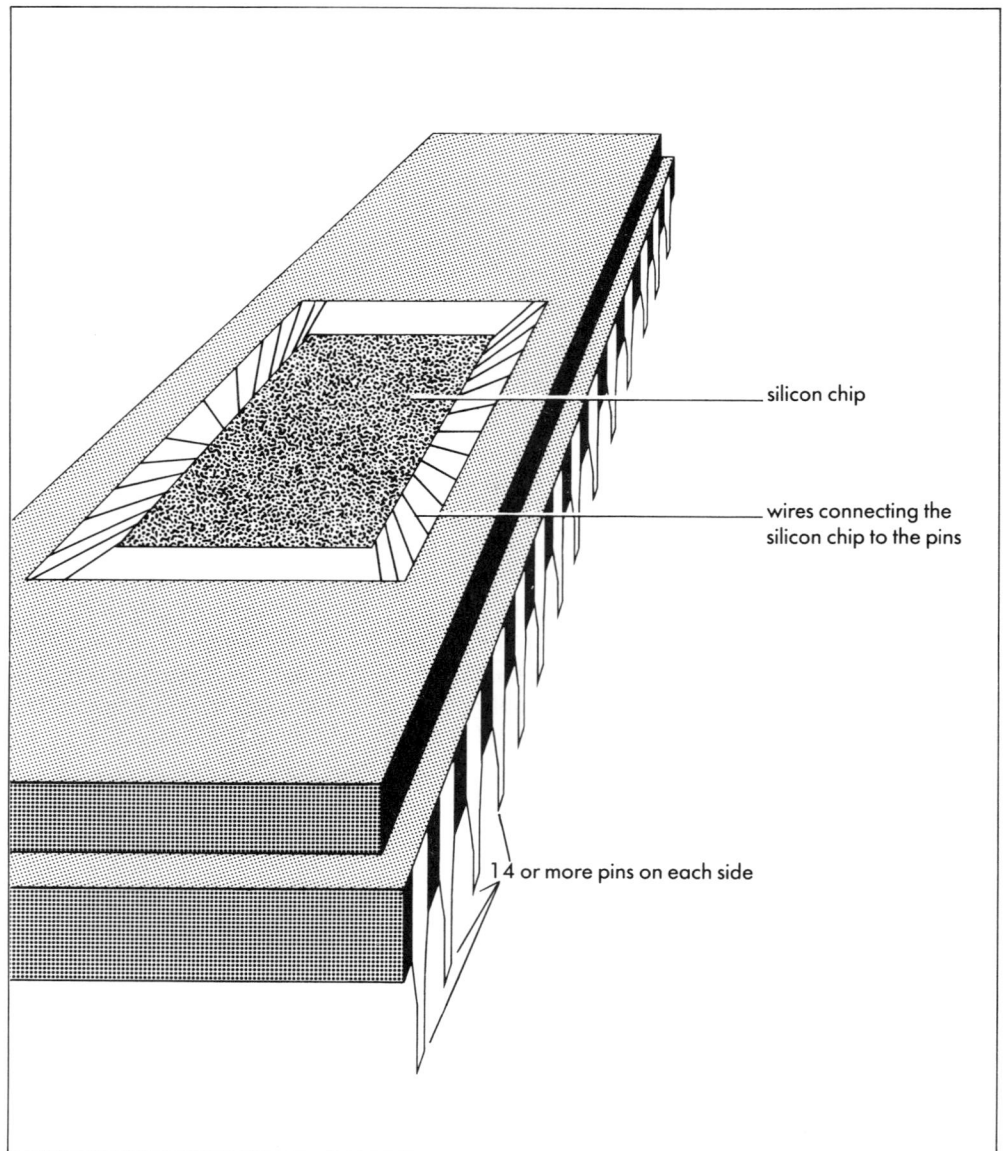

- silicon chip

- wires connecting the
  silicon chip to the pins

14 or more pins on each side

Fig. 7.2 A microprocessor

---

3 > **HIGH LEVEL
      LANGUAGES**

**Advantages of high
level languages**

Machine code and assembly languages are difficult to understand and write. They are machine orientated, not relocatable in memory, and not portable from computer to computer. High level languages attempt to overcome these difficulties. Programs in **high level languages** are easier to understand, as the program instructions are closer to English than low level languages.

High level language programs are **problem orientated**, that is, they relate more to the type of problem being solved than to a particular computer. A high level language program written for one computer may run on another computer with only minor alterations, provided they are running the same operating system.

The following are some of the wide variety of high level programming languages available. A short example program is given for each language, to give some idea of what the language 'looks like'. No attempt is made to demonstrate all the facilities available in each language.

BASIC: Beginners All-purpose Symbolic Instruction Code

A language designed to be easy to learn. It is widely used in education and is often the first programming language learnt. BASIC is almost always the main language supplied and used with home microcomputers.

Because of its popularity and wide availability, BASIC has been extended since its introduction, so that it is now a powerful, flexible language used for a wide variety of commercial and scientific applications.

❝A BASIC program❞

```
10   REM *************** Sample BASIC program ***************
20   REM This is a Menu driven program to calculate areas
30   PRINT "Menu"
40   PRINT "A. Area of Rectangle"
50   PRINT "B. Area of Circle"
55   PRINT "C. Finish"
60   PRINT "Please input your option choice (A, B or C)"
70   INPUT A$
80   IF A$ = "A" THEN GOTO 110
90   IF A$ = "B" THEN GOTO 180
95   IF A$ = "C" THEN GOTO 999
100  GOTO 30
110  REM ******** Calculate the area of a Rectangle *********
120  PRINT "Input the length of the rectangle"
130  INPUT L
140  PRINT "Input the breadth"
150  INPUT B
160  PRINT "The area of the rectangle is"; L*B
170  GOTO 30
180  REM ********* Calculate the area of a Circle *********
190  PRINT "Input the radius of the circle"
200  INPUT R
210  PRINT "The area of the circle is"; 3.14*R*R
220  GOTO 30
999  END
```

Fig. 7.3 Blaise Pascal, the French mathematician

PASCAL: (Named after the French mathematician Blaise Pascal)

Pascal is often the second language learnt by students of computing. It is used extensively in colleges, universities, scientific computing and commerce. Pascal is available for most microcomputers and almost all mainframes.

Pascal is a *structured* language. It was designed as a teaching language to encourage good program design and a clear structure. Procedures are used to make programs easier to write, read and understand. Any variables used must have their type declared before they are referred to. There are a range of facilities that make programming easier and more convenient.

❝A PASCAL program❞

```
program swap (input, output);
(* sample pascal program: two numbers are input in order,*)
(* their order swapped and then they are printed         *)
var first, second : integer;
(* ************************************************** *)
procedure numbersin;
begin
     write ('This program inputs two integers');
     writeln ('and prints them in reverse order');
     writeln ('Input the first number');
     readln (first);
     writeln ('Input the second number');
     readln (second);
end;
(* ************************************************** *)
procedure switch;
var temporary : integer;
begin
     temporary := first;
     first := second;
     second := temporary;
end;
(* ************************************************** *)
procedure printout;
begin
     write ('In reverse order the numbers input are');
     writeln (first, 'and', second);
end;
(* ************************************************** *)
(* the main program which calls the procedures       *)
begin
     numbersin;
     switch;
     printout;
end.
```

COBOL : COmmon Business Orientated Language

Is used widely in data processing applications throughout business and commerce. It is particularly useful in data processing because files, records and fields are easily defined and manipulated. COBOL instructions read very like English in comparison with other languages.

COBOL has been the most popular commercial language for at least twenty years. It has been regularly updated with extra features, so that it can cope with the changes in computer technology that have taken place during that time. The death of COBOL is frequently predicted by the computer press. However, it has survived, probably because of its enormous popularity! COBOL is available for all mainframes and the more powerful personal microcomputers.

❝❝ A COBOL program ❞❞

```
IDENTIFICATION DIVISION.
PROGRAM-ID. RESULTS.
PURPOSE. PRINTS OUT GCSE RESULTS.
PROGRAMMER. A. HOULBROOKE.

ENVIRONMENT DIVISION.
INPUT-OUTPUT SECTION.
FILE-CONTROL.
SELECT RESULT-FILE
ASSIGN DK ACCESS DYNAMIC ORGANISATION INDEXED.
SELECT PRINT-FILE
ASSIGN PROUT.

DATA  DIVISION.
FILE  SECTION.
FD    RESULT-FILE
      BLOCK 12 RECORDS
      DATA RECORD RESULT-DETAILS
      LABEL RECORD STANDARD.

01    RESULT-DETAILS.
      03 ID-NO           PIC   X(5).
      03 NAME            PIC   X(50).
      03 SYLLABUS-CODE   PIC   999.
      03 EXAM-GRADE      PIC   X.

FD    PRINT-FILE
      DATA RECORD PRINT-LINE
      LABEL RECORD OMITTED
      LINAGE 60 FOOTAGE 60 TOP 3 BOTTOM 3.
01    PRINT-LINE    X(132).
WORKING STORAGE SECTION.
01    PRINT-IMAGE.
      03 DUMMY-1         PIC X(28)
            VALUE " RESULT FOR CANDIDATE, NAME ".
      03 PRINT-NAME      PIC X(50).
      03 DUMMY-2         PIC X(12)
            VALUE ", ID NUMBER ".
      03 PRINT-CODE      PIX 999.
      03 DUMMY-3         PIC X(4)
            VALUE " IS ".
      03 PRINT-GRADE     PIC X.

PROCEDURE DIVISION.
OPEN INPUT RESULT-FILE.
OPEN OUTPUT PRINT-FILE.
READ-LOOP.
      READ RESULT-FILE NEXT END GO TO END-ROUTINE.
      MOVE ID-NO TO PRINT-NAME.
      MOVE NAME TO PRINT-NAME.
      MOVE SYLLABUS-CODE TO PRINT-CODE.
      MOVE EXAM-GRADE TO PRINT-GRADE.
      MOVE PRINT-IMAGE TO PRINT-LINE.
      WRITE PRINT-FILE BEFORE ADVANCING 1 LINE.
END-ROUTINE.
      CLOSE RESULT-FILE.
      CLOSE PRINT-FILE.
      EXIT.
```

FORTRAN : FORmula TRANslation

FORTRAN is a language designed for scientific computing. It was one of the first high level languages and came into use nearly thirty years ago. FORTRAN is relatively difficult to understand and use. It is still widely used, especially for 'number crunching' programs. Scientists and mathematicians are likely to use FORTRAN. It is available on most mainframes and some microcomputers.

A FORTRAN program

```
100C        MASTER /S/CD31SRCE
110C        AUTHOR R ALLAN
120C        CHANGES DATES FROM MMDDYY TO DD/MM/YY
130         CHARACTER DMY*8,MM*2,DD*2,YY*2,DAT*8
140         CALL DATIM(DMY,T)
150         DECODE (DMY,05)MM,DD,YY
160 05      FORMAT(A2,1X,A2,1X,A2)
170         ENCODE (DAT,06)DD,MM,YY
180 06      FORMAT (A2,1H/,A2,1H/,A2)
190         STOP
200         END
```

LOGO : (from the Greek word LOGOS, which means "word")

Logo is a dialect of LISP, which is a powerful language used in research into artificial intelligence. Logo was designed to manipulate language, i.e. words and sentences. It is understood and used by many children in primary school and by research workers in computer science projects in universities. It is a simple, but powerful, language. It is famous for its 'turtle graphics' and the various 'microworlds' that can be constructed for users to experience. Logo is a widely available language on microcomputers and is mainly used in education.

A LOGO program

```
TO FAN.CLUB
LOCAL "NAME
PR [HI, WHAT'S YOUR NAME?]
MAKE "NAME RL
TEST EQUALP :NAME JOE DAVIES
IFTRUE [PRINT [WOW, CAN I HAVE YOUR AUTOGRAPH?]]
IFFALSE [PRINT SE [OH, HELLO,] FIRST :NAME]
END
```

High level languages have several common features that make programming in them easier. They allow the programmer to use expressions very much like the algebra and arithmetic used in maths, e.g. A = (3 * B + C).

Key words, that is, words that define an operation, e.g. PRINT (in BASIC), are universally used. Labels are used for branching to other parts of the program. Sometimes the labels will be words or simply line numbers as in BASIC. Structures such as procedures, subroutines, functions and loops are often available. Loops are typically FOR/NEXT, WHILE/WEND or REPEAT/UNTIL. Conditional branching is possible using IF/THEN/ELSE statements and unconditional branching using GOTO.

However, before a high level language program can be run, it must be converted to machine code. Each high level language instruction will be translated to several machine code instructions. The resulting machine code program is unlikely to run as fast as a program originally written in assembly language or machine code.

High level language programs allow more flexibility in use for several reasons:

■ They are relocatable in memory and portable from one computer to another.

■ They are easier to understand than machine code or assembly language and designed to be problem orientated.

■ Designing and writing high level language programs is fast and relatively easy.

■ If programs have 'bugs', i.e. mistakes, in them, these can be found quickly.

■ A program written in a high level language by one programmer is more easily understood by another programmer.

For these reasons, the use of high level languages reduces the cost of software development and maintenance.

4 > TRANSLATING TO MACHINE CODE

All high level languages have to be *translated to machine code* before they are run. A computer can only execute machine code. It cannot execute any other language.

INTERPRETERS

An **interpreter** converts a program written in a high level language into machine code (see Fig. 7.4). It does this one instruction at a time as the program is run. The **source code**, i.e. the high level language program, is saved on backing storage. This is loaded into the memory of the computer and run. As the program is run, the interpreter converts one instruction in the source code to machine code, then executes it.

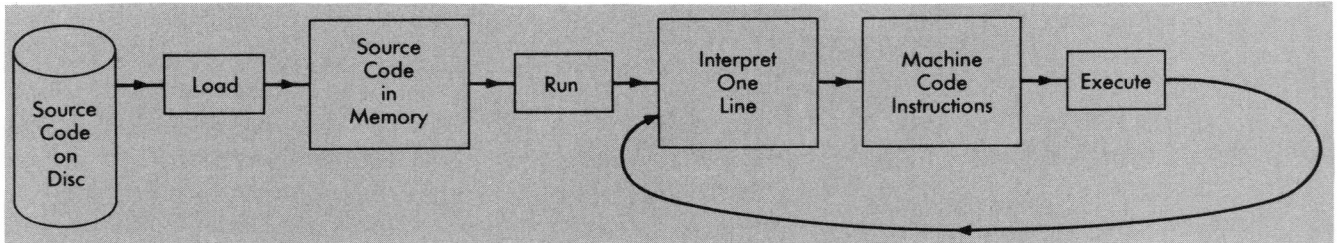

Fig. 7.4 How an Interpreter works

Before an instruction is converted to machine code, it is checked for syntax errors. **Syntax errors** are errors resulting from incorrect use of the rules governing the structure of the language, e.g. using PRONT instead of PRINT in BASIC would result in a syntax error. As the program is run, execution errors may be detected. An **execution error** is an error that occurs while the program is running, e.g. division by zero.

The interpreter does not, and cannot, check for **logic errors**. These are errors in the logic of the program. The syntax may well be correct and the program may run and produce output but because the program logic is incorrect, the required processing will not be done. Consequently the output will be faulty.

The most frequently used interpreted language is BASIC.

COMPILERS

A **compiler** converts a program written in a high level language into machine code (see Fig. 7.5). The source code is saved on backing storage. This is loaded into the memory of the computer and compiled. The compiler converts the whole of the source code program into machine code. This machine code program is known as the **object code**. The object code is an independent machine code program which can be saved on backing storage. A compiled language is not run from the source code. To run the program, the object code is loaded into memory and executed.

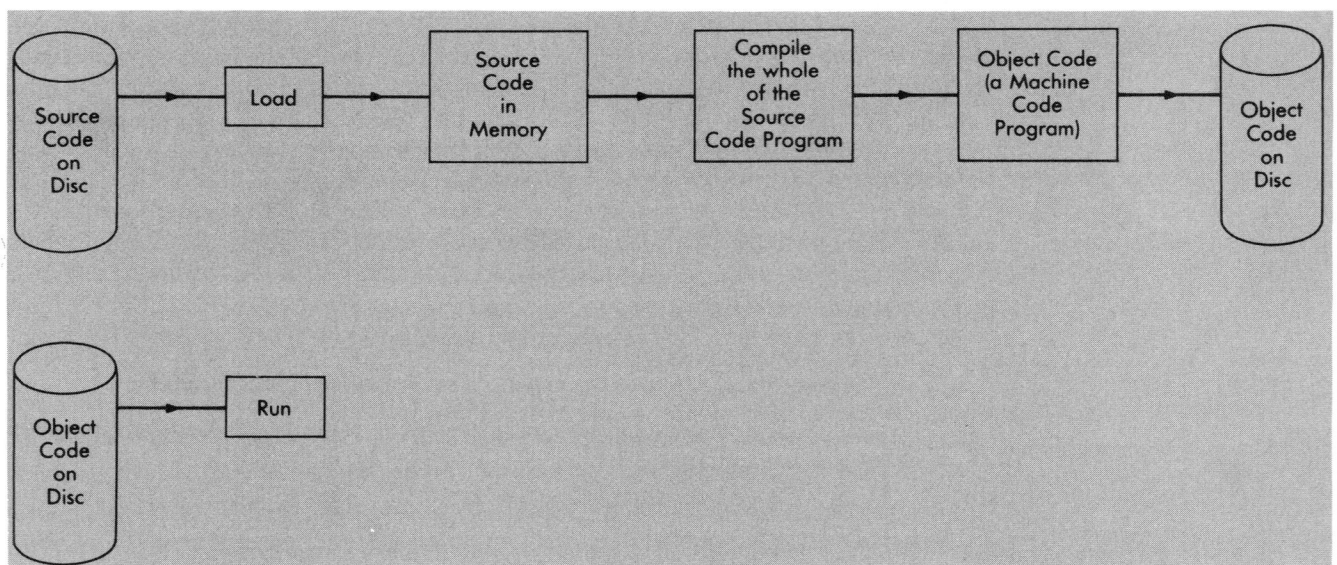

Fig. 7.5 How a compiler works

During compilation the source code is checked for syntax errors and while the object code is run, execution errors are reported. Almost all high level languages are compiled languages. PASCAL, COBOL and FORTRAN are all compiled languages.

Interpreted languages run slowly because they are converted to machine code as they run. Compiled languages run from the object code which is a machine code version of the program, output from the compiler. Consequently programs written in a compiled language run much faster than programs written in an interpreted language. If the source code program needs to be changed, it will be necessary to re-compile a compiled language to produce a working object code. With an interpreted language, changes to the source code immediately affect program execution. For this reason, program development is faster in an interpreted language. Any changes to the source code can be tested very quickly, to see if they work. This is one of the reasons why BASIC is an easy language to learn.

Since interpreted languages encourage faster program development and compiled languages run faster, it would be helpful to have an interpreter and a compiler for the same language. Programs could be developed using the interpreter, and the final version could be compiled to obtain a faster, executable version. Unfortunately, this is not often possible, as either an interpreter or a compiler is available, but not both. Some of the more recent versions of BASIC do have both an interpreter and a compiler available.

Interpreters and compilers are programs. They are somewhat different from most programs in that their input is a source code program and their output is machine code. However, as they are programs they can be saved onto disc and loaded into RAM memory when required. If there is plenty of room in RAM memory for the interpreter or compiler and the source code program, this is not a problem. Unfortunately, on microcomputers with very small RAM memory the interpreter or compiler will often be so large that it will not fit in memory with a source code program. In this case, the translation program will be supplied in a ROM microchip. This does not use any RAM memory and can be permanently installed in the microcomputer. As interpreters tend to be smaller than compilers, the translation program used is likely to be an interpreter. This is why the language used with the majority of home microcomputers is BASIC, supplied on a ROM microchip.

EXAMINATION QUESTIONS

MULTIPLE CHOICE QUESTIONS

1 A program is written in high level language. Which one of the following statements is true?
   A   Each instruction in the program represents a number of machine instructions.
   B   It is written in binary.
   C   It does not need to be translated before execution.
   D   It is translated by an assembler before execution.
   E   The language is called 'high-level' because it is difficult to learn.   (NEA; 1988)

2 Which of the following is most likely to be PORTABLE?

   a)   A machine code program.
   b)   A program in PASCAL.
   c)   A game for a home microcomputer.
   d)   A program in an assembly language.
   e)   A washing machine program.

3 A pupil has written a program. As it is in a computer language why does it need to be translated before the computer can execute it?　　　　　　　　　　　(LEAG; 1988)

4 a) Figure 1 shows the flow of data in a computer system. In which part would you expect to find the Immediate Access Store?

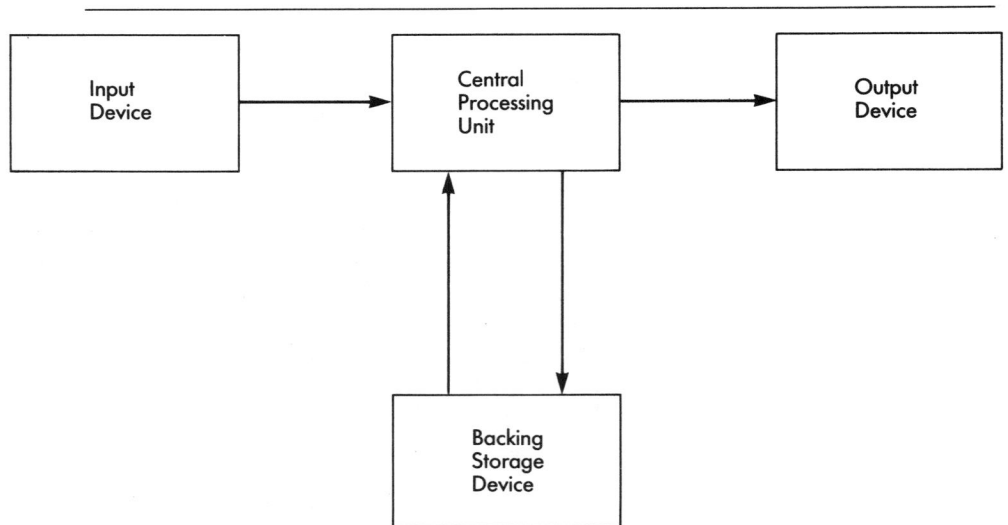

_____

```
┌──────────────┐        ┌──────────────┐        ┌──────────────┐
│  Input       │───────▶│  Central     │───────▶│  Output      │
│  Device      │        │  Processing  │        │  Device      │
│              │        │  Unit        │        │              │
└──────────────┘        └──────────────┘        └──────────────┘
                          ▲          │
                          │          ▼
                        ┌──────────────┐
                        │  Backing     │
                        │  Storage     │
                        │  Device      │
                        └──────────────┘
```

Fig. 1

b) Give one use for the Immediate Access Store.

_____

_____

c)　　i) An instruction word has been copied from the Immediate Access Store under the direction of the control unit. Where would it have been copied to?

_____

_____

　　ii) What part does the Program Counter play in the above event?

_____

_____

d) Some instructions make use of the accumulator. Describe briefly one use of the accumulator.

_____

_____

　　　　　　　　　　　　　　　　　　　　　　　　　　　　　　　(LEAG: 1988)

5 The T40 microcomputer system has a high level language interpreter.

a) i) Explain how a syntax error can occur.

_____

_____

　　ii) Explain how you would find the syntax error.

_____

_____

b) i) Give and explain an example of a logical error.

_____

_____

　　ii) Explain how to find the logical error.

　　　　　　　　　　　　　　　　　　　　　　　　　　　　　　　(LEAG; 1988)

6   a) Name a commonly used high-level computer language.

_____

(1)

   b) Name the two different types of translators used with a high-level language.

   Type 1: _____

(1)

   Type 2: _____

(1)

   c) Explain the main difference between the methods of operation of these two types of translator. (4 lines available)

   d) What type of translator is used for a low-level language?

_____

(1)

   e) What is the name for the type of instructions that the computer hardware actually uses?

_____

(2)
(SEG; 1988)

7   The following instructions taken from different computer programs are in one of a high level language, machine code or an assembly language. In each case say what type of language is used:

   a)   0010 0000 1011
   b)   20 IF ANSWER = 'YES' THEN 600
   c)   STA 15

O U T L I N E   A N S W E R S

MULTIPLE CHOICE QUESTIONS

1   Key A

2   b) A program in PASCAL.

SHORT STRUCTURED QUESTIONS

3   It is probable that the program written by the pupil is in a high level language, e.g. BASIC. Computers can only execute instructions in machine code. Hence the pupil's program must be translated to machine code before execution.

4   a) In the Central Processing Unit
   b) The IAS stores programs while they are executed and data while it is being processed.
   c) i) To the Current Instruction Register.
       ii) The Program Counter contains the memory address of the next instruction to be executed.
   d) The accumulator is used when doing arithmetic, e.g. addition.

5   a) i) A syntax error is an error in the format of an instruction, e.g. in BASIC

   10 PRONT " NAME AND ADDRESS"

       would cause a syntax error as the word PRINT should have been used instead of PRONT
       ii) The interpreter would give the location of the syntax error, e.g. SYNTAX ERROR AT LINE 10, when the program is run.
   b) i) A logical error is a mistake in the logic of the program.
       For example WAGE = HOURS * WAGE is a logic error.
       It should read WAGE = HOURS * HOURLY RATE.
       ii) A logical error is found by testing the program and carefully checking the output.

6 a) BASIC, COBOL, PASCAL, etc.
    b) Type 1: Interpreter
       Type 2: Compiler
    c) An interpreter translates one line of the high level language to machine code at a time when the program is run and then executes it. The program is only saved as a high level language program.
       A compiler converts the whole of the high level language program to machine code. The program is stored in both high level language and machine code. The program is executed from the machine code version.
    d) Assembler
    e) Machine code

7 a) Machine code.
    b) High level language.
    c) Assembly language.

A STUDENT'S ANSWER WITH EXAMINER'S COMMENTS

QUESTION

The T90 microcomputer system has a compiler for its main high level language.

a) Use the terms **'source code'** and **'object code'** to complete the spaces in the following sentences.
'A compiler produces _____ and error messages as it translates. The input to the compiler is the _____.'

b) Compilers and interpreters both translate high level languages but use a very different approach. Give **two** differences you would notice in *your* method of writing and testing a program if you changed from using an interpreter to using a compiler.

(LEAG; 1988)

A STUDENT'S ANSWER

a) 'A compiler produces __*object code*__ and error messages as it translates. The input to the compiler is the __*source code*__.'

b)(i) Using an interpreter is faster than using a compiler.

(ii) A compiler is harder to understand and is used with more difficult languages.

Examiners comment
a) correct.
b) i) Reason too vague. An interpreter runs from the source code, so program development is faster. A compiled language must be re-compiled after every alteration so this slows down writing and testing. However, a compiled language runs much faster than an interpreted language as it is run from the machine code version.
      ii) Incorrect. See the answer to part (i) for the second difference.

OPERATING SYSTEMS AND NETWORKS

OPERATING SYSTEMS

STANDALONE MODE

WINDOWS, ICONS, MOUSE, POINTER (WIMP)

NETWORKS

GETTING STARTED

The **Operating System** (OS) is a program that supervises the running of other programs and helps the user manage the computer system. The operating system provides a standardised environment in which programs can easily access the hardware, making them *portable* between different computers running the same OS.

An Operating System will also maintain security by checking **User Identification Numbers** and the corresponding *passwords*. However large or small a computer, in order to use it an operating system must be available.

Programs may be run **interactively** on a microcomputer, or on a mainframe using a *terminal* connected *on-line* via a *modem* and a telephone line. A microcomputer can be used as a terminal if **communications software** is available.

It is possible to run more than one program at the same time on some computers. This is known as *multitasking* or *multiprogramming* .

Microcomputers are often used in *standalone mode* although they may also be connected together to form a *network*. Mircocomputers attached to a network or terminals used to access a mainframe computer are examples of **network stations**.

There are several ways in which network connections can be made. The shape of the network chosen is determined by the way in which the links are made and the size of the computers attached to the network. A mainframe computer and its terminals form a **star network**; microcomputers can be connected to form a **line network** or a **ring network**. A **Local Area Network (LAN)** has permanent cable links between all the network stations and other hardware connected to the network, whereas a **Wide Area Network (WAN)** will make use of temporary links, such as telephone lines, to make network connections. LANs will be confined to a building or room in contrast to WANs, which may be international.

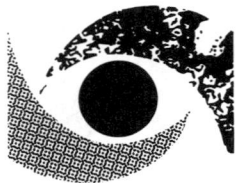

ESSENTIAL PRINCIPLES

1 ▷ OPERATING SYSTEMS

WHAT IS AN OPERATING SYSTEM?

The **Operating System (OS)** is a program. It must be available in memory when a user program is run. Unless an OS is present a computer cannot normally be used. In the vast majority of computers the operating system is loaded into the memory from disc. In some microcomputers with relatively small RAM memory the OS is present in a ROM chip, thus leaving all the RAM memory free for user programs and data.

IBM PCs and compatibles, such as RM Nimbus computers, use the MS-DOS operating system. Another OS commonly used with microcomputers is CP/M, which is used on the Amstrad PCW series and the Atari ST range. UNIX is an increasingly popular OS for mainframe computers.

▋▋ **Types of Operating System** ▋▋

WHAT DOES THE OPERATING SYSTEM DO?

- **The OS supervises programs while they are running.** The operating system looks after programs while they are being run, making sure no problems arise and helping to overcome them if they do. The OS tries to keep programs running if at all possible.

- **The Operating System makes the hardware easy to use.** User programs run on the OS, which runs between the user program and the hardware (see Fig. 8.1), making it possible for the user program to access the hardware using simplified standard routines provided by the OS. For example, when you press a key on the keyboard a very complex process involving electronics and Operating System software leads to that character appearing on the screen. We would find it tedious to have to directly program this process every time we press a key. The computer would be practically unusable without standard OS routines to ensure key presses resulted in corresponding character displays on the screen.

▋▋ **Functions of the Operating System** ▋▋

  All access to the hardware from the user programs should be through the standard routines provided by the operating system.

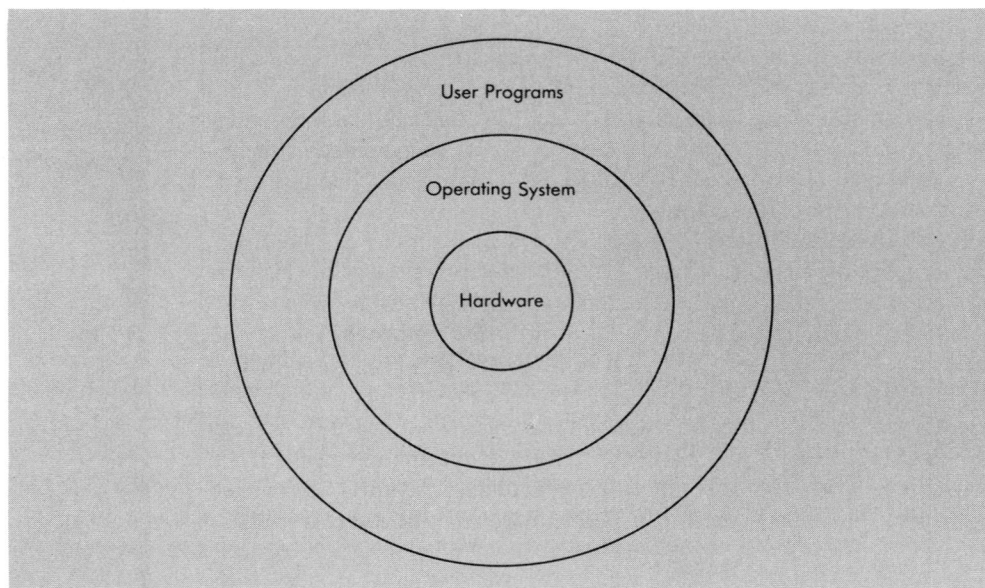

Fig. 8.1 The OS runs between the user programs and the hardware

- **The OS helps the operator decide what to do.** The operating system supervises the running of user programs and will display messages telling the operator what to do. For example, if the printer has run out of paper the OS will attract the operator's attention to this; if the program needs some data, the OS will display a message on the operator's console asking for the data to be provided and may tell the operator which file and which disc is needed. A **console** is a special terminal in the computer room which displays information about the running of the computer and which the operator uses to control the computer.

■ **The OS makes programs portable from one computer to another.** Operating Systems provide a standardised environment, enabling user programs to use peripherals, such as disc drives, by giving the same instructions on any computer running that Operating System. The disc drives could be of different makes and work differently and the computers could also be different, but still the OS would allow standard instructions to be used. Ideally, this makes programs **portable**, in other words, they should run on any computer running the OS they were written to be run on. In practice this ideal is not often achieved.

■ **The Operating System provides utilities to manage the computer system.** When using any computer system it is important to be careful and tidy so that, for example, you do not lose files or get one file confused with another. The OS provides the necessary utilities to enable the system to be well managed.

For discs, there will be instructions to **format** the disc and to **delete**, **rename** or **copy** files saved on the disc. When a disc is *formatted* a skeleton framework is set up of the sectors and blocks on the disc in which data and programs will later be saved. On a new (unformatted) disc this framework is not present. The disc must be formatted before it can be used.

A file is *deleted* by removing it from the disc. A *renamed* file will have its filename changed, but not the data in the file. A file can be *copied* from one disc to another, so that a copy of the file exists on both discs.

The OS will maintain a **directory** (or *catalogue*) of a disc, which is simply a list of the filenames of all the files on a disc. This directory is itself saved on the disc.

■ **Operating Systems optimise the use of resources.** In larger computers the OS will arrange the use of hardware and software resources, so that maximum use is made of them and all users get a fair share. Users can be given **priorities**, so that if resources are in short supply the operating system can restrict access to users with a *low* priority and make the resources available to those with a *high* priority. A **log** will be kept by the OS which records *who* is using the computer, *how long* they used it and *what* they did. This gives enough information so that users can be charged for the resources they have used.

■ **The OS maintains security.** On larger computers and networks each person who is allowed to use the computer will have a User Identification Number usually known as the **User Id**. Each user also has a **password** which is known only to the user. The OS keeps a register of all the User Ids and passwords and will only allow registered users who give the correct password to use the computer.

Hackers, who are not registered users, will sometimes discover how to break into the system, often by guessing a User Id and the password. However, their activities will be recorded on the log by the OS and they can usually be traced and identified.

2 ▷ STANDALONE MODE

Microcomputers which are not linked to other computers are being used in **standalone mode**. Often, they will have peripherals, such as printers and disc drives, attached to them but they will not be linked to other computers most of the time.

When a program is being run on a computer and the program requires the user to enter data *while the program is running*, this is **interactive** processing. Most programs that are run on standalone microcomputers are interactive. Interactive processing can also be done on a terminal connected to a mainframe computer. A terminal is not a standalone computer. Standalone computers will usually be used interactively, but interactive processing is possible in other situations.

In general, microcomputers run one program at a time, but it is becoming common for a computer to run several programs at the same time. On a microcomputer, running several programs at the same time is called **multitasking**, but on a mainframe this is referred to as **multiprogramming**. For example, when using my wordprocessor I may wish to refer to a database to extract information to be put in an article I am writing. If the microcomputer I am using will only run one program at a time I have to save the article on disc, exit from the wordprocessor, load the database, extract the information, print the information, exit from the database, load the wordprocessor, get the document I was using and type in the information I extracted from the database! A lengthy process!

If the microcomputer supports multitasking, I simply load the database, extract the information and transfer it into the article. I am able to do this because the wordprocessor and the database will run on the same computer at the same time.

3 > WINDOWS, ICONS, MOUSE, POINTER (WIMP)

WIMP systems have been developed to make it easier for users to make use of a computer. They enable the OS and other programs to be run without the need to type in complex text operating system commands. OS commands are often difficult to remember and it is easy to make mistakes when typing them in at the keyboard. WIMP user interfaces bypass these problems by avoiding the keyboard.

WINDOWS

Windows are rectangular areas of the screen which contain information relating to one task (see Fig. 5.11). If a microcomputer supports multitasking, it is possible to run different tasks in different windows, displaying the results on the screen at the same time. For example, a wordprocessor can be run in one window and a database in another, at the same time. This allows data to be transferred from, say, the database to the word-processor, by moving it between the windows. It is also possible to open windows on different parts of the same task, for example, different parts of a wordprocessing document and transfer text between them.

> **Features of WIMP systems**

ICONS

Icons are pictures that represent operations that can be performed, e.g., a picture of a dustbin may be used to allow files to be deleted. Operations are also made available through **pull-down menus**. These are menus that can be pulled down from the top of the screen. They contain lists of menu options that can be chosen.

POINTERS

Pointers are used to point at icons and menu options. They are controlled by moving a **mouse** about a flat surface. The movement of the pointer on the screen corresponds to the movement of the mouse on the flat surface. An icon or menu option can be selected by *pointing* at it and *clicking* one of the buttons on the mouse. When an icon or menu option is selected, the operation it represents is performed. Usually all the operations available can be accessed using a mouse, without the need to type in text OS commands at the keyboard.

WIMP systems are available for many standalone microcomputers, in particular the Apple Macintosh and the Atari ST microcomputers. However, they are so clear and easy to use that they are now becoming available on networks and mainframe computers.

4 > NETWORKS

Computers can be linked together to form **networks**. There are several ways in which these connections can be made. The shape of the network chosen is determined by the way in which the links are made and the size of the computers attached to the network.

STAR NETWORK

A **Star Network** is common when a mainframe computer is being accessed by many users (see Fig. 8.2). When many users access a computer at the same time, this is known as **multiaccess**.

Networks are accessed using **network stations** connected to the computer. Network stations consist of the hardware necessary to access the network. They may be terminals or microcomputers being used as terminals.

Terminals and Modems

> **Hardware and Software used in a *Star Network***

Terminals usually consist of at least a **Visual Display Unit** (VDU), which is a keyboard and a monitor screen. VDUs cannot operate in standalone mode. They are *not* microcomputers and have no processing power of their own. They are connected to a central computer and give the user access to its processing power.

A microcomputer can also be used as a terminal. To do this, communications software and a **modem** are required. A modem (*modulator/demodulator*) converts the digital signal

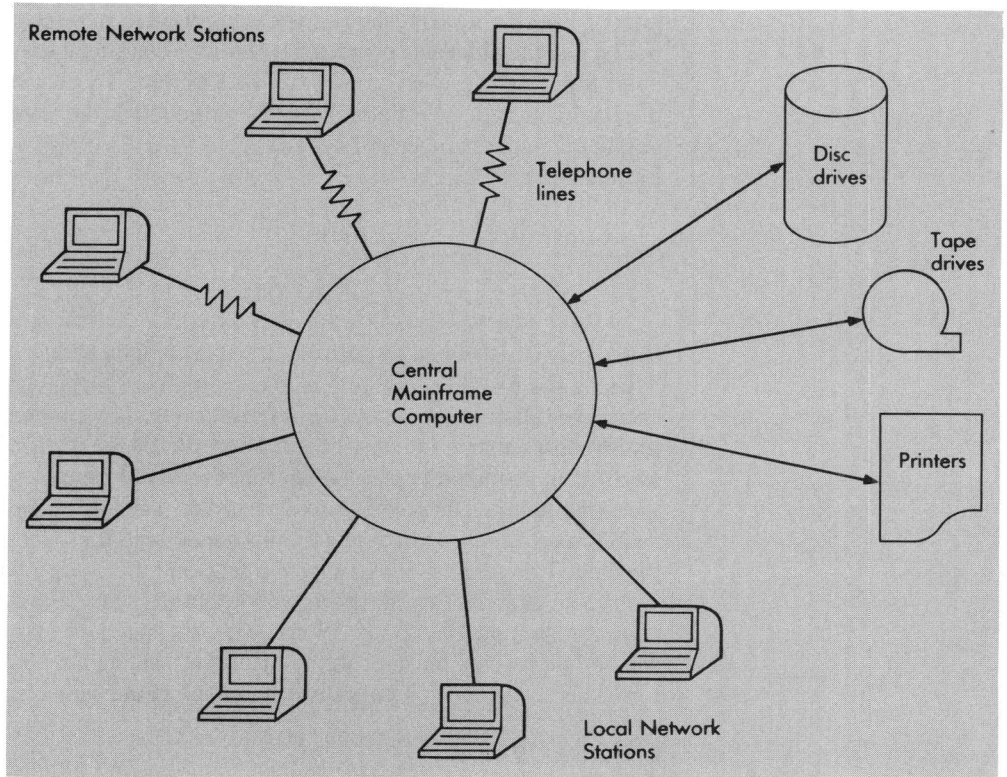

Fig. 8.2 A Star Network

output by the microcomputer to a signal that can be transmitted along the telephone lines. A modem also converts signals sent along the telephone lines to digital signals that the computer can process (see Fig. 8.3). The diagram shows two similar microcomputers communicating but, in fact, provided the appropriate communications software is available, any two computers can communicate.

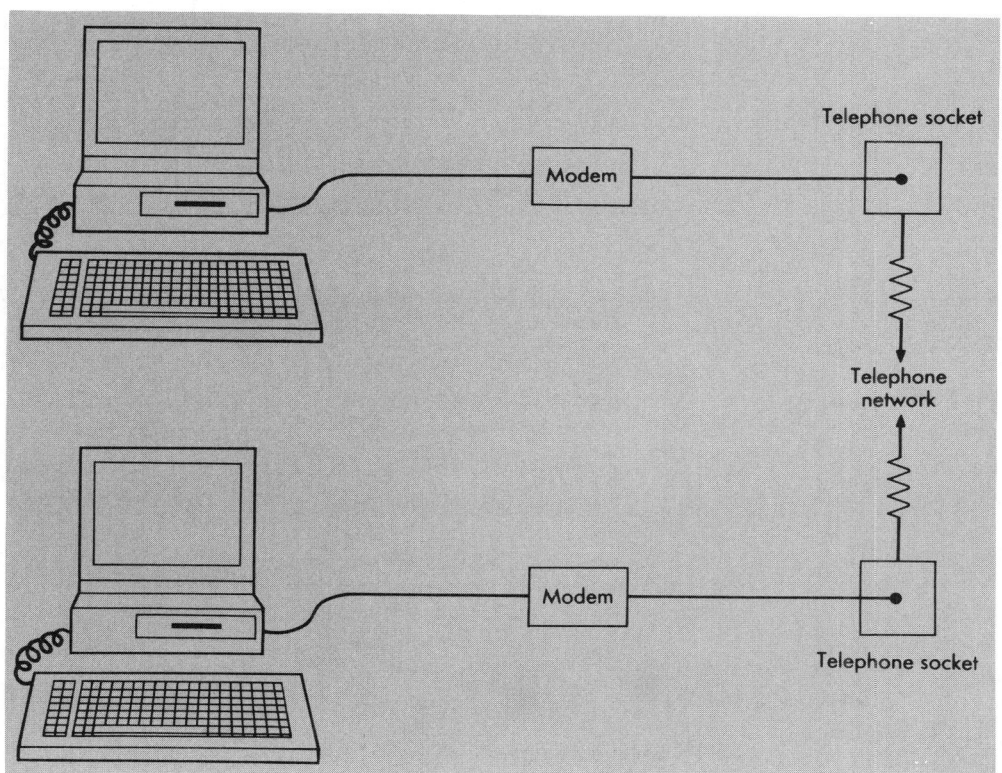

Fig. 8.3 Computers communicating using the telephone network

Communications software

Communications software is a program that can transmit and receive data via the modem and the telephone system. The telephone system is not a reliable means of transmitting data, so when the data is transmitted, it is checked. The modem does a

parity check automatically as the data is received. To perform a parity check using **even parity**, all the bits representing the received character are added up. If the number of 1s is even the data has been transmitted accurately. To ensure the number of 1s is even, a **parity bit** is added to the bit pattern representing the character. This extra bit is set at 1 or 0 to make the number of 1s even.

For example:

even parity bit	bit pattern
1	101 0010
0	011 0011

Odd parity is also used. In this case, the parity bit is set to make the number of 1s odd.

Using the telephone system is expensive as a charge is made for the length of time the network station is connected to the mainframe. A VDU must be **on-line**, i.e. connected, to the central mainframe computer in order to be used, as it has no processing power of its own. A microcomputer can be used both as a terminal and in standalone mode. Using a microcomputer, it is possible to access the mainframe computer, transfer data from the mainframe to the microcomputer, disconnect and then use the microcomputer to process the data. This reduces the connection time and the costs involved in communications.

In most Star Networks there will be both terminals and micromputers connected to a central mainframe computer. Some will be connected via the telephone network, others will be in the same building as the mainframe and connected directly to it. Not all of these terminals and microcomputers will be on-line at the same time.

LINE NETWORK

A **Line Network** is used to link several microcomputers, allowing them to communicate with each other and to share data and peripherals (see Fig. 8.4). Each microcomputer uses its own processing power and it is likely that each will be running a different program.

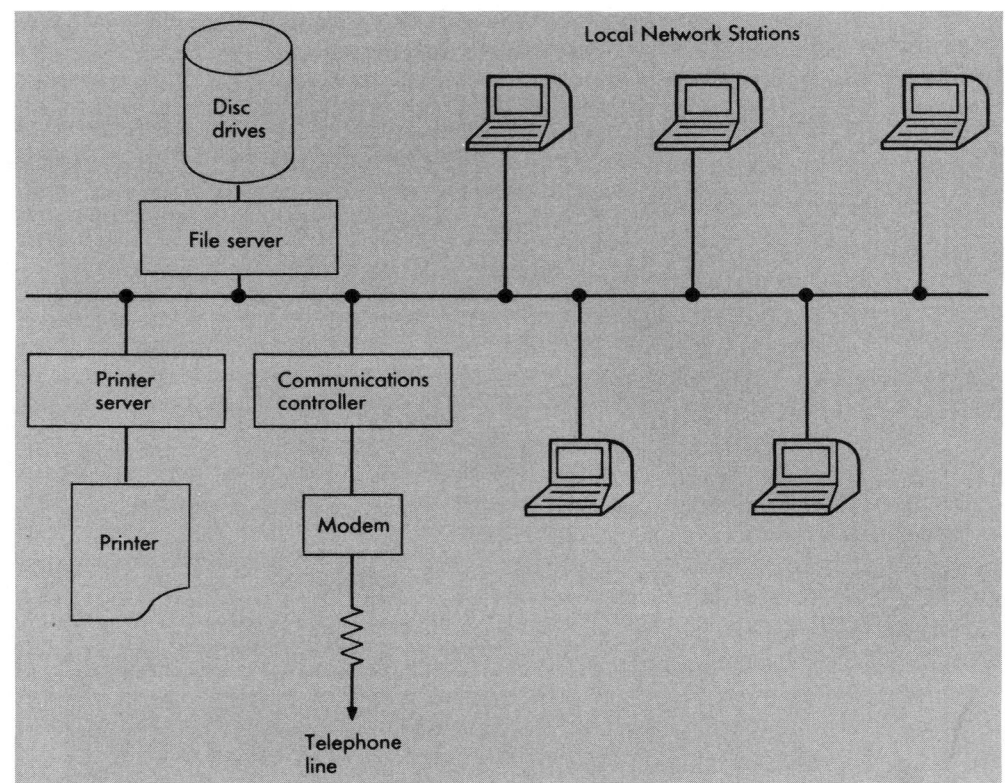

Fig. 8.4 A Line Network

File server

On most line networks there will be a **file server**, i.e. a computer that organises the sharing of files saved on backing storage by all computers connected to the network. Files will be stored on a hard disc capable of storing very large volumes of data and accessing it very quickly. By sharing a hard disc, each network station is given access to greater volumes of on-line data at a more economic cost. Most of the programs run by

Hardware and software used in a _Line Network_

microcomputers connected to the network will also be stored on the hard disc and loaded and run as required.

Printer server

The **printer server** organises the use of a printer connected to the network. A printer server is a microcomputer attached to a printer that can run the appropriate software to allow the printer to be shared by all the network stations. By using a networked printer it is possible to have a share of a high quality printer, rather than full use of a basic printer at each network station, for approximately the same cost. However, only *one* file can be printed at a time, so sharing a printer means that it will be necessary to **queue** the files to be printed.

When a user at a microcomputer connected to the network requires printed output, a file containing the data to be printed is sent to the printer server. The printer server checks to see if the printer is being used. If it is free the file is printed immediately. If the printer is in use, the file is put in the printer queue. The printer continues printing until there is no more printing to be done. The user can run other programs on the computer as soon as the file is put in the printer queue, but will not be able to collect the printout until it is printed some time later. The advantage of sharing a printer on a network is that a better quality printer can be available; the disadvantage is that it may be necessary to wait some time for printouts.

Communications controller

Microcomputers connected to the network may also wish to *communicate* with other computers that are not on the network using a shared modem and telephone lines. A **communications controller** will be necessary to ensure that data is sent to the appropriate network station. In some Line Networks the file server, printer server and communications controller may be a single micrcomputer doing all of these tasks. The RM Nimbus networks that are widely used in education are examples of Line Networks.

RING NETWORKS

A **Ring Network** is similar to a Line Network, except that the ends of the line are joined to form a ring (see Fig. 8.5).

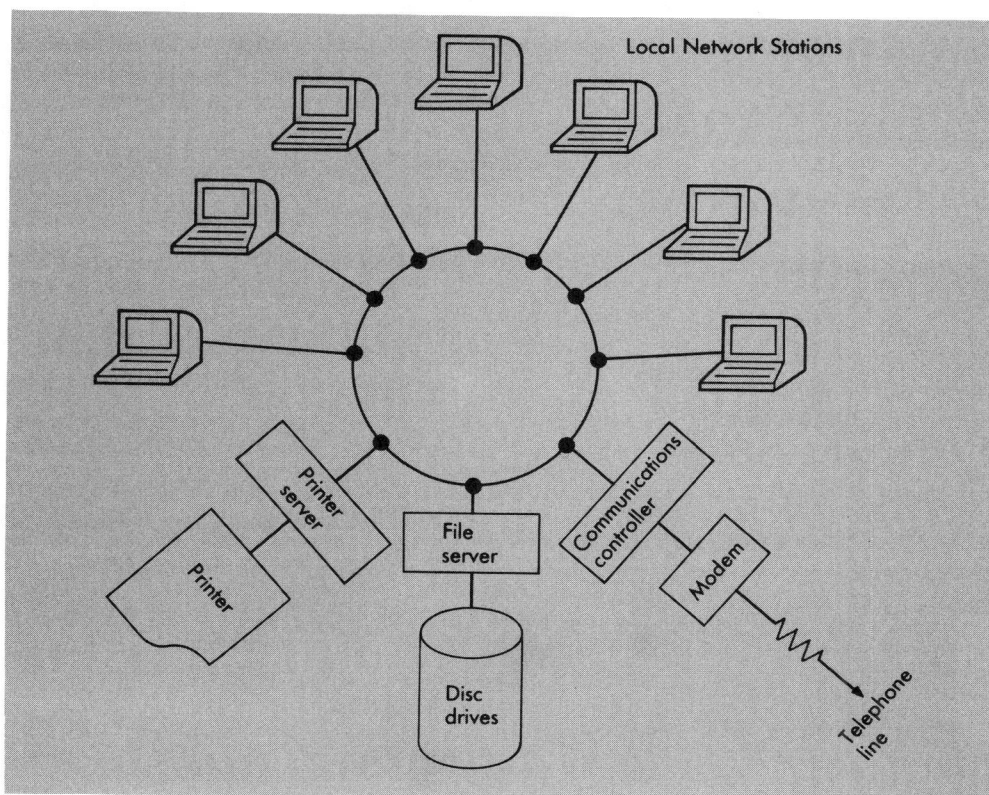

Fig. 8.5 A Ring Network

On a line network data are sent in both directions along the network whereas on a ring network data are sent in one direction only. Consequently ring networks generally

❝❝Features of a *Ring* Network❞❞

communicate faster. However, it is often easier to extend line networks as only a single cable is needed to each new network station. This is useful where the complete network cannot be planned in advance because of the need for possible future expansion or where network stations are widely dispersed.

LOCAL AREA NETWORKS (LAN)

❝❝Features of a *Local Area Network*❞❞

A **Local Area Network** or LAN is a network where all the different hardware connected to the network is permanently linked by a cable, so that there is no need to use a modem and telephone line to access peripherals attached to the network or to communicate with other network stations. LANs are likely to be Line Networks or Ring Networks. A LAN will be located on one site, possibly in a building such as a school or an office block, perhaps even in a single room.

WIDE AREA NETWORKS (WAN)

❝❝Features of a *Wide Area Network*❞❞

A **Wide Area Network** or WAN is a network where all the hardware on the network is not permanently linked, perhaps due to the wide geographical distribution of network stations. WANs are likely to make use of a modem and telephone lines for regular communications with other parts of the network. A common example of a WAN is a mainframe computer that is accessed from terminals via the telephone system in a Star Network.

Since the telephone network is world wide, it is possible and not uncommon for WANs to be international. For example, a newspaper reporter can write articles on a word-processor running on a lap-top computer powered from a car battery while sitting in a car parked at a remote location (see Fig. 8.6). The article can be saved as a wordprocessing document on a disc. When it is possible to use a telephone, perhaps from a public call box, the reporter can use the telephone system to make a temporary connection between the lap-top computer and the WAN used by the newspaper. Once connected, the reporter can send one or more articles, previously prepared for publication, in a few seconds.

Fig. 8.6 A reporter making use of a Wide Area Network

This method of working has changed the job of a reporter. There is less need to work from a centralised office. All work can be done in any location from where the telephone network can be accessed. Reporters can now work at home. On the other hand, they may also be required to spend long periods away from home when working on assignments. The cost to the newspaper owner is greater investment in computer technology but this is offset by savings on office accommodation and clerical staff. There may be greater profits due to the increased speed at which news is reported. Customers may well be attracted to a paper that prints news ahead of its rivals.

THE ADVANTAGES AND DISADVANTAGES OF NETWORKS

It is cheaper to buy a few complete standalone microcomputer systems, than to set up a network with two or three stations. However, once the initial cost of setting up a network has been paid, it is cheaper to add extra stations to a network than buy standalone systems. Expensive peripherals can be shared on a network where the cost of purchase for a standalone system might be too great, e.g. laser printer, hard disc, graph plotter.

Programs and data stored on a hard disc connected to the network can also be shared. This may be more economic than buying single copies of software packages for a number of standalone systems. Networks enable users to share data. If this data is kept up-to-date, then they will coordinate their work better and it will be of a higher standard.

SECURITY PROBLEMS

However, networks create security problems because of the increased number of users sharing the system. These problems can be overcome in several ways.

- Using User Ids and passwords to restrict access to the use of the software and data stored on the network;

- Physical access to network stations should be restricted by employing security guards and door locks operated by magnetic stripe cards, or by entering a password on a key pad;

How to overcome security problems

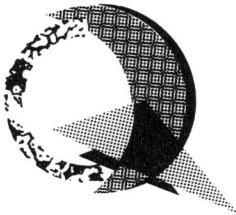

- The network cable should be shielded to prevent unauthorised connection and the data on the network should be encoded to obscure its meaning (i.e. data encryption);

- The Operating System should keep a log of users and their activities so that hackers can be detected and traced.

All these measures should be used to deter unauthorised use of the network.

EXAMINATION QUESTIONS

MULTIPLE CHOICE QUESTIONS

1   Which one of the following is a systems program?
   A   A stock control program
   B   A spreadsheet program
   C   A file-copying program
   D   A graphics package
   E   A program for a computerised personnel system   (NEA; 1988)

2   Which one of the following devices is most likely to be used off-line to a main computer?
   A   Magnetic tape unit
   B   Disc drive
   C   Key-to-disc
   D   Operator's console
   E   Graphical display unit   (NEA; 1988)

SHORT STRUCTURED QUESTIONS

3   Some schools and colleges have networks of computers.

   a)   Give **two** advantages of a network of computers.
      i)   _One printer can be used for all the computers._
      ii) _As many computers as you want can be used._

   b)   Give **one** disadvantage of using a computer network.
      Because there are so many computers, it will be slow.   (6)

                                                                         (WJEC; 1988)

4   Write down **two** functions of a computer operating system.

*Function 1:*_____

_____

*Function 2:*_____

_____ *(2)*

(MEG; 1988)

5   a)   An operating system is an essential feature of any general purpose computer system. This is true whether the computer system is a central mainframe with many users, some using remote terminals, or a personal computer with only one user.
Describe **three** of the jobs that need to be done by the operating system.   *(9)*

b)   Any computer system that holds personal, commercial, or military information needs protection from unauthorized access or use.
i) For a central mainframe computer system there are many different ways in which it is possible to restrict access. Describe briefly **three** of the methods that might be used.   *(9)*
ii) For a personal computer state **two** precautions not already given in your answer to part b) i).   *(2)*

(LEAG; 1988)

6   A journalist writes about the news for a newspaper. The news stories are written on a small computer using wordprocessor software. They are sent to the editor using a modem and telephone. The editor checks the story and makes any changes that are needed. The story is then sent to a printing machine by another telephone link.

a)   Give an advantage to the journalist.

_____ (2 lines available)

b)   Give an advantage to the newspaper owner.

_____ (2 lines available)

c)   Give a disadvantage to the journalist of working from home in this way.

_____ (2 lines available)

(LEAG; 1988)

OUTLINE ANSWERS

MULTIPLE CHOICE QUESTIONS

1   C.

2   C.

SHORT STRUCTURED QUESTIONS

3   a)   i) Peripherals, such as a hard disc and a printer, can be shared by all the network stations.
ii) Programs and data saved on the hard disc can be shared by all the users of the network.

b)   Security is more difficult to maintain as more users have access to the network. It is also possible for a hacker to break into the network by making an unauthorised connection to the network cable.

4   Refer to the answer for 5a) below.

5   a)   The operating system:
i) Supervises programs while they are run making sure no problems arise and helping overcome them if they do.

ii) Helps the operator decide what to do by displaying messages on the operator's console. For example, a message telling the operator that the printer has run out of paper.

iii) Provides utilities to manage the computer system, e.g. delete files, copy files, screen dump, etc.

iv) Makes the hardware easier to use, e.g. when a key is pressed a character appears on the monitor screen.

b) i) *Method 1*: Restrict areas to the use of the network by requiring a user identification number and password to be entered before access is granted.
Method 2: Shield the network cable to prevent unauthorised connection.
Method 3: When data is transmitted along the network cable it should be in a special code. This is known as data encryption.

ii) *Precaution 1*: Restrict physical access by placing all computer equipment in a locked room. The lock should be a combination lock, or require a password to open it. The room may also be guarded by security staff.
Precaution 2: Keep hardware and software separate when not in use. Software should be locked in a safe in another room.

6 a) The journalist can work at home or in any other location where the computer can be used, e.g. on location abroad.

b) There is no need to provide as much office space or typists to type up the reporter's notes. This saves the newspaper owner money.

c) The journalist may become isolated from his colleagues and unaware of developments taking place at the newspaper's head office.

A STUDENT'S ANSWER WITH EXAMINER'S COMMENTS

QUESTION

A remote terminal is connected to a central mainframe computer using the telephone lines.

a) What device is needed at each end of the telephone line?

A modem

b) What job does this device do?

Sends the information down the telephone line

c) Here is part of a message that is being sent from the terminal to the central mainframe.

Typed letter	Binary pattern sent	Binary pattern received	Letter displayed
I	00001001	00001001	I
space	00000000	00000000	space
A	10000001	10000011	C
M	10001101	10001101	M
space	00000000	00000000	space
J	00001010	00001010	J
O	00001111	00001111	O
H	10001000	10001000	H
N	10001110	10001111	O

Even parity bit   Letter code

i) What is a group of 8 bits that represents one of the letters called?

a character code

ii) What is even parity?

        when all the bits are even

iii) How does the mainframe computer know that the message is wrong?

        the N is now an O

(LEAG; 1988)

Examiner's comment:

a) correct

b) The modem (modulator/demodulator) converts digital signals used by the computer to analogue signals that can be sent down the telephone line and vice versa. The answer is only partially correct.

c)   i) correct

    ii) When even parity is used the parity bit is set to 1 to make the total number of bits set to 1 even.

      The answer is only partially correct.

   iii) This misses the point entirely. The computer knows the message is wrong because the number of bits that are set to 1 is even before transmission (N) but odd after transmission (O).

CHAPTER 9

MICRO-ELECTRONICS: LOGIC AND CONTROL SYSTEMS

GETTING STARTED

Truth tables are used to illustrate the inputs and the outputs of **binary logic**. Three **logic gates**, i.e. **AND**, **OR** and **NOT**, are described. These are used to construct **logic circuits**, which are used in very complex combinations to make computers. A **decoder**, used to decode binary signals, a **control switch**, used to switch data lines on and off, a **half adder** and a **full adder**, used in binary addition, are given as examples of the type of logic circuits used to build computers.

Logic circuits can also be used independently, built into machines and other devices to monitor and control various processes. A typical **fault detection** system for an industrial machine is described and a simplified **traffic light controller** is discussed.

Binary logic is also used when a computer is part of a larger system designed to control a process. **Sensors** attached to the computer monitor the environment, giving the computer information. The computer responds to this information by sending signals to activators that control devices to change environmental conditions. The sensors, in turn, respond to these changed conditions. This is known as a feedback loop. A **lift control** system and a computer controlled **greenhouse** are used as illustrations.

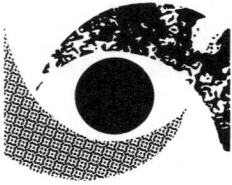

E S S E N T I A L   P R I N C I P L E S

Although the electronic components used in computers are very complex, they are made up of very simple basic elements. The complexity lies in the ways in which these basic elements are combined together. The basic elements used in the design of computer systems are **logic gates**.

You are not going to be able to make a computer for your GCSE project, though if you have a knowledge of electronics, a program to monitor a heat or light sensor is a possibility. However, you are expected to know how the logic gates and some logic circuits work.

1 > TRUTH TABLES

Constructing a Truth Table

Truth Tables are a convenient way of expressing the possible input conditions affecting a decision based on well defined rules and the results of it. Look at Figure 9.1. There are two inputs, 'On holiday' and 'A weekday' that are combined to give four different input conditions. 'False' means Paul is *not* 'On holiday' and 'true' means he *is* 'On holiday'. Each input condition has a result defined by the rule given.

Rule: Paul has decided that he will go fishing if he is on holiday OR if it is NOT a weekday.

Inputs		Output
A weekday	On holiday	Goes fishing
FALSE	FALSE	TRUE
FALSE	TRUE	TRUE
TRUE	FALSE	FALSE
TRUE	TRUE	TRUE

Fig. 9.1 A rule defining a Truth Table

SWITCH CIRCUITS

Truth tables can be used to describe how electrical circuits containing switches work. Look at Figure 9.2. This shows a **switch circuit** and the corresponding truth table. There are three switches labelled, A, B and C, in the circuit. Since there are three inputs, these combine to make eight different input conditions. In order for the light bulb to come on, either switch C must be on or switches A and B must both be on.

Fig. 9.2 A switch circuit and the corresponding truth table

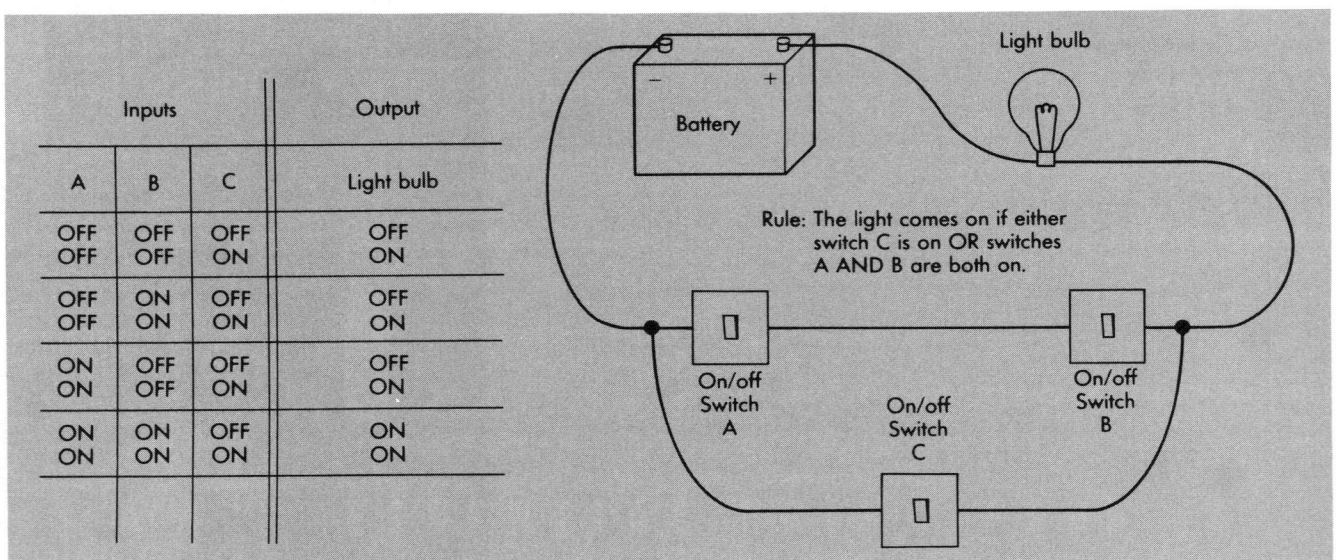

Inputs			Output
A	B	C	Light bulb
OFF	OFF	OFF	OFF
OFF	OFF	ON	ON
OFF	ON	OFF	OFF
OFF	ON	ON	ON
ON	OFF	OFF	OFF
ON	OFF	ON	ON
ON	ON	OFF	ON
ON	ON	ON	ON

Battery

Light bulb

Rule: The light comes on if either switch C is on OR switches A AND B are both on.

On/off Switch A

On/off Switch C

On/off Switch B

BINARY LOGIC

In both of the above examples we see **binary logic** being used. If we consider '1', 'true' and 'on' to be equivalent and similarly with '0', 'false' and 'off', we get the truth tables shown in Figure 9.3 (a) and (b). These are binary logic truth tables, because only *two* possible states are possible for each individual condition. These states are represented using a '1' or a '0'. In electronic binary logic circuits '1' is represented by a voltage level of 5 volts, '0' is represented by 0 volts. Notice that the different input conditions shown in the truth tables could be generated by counting in binary starting at zero.

(a)

Inputs		Output
a weekday	on holiday	goes fishing
0	0	1
0	1	1
1	0	0
1	1	1

(b)

Inputs			Output
A	B	C	Light bulb
0	0	0	0
0	0	1	1
0	1	0	0
0	1	1	1
1	0	0	0
1	0	1	1
1	1	0	1
1	1	1	1

Fig. 9.3 Binary logic truth tables

LOGIC GATES

Logic Gates and Truth Tables

In both of the above examples, the rule expressing the relationship between the inputs and the output uses the terms AND, OR and NOT. These are basic logical relationships. **Logic gates** are electronic components whose function can be described using the logical AND, OR or NOT terms. The operation of each of these logic gates can be fully described in a truth table (see Fig. 9.4).

AND gate

Inputs		Output
0	0	0
0	1	0
1	0	0
1	1	1

The output is 1 only if both inputs are 1

OR gate

Inputs		Output
0	0	0
0	1	1
1	0	1
1	1	1

The output is 1 if either input is 1

NOT gate

Input	Output
0	1
1	0

The output is 1 if the input is 0
The output is 0 if the input is 1

Fig. 9.4 AND, OR and NOT logic gates

2 | **LOGIC CIRCUITS**

Logic Circuits and Truth Tables

Logic gates can be combined to make **logic circuits**. These circuits can be designed to do the variety of tasks needed in a computer system. A computer is built up from many different logic circuits. They can also be built into machine tools, washing machines, etc. to perform the simple logic required for some monitoring and control tasks.

The example shown in Figure 9.5 is not a useful circuit. It is an example to show how the output from a logic circuit can be worked out from the inputs. Once you have the diagram of the logic circuit, you must make sure that all the outputs from every logic gate have been labelled with a letter. In the example, A, B and C are the inputs; E and F are intermediate processing states; X is the output.

The truth table is worked out by first entering all the different input conditions. Since there are three inputs, there will be eight different input conditions. These can be listed by counting in three bit binary from zero to seven. The intermediate processing state, E, is the result of A AND B; F is the result of NOT C. The output, X, is given by E OR F.

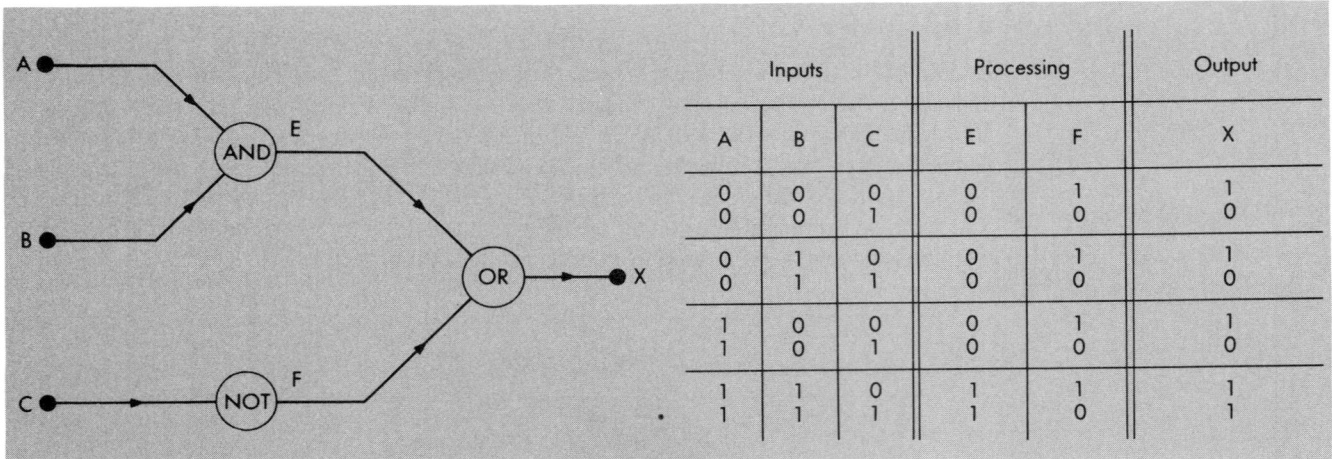

Inputs			Processing		Output
A	B	C	E	F	X
0	0	0	0	1	1
0	0	1	0	0	0
0	1	0	0	1	1
0	1	1	0	0	0
1	0	0	0	1	1
1	0	1	0	0	0
1	1	0	1	1	1
1	1	1	1	0	1

Fig. 9.5 A logic circuit and the corresponding truth table

A DECODER

A **decoder** is used to select a single output from a range of possible outputs in response to the binary code input. A two bit decoder is shown in Figure 9.6. Notice that only one of the four outputs is selected, i.e. has a value of 1, depending on the input binary code. For example, if 01 is input then B is the only output that has a value of 1, that is, an input of 01 selects output B.

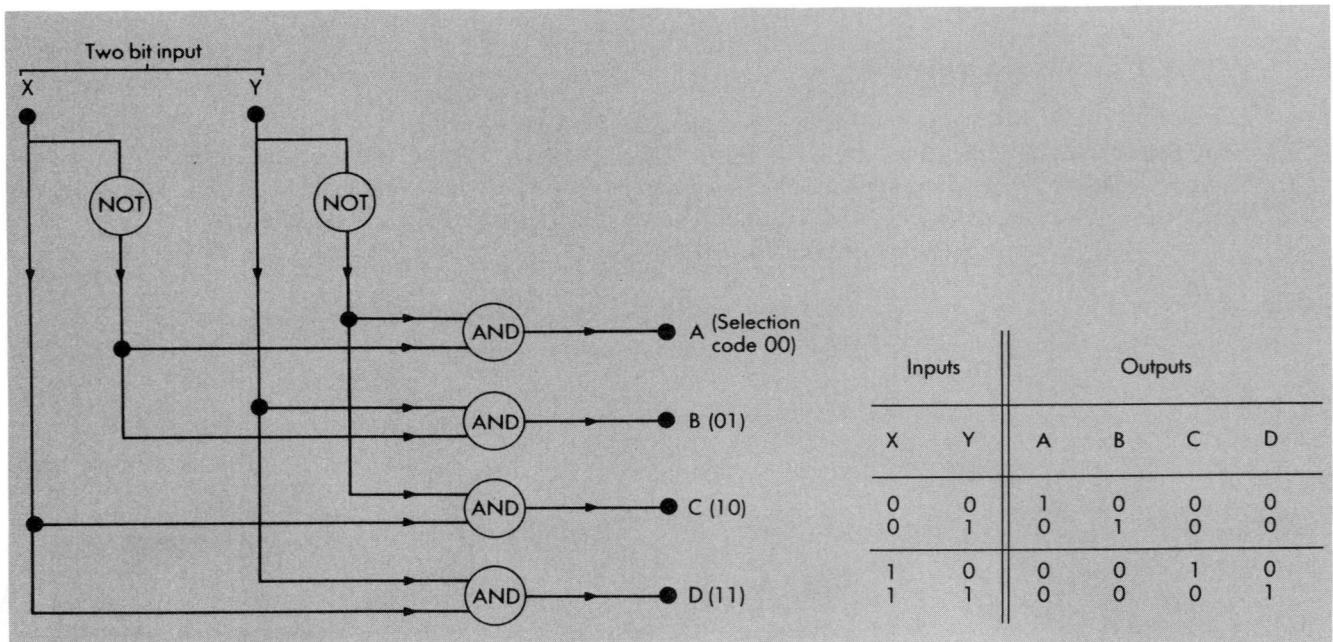

Inputs		Outputs			
X	Y	A	B	C	D
0	0	1	0	0	0
0	1	0	1	0	0
1	0	0	0	1	0
1	1	0	0	0	1

Fig. 9.6 A two bit decoder and the corresponding truth table

A CONTROL SWITCH

A **control switch** is used to allow or prevent data from passing down a data bus. A **data bus** is a set of parallel lines that carry binary data. In Figure 9.7 a control switch is being used on a four bit data bus. If the control switch is set at 0, the switch is off and the output from all data lines is 0; if the control switch is set at 1, the switch is on and whatever is input is output, i.e. if 0 is input then 0 is output, if 1 is input then 1 is output.

A HALF ADDER

The logic circuit for a **half adder** and the corresponding truth table are shown in Figure 9.8. The two input bits are added together to give the sum in binary shown as the two bits X and Y. For example, in binary, 1 + 0 = 01. Similarly, 1 + 1 = 10. X is known as the **carry bit** and Y is known as the **sum bit**.

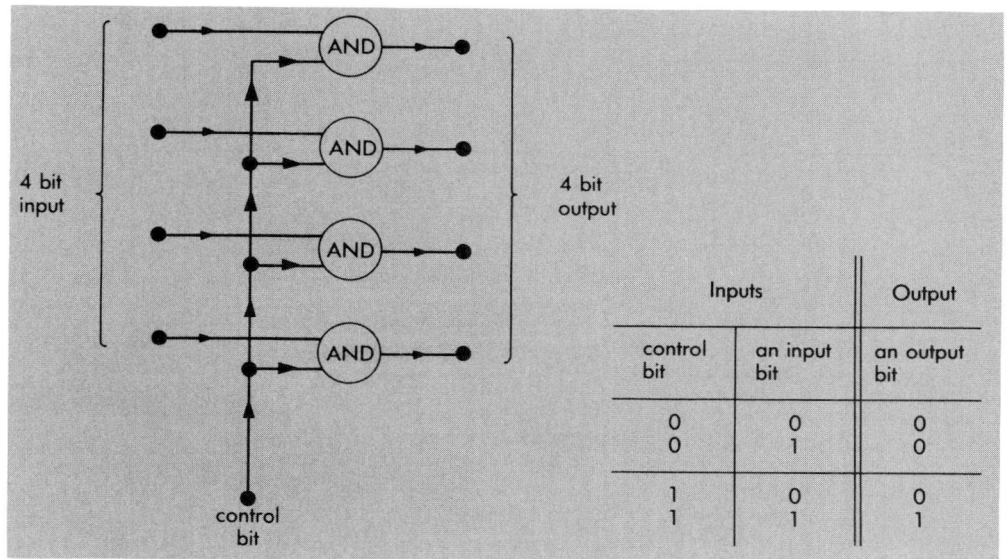

Fig. 9.7 A control switch and the truth table showing the effect on a single input bit

Inputs		Output
control bit	an input bit	an output bit
0	0	0
0	1	0
1	0	0
1	1	1

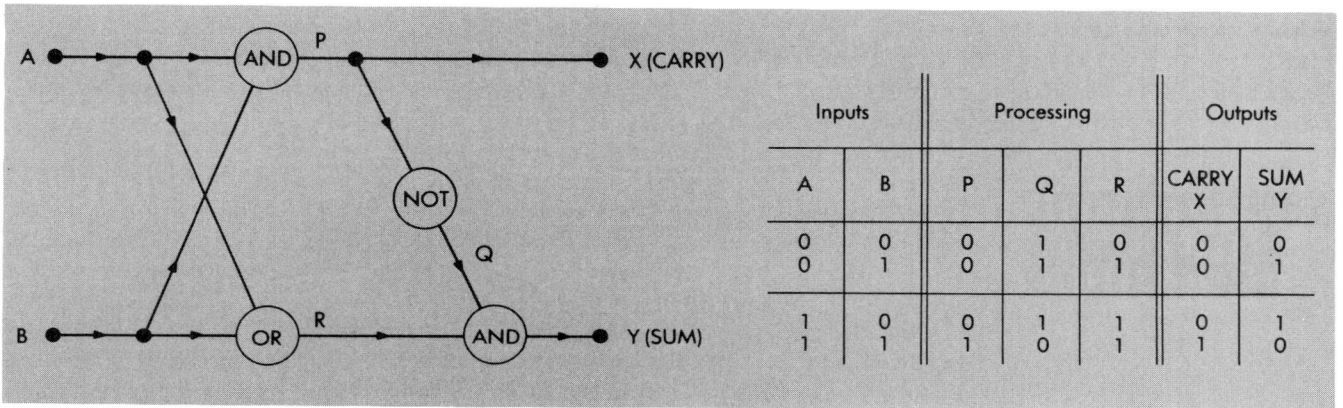

Fig. 9.8 A half adder and its truth table

Inputs			Processing			Outputs	
A	B		P	Q	R	CARRY X	SUM Y
0	0		0	1	0	0	0
0	1		0	1	1	0	1
1	0		0	1	1	0	1
1	1		1	0	1	1	0

Half Adder logic circuit and *Truth Table*   This circuit is called a half adder because it cannot be used for full addition of two binary numbers. It can only add two bits at a time. In order to add two binary numbers together we need a circuit that can input and add together a bit from each number and a carry bit from a previous addition, i.e. three input bits.

A FULL ADDER

Full Adder logic circuit and *Truth Table*   A **full adder** can be made using two half adders (see Fig. 9.9). It has the ability to add three input bits, two from the binary numbers being added together and a carry bit from a

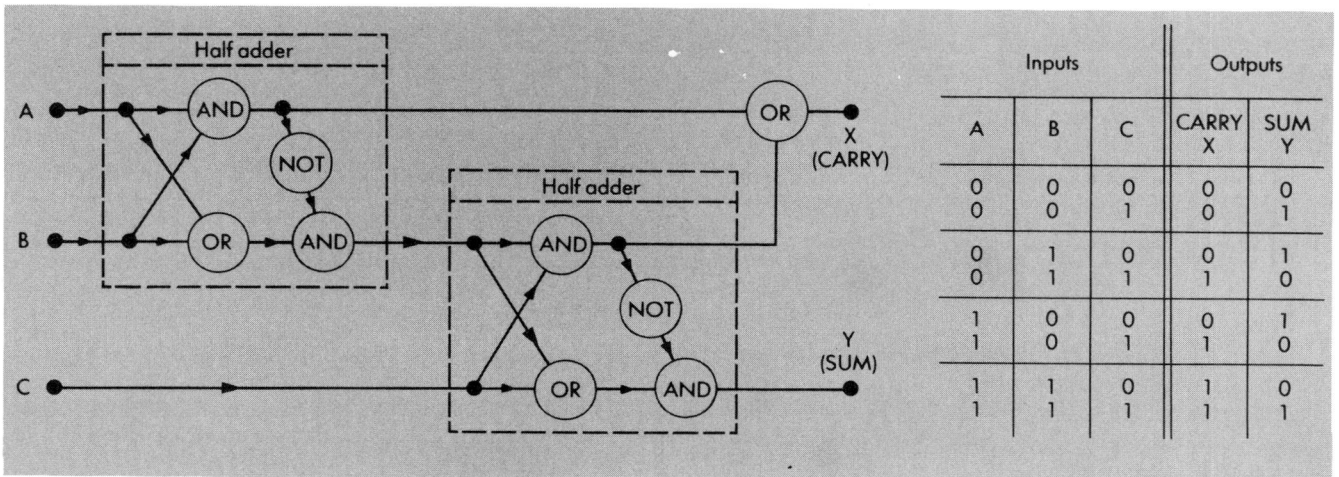

Inputs			Outputs	
A	B	C	CARRY X	SUM Y
0	0	0	0	0
0	0	1	0	1
0	1	0	0	1
0	1	1	1	0
1	0	0	0	1
1	0	1	1	0
1	1	0	1	0
1	1	1	1	1

Fig. 9.9 A full adder, made using two half adders, and its truth table

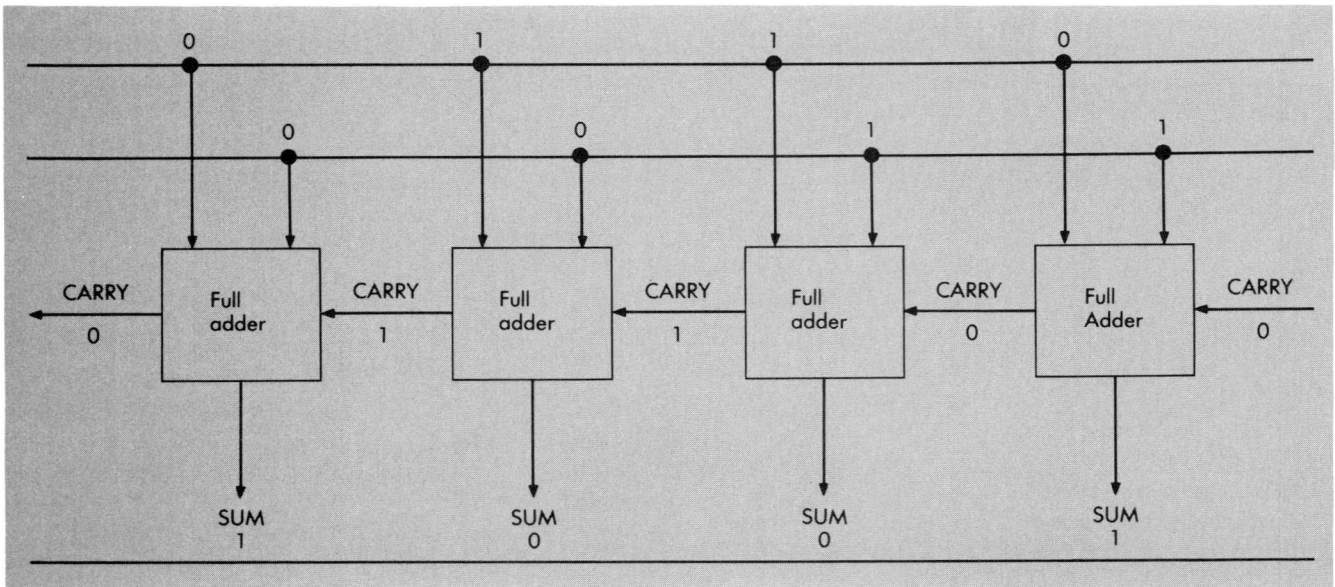

Fig. 9.10 The addition of two four bit binary numbers using full adders.
The sum 0110 + 0011 = 1001 is shown.

previous addition. The three input bits are added together to give a sum bit and a carry bit. Figure 9.10 illustrates the addition of two four bit binary numbers using four full adders. The Arithmetic and Logic Unit in the CPU will contain full adders to enable it to do any additions required.

3 ▷ A FAULT DETECTION SYSTEM

All industrial machines should have automatic systems for monitoring their performance. This is essential for good quality manufacture and safety. Logic circuits can be designed to detect breakdowns, etc. as they occur. The following describes a typical arrangement.

An industrial machine has its own monitoring system which sets a 'fault detect' signal light when the machine breaks down. When a breakdown happens, a green light which is normally *on* is turned *off*, a *red light* comes on and a *bell* rings. The machine operator can use an over-ride switch to turn the bell off but the red light stays on until the fault is cleared. This type of arrangement is a fairly common safety system for machine tools and other industrial machines. Figure 9.11 shows a logic circuit that could be used.

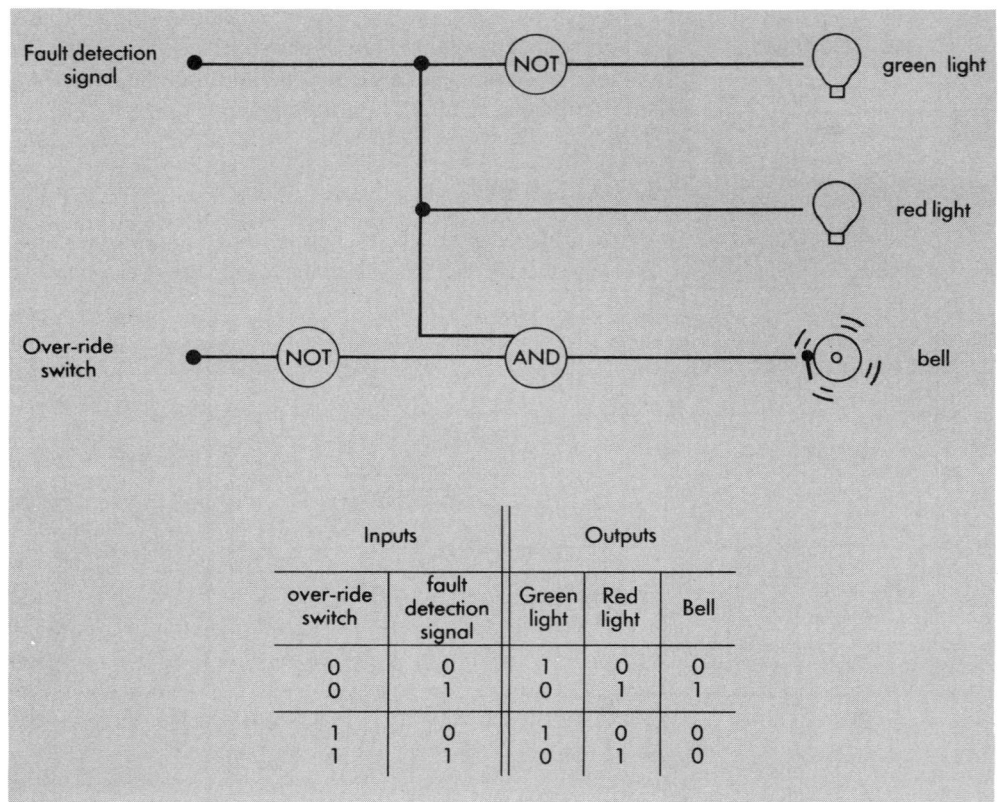

Inputs		Outputs		
over-ride switch	fault detection signal	Green light	Red light	Bell
0	0	1	0	0
0	1	0	1	1
1	0	1	0	0
1	1	0	1	0

Fig. 9.11 A safety system for industrial machines

<table>
<tr><td>4</td><td>A TRAFFIC
LIGHT
CONTROLLER</td></tr>
</table>

Logic circuits can be used to control the operation of traffic lights. For example, a traffic light may be controlled by a timing system (see Fig. 9.12). The timing system has a two bit output that sets the four states used in a basic traffic light system. The timer controls the duration of each state and its output determines which combination of lights is selected.

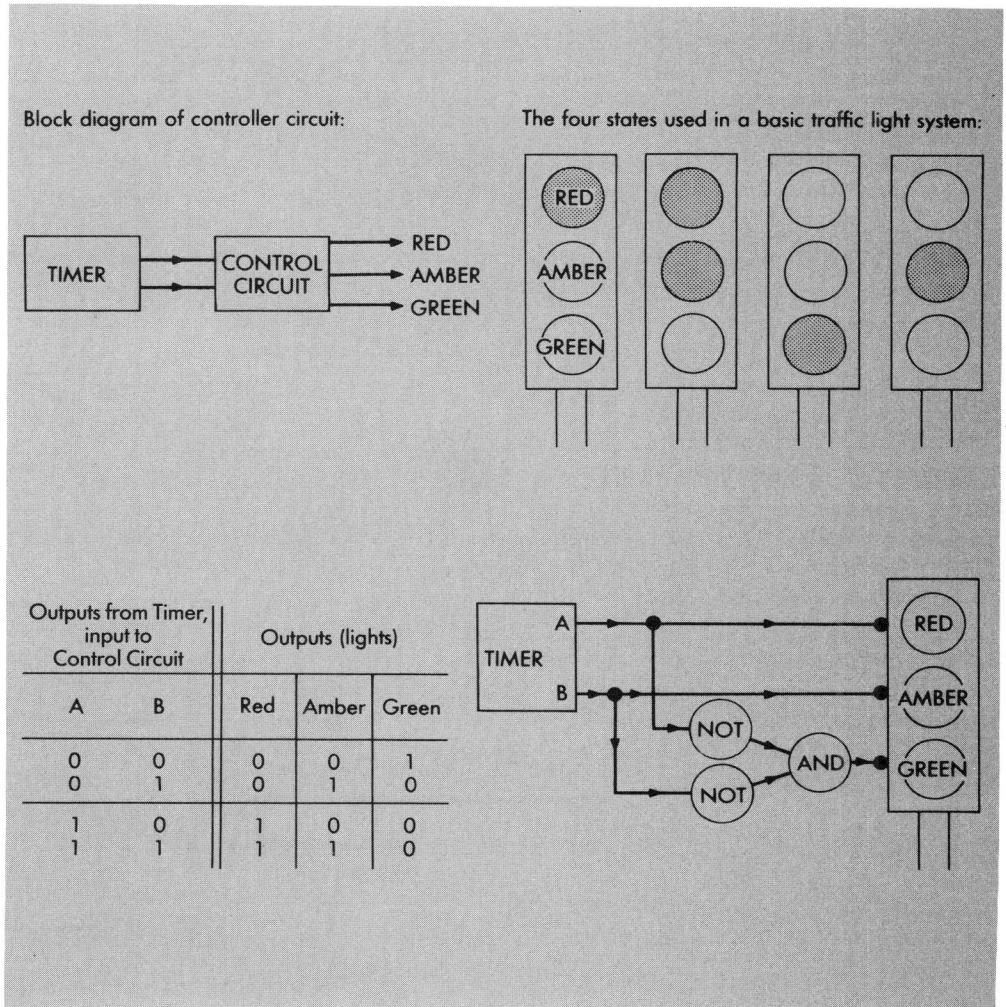

Block diagram of controller circuit:

The four states used in a basic traffic light system:

Outputs from Timer, input to Control Circuit		Outputs (lights)		
A	B	Red	Amber	Green
0	0	0	0	1
0	1	0	1	0
1	0	1	0	0
1	1	1	1	0

Fig. 9.12 A traffic light controller

<table>
<tr><td>5</td><td>A LIFT
CONTROL
SYSTEM</td></tr>
</table>

Computer systems can replace logic circuits in more complex control applications. Part of a lift control system is shown in Figure 9.13. In this case sensors, activators and a microcomputer are used.

A **sensor** is a device which responds to a particular environmental condition by outputting a voltage in proportion to the magnitude of the condition sensed. In the case of the lift control, system sensors A and B will normally output 0 volts. If the infra red beam attached to the base of the lift shines on them, they output 5 volts. The *Analogue to Digital Convertors (ADCs)* convert the analogue voltage to a digital signal which can be input by the computer.

An **activator** is a device which inputs control signals from a computer, interprets them and initiates the required actions. The lift motor activator will control whether the motor is on or off regardless of the direction it turns.

As the lift is moving upwards the infra red beam attached to the bottom of the lift passes sensor B, which sends a signal to the computer. If the lift has to stop at a particular floor the computer will signal the lift motor activator to stop the motor and the lift will slow down and stop. However, if sensor A is passed while the lift is slowing down, then the floor of the lift will be too far above the level of the floor of the building. In this case the computer will reverse the lift motor and the lift moves downwards. As sensor A is passed by the lift going downwards, the computer detects this and stops the lift motor so that the lift slows down and stops. However, if sensor B is passed the floor of the lift will be too far below the level of the floor of the building! The computer senses this and reverses the lift motor so that the lift is moving upwards again. This process is repeated until the floor of the lift comes to rest between sensors A and B. This cycle of sensing and reaction is known as a

feedback loop. Feedback loops are an essential part of most computer control systems.

A computer is used to control the lift because the logic is complex. This is only part of a larger system that may involve selection of floors from inside or outside the lift and scheduling of several lifts. The logical decisions involved can be easily expressed in a computer program.

Fig. 9.13 Part of a computer control system for a lift

6 A COMPUTER CONTROLLED GREENHOUSE

Figure 9.14 is an illustration of a computer control system for a greenhouse. The aim of such a system is to regulate temperature and humidity, so that optimum plant growth is achieved. The temperature and humidity sensors monitor the environmental conditions in the greenhouse and the heater, window motor and overhead spray activators are used to control it.

The humidity sensor generates a voltage that is proportional to the amount of water vapour in the air. Voltage is an analogue signal. This signal is input to the ADC which converts it to a binary number. If the humidity is low, the voltage is low and the binary number is also low. The size of the binary number output from the ADC and input to the computer is proportional to the humidity in the greenhouse.

The computer is programmed to respond to low humidity by turning on the overhead spray and closing the windows. This is done by sending control signals to the window motor activator and the overhead spray activator. These turn on the overhead spray and the motor to close the windows. This has the effect of increasing the humidity. As the humidity increases, the sensors sense this and the system responds until an *equilibrium state* is reached. This is another example of a feedback loop.

If necessary, temperature and humidity data can be recorded at regular intervals so that

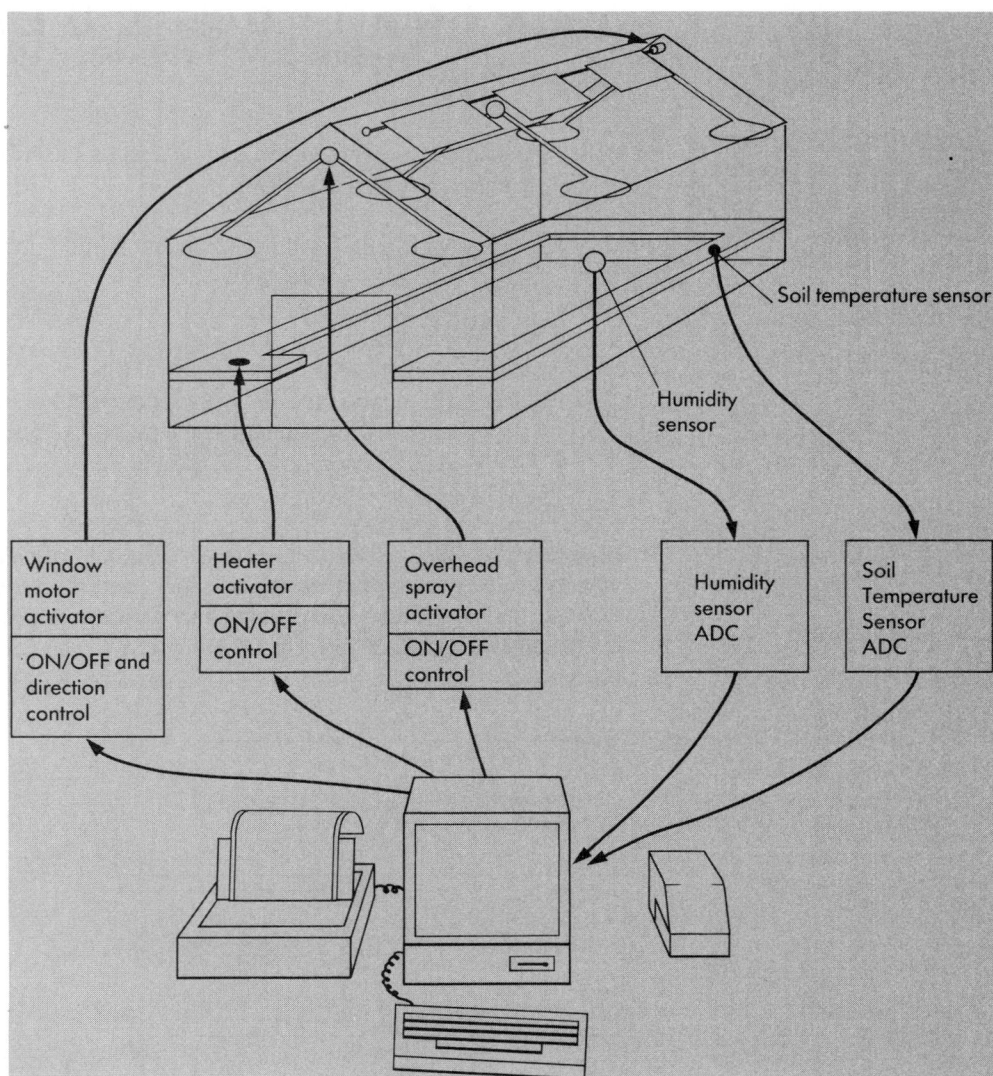

Fig. 9.14 A computer control system for a greenhouse

a record of the environmental conditions in the greenhouse is kept. This data would be saved on backing storage, in this case, floppy discs. The process of reading and saving environmental data is known as **data logging**. Data logging is done so that we can analyse the recorded data at a later date.

A computer control system for a greenhouse is only justified if the business is large enough for the improved quality and quantity of produce grown to pay for the computer system. In practice, one computer would control several greenhouses.

In a large business with several greenhouses the advantages of a computer control system lie in its ability to *precisely* control temperature and humidity in all the greenhouses at all times. Each greenhouse will have its own program of temperature and humidity settings stored in the computer. These can be set at different levels depending on the time of day. To alter the settings it is only necessary to enter new values at the keyboard. The computer will automatically change the environment in the greenhouse to these new settings. The control system constantly monitors the environment day and night. It responds immediately to any variation from the required settings. The entire system can be controlled from the computer. Other sensors and activators could be fitted to control lighting, shade and other factors if needed.

E X A M I N A T I O N   Q U E S T I O N S

In Questions 1 and 2 a common computing term is described. You are required to write down the term that has been described.

1   *Description:* A logic gate with two inputs and one output. The output is logic 1 only when both inputs are logic 1.

    Term: _____

(NEA; 1988)

2   *Description:* The action involved in collecting data for a particular computer process, such as the continuous collection of temperatures in a chemical process.

    Term: _____

(NEA; 1988)

3   A microprocessor system is used to control the heating in a house. The heating can be set to come on and off at particular times, and the temperature in each room can be individually set. Within each room there is a temperature sensor, and an electrically controlled valve to turn the radiators on and off.

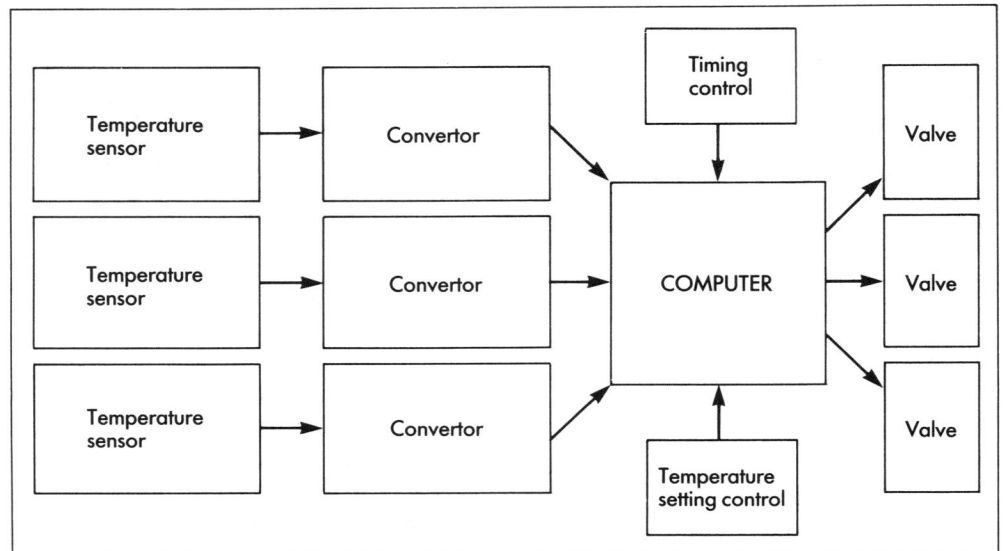

   a) Explain why the convertors are needed. (3 lines available)

(3)

   b) Discuss the advantages and disadvantages of using a computer controlled system compared with other control systems. (10 lines available)

(8)

   c) Describe briefly another way in which a computer might be used in the home to assist the householder. (15 lines available).

(8)

(SEG; 1988)

4   A runner is training for a 1500 m race. The coach is worried about the effects of running on the athlete's heart and lungs. To monitor the runner there is a microcomputer system worn on a belt around her waist. There are sensors that will measure the following:
    1 breathing rate;
    2 heart rate;
    3 stepping rate.
These sensors are connected to the microprocessor. The microprocessor is connected to a radio transmitter. The transmitter sends the information collected to a track side computer system. This is shown in the diagram on the next page.

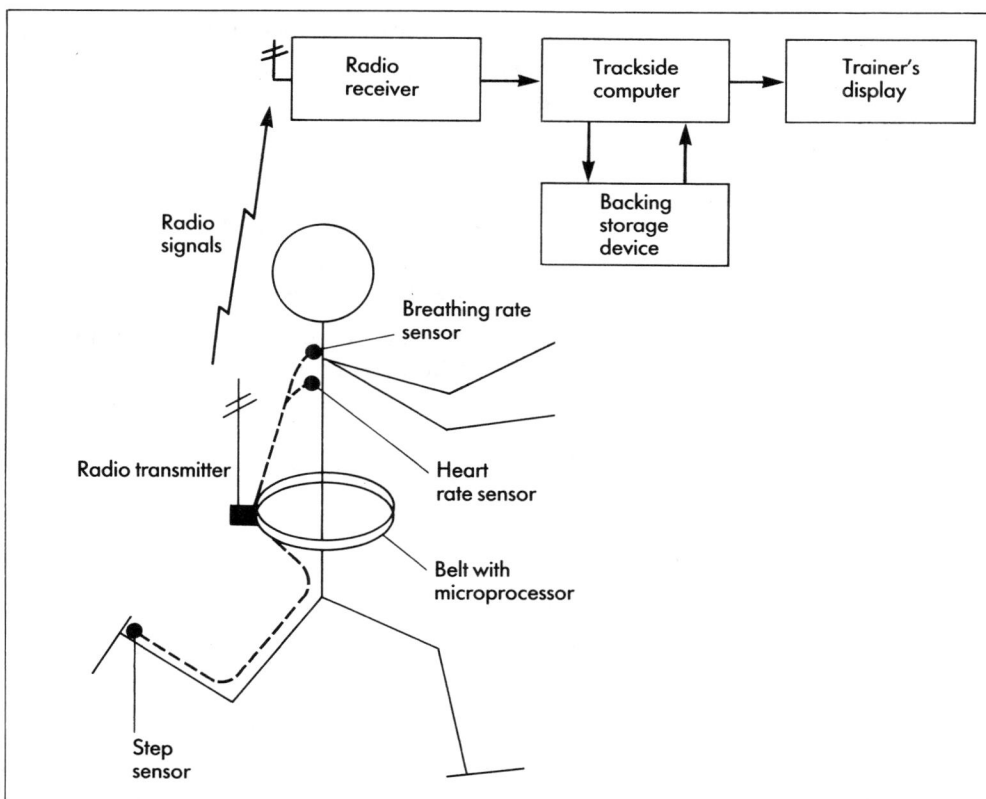

a) What inputs are required for this data logging system?

_____

b) There is an output device connected to the belt microprocessor. This output device is not shown on the diagram. It gives urgent information to the runner.
   i) Describe or name a suitable device.

   _____

   ii) Give one use for this device

   _____

c) The track side computer system also has an output device.
   i) Describe or name a suitable device.

   _____

   ii) Give one use for this device.

   _____

d) Give one reason why there is a backing storage device provided on the track side computer.

(LEAG; 1988)

5 An automatic car wash offers a number of alternative programs. It is controlled by a microprocessor. The microprocessor is connected to a number of sensors and activators.

a) What is the purpose of

   i) a sensor? _____

   _____

   ii) an activator? _____

   _____

b) The algorithm below describes briefly how a customer operates the car wash.

> select a program for the car wash and pay
> REPEAT
>   drive forward into the car wash
> UNTIL a red light comes on
> REPEAT
>   wait for the car to be washed
> UNTIL a green light comes on
> drive out of the car wash

Give **two** types of sensor that the car wash might include and in each case give a reason why the sensor is needed.

Sensor 1: _____

Reason: _____

_____

_____

Sensor 2: _____

Reason: _____

(NEA; 1988)

6   A computer-controlled car park issues tickets as cars arrive. When the time comes to leave the driver inserts the ticket into a payment device. The computer calculates and displays the fee. The driver inserts coins into the device to pay the fee. If necessary the machine will give change. The payment device then issues an "exit" ticket. The driver now has a short time in which to drive the car to the exit barrier and insert the exit ticket. When the exit ticket is inserted the computer raises the barrier.

  a) State a suitable machine-readable method for encoding the arrival time on the parking ticket the machine issues.   (1)

  b) Identify **three** different output devices that would be connected to the car park computer system. Say **briefly** what they would be used for.   (3)

  c) The control program that runs the car park system has many parts. One part works out which coins need to be ejected when change is required. For example, if the computer has calculated that the driver needs 37p in change, which coins are to be ejected?
    One answer would be:
      1 – 10p coin
      5 – 5p coins
      2 – 1p coins
    i)   Give another possible answer that uses fewer coins.
    ii) Give another possible answer if there are no 20p coins or 5p coins left in the payment device.   (2)

  d) The payment device accepts 1p, 2p, 5p, 10p, 20p, and 50p coins. It will use all except the 50p coin in giving change. The device issues change using the least number of coins possible.
    i)   Assuming that there are always enough of each type of coin to give the required coins in change, design an algorithm that would work out how many of each of the five types of coin to eject. You may explain your algorithm using a diagram or words.   (7)
    ii) Dry run your finished algorithm with 37p as the change required.   (1)
    iii) Give a revised algorithm that will take account of some coins having run out.   (6)

(LEAG; 1988)

OUTLINE ANSWERS

1   *Term:* AND gate.

2   *Term:* Data logging or data capture.

3   a) Convertors, i.e. Analogue to Digital convertors, are needed to change the analogue voltage output by the sensors to digital data, i.e. binary numbers, that can be input and processed by the computer.

   b) **Advantages:**
      i)   Constant monitoring of temperature.
      ii) Immediate response to temperature change.
      iii) Computer can be programmed to maintain different temperatures at different times of the day.
      iv) Entire system can be controlled from one place.

   Disadvantages:
      i)   Expensive to install.
      ii) If the computer malfunctions then the entire system goes wrong.
      iii) Specialist skills are needed to set up and run the system. People with these skills might not be available.

   c) Computers can assist the householder by helping with the running of household finance. Software packages are available to help with budgeting, paying bills and saving. They give detailed breakdowns of past spending and can be used to estimate future expenditure.

4   a) Heart beat;
      Air intake;
      Steps taken.

   b) i) Loudspeaker
      ii) The loudspeaker is used to tell the runner if the heart rate is so fast it is dangerous. If the loudspeaker made a beep for every heart beat, then the runner could use this information to increase or decrease running speed to match the stress on the heart.

   c) i) Monitor
      ii) The monitor is used to display the input data as it is recorded so that the trainer can monitor the performance of the runner from the trackside.

   d) The backing storage device is used to record the data for each training session. This can later be analysed so that ways of improving the runner's performance can be found.

5   a) i) A sensor is a device that responds to some environmental condition, e.g. temperature, by outputting a voltage proportional to the level of the condition sensed.
      ii) An activator turns some device on or off, e.g. a valve.

   b) i) *Sensor 1:* A touch sensor in the floor.
      Reason: To detect if the car is far enough into the car wash.
      Sensor 2: A temperature sensor
      Reason: To ensure the water used is at the right temperature.

6   a) The time could be recorded on a magnetic stripe on the ticket.

   b) i)   A write head to record the time on the magnetic stripe.
      ii) A small monitor screen or an LED display to show the fee payable.
      iii) Activators to release the coins given as change.

c) i) 1 – 20p
    1 – 10p
    1 – 5p
    1 – 2p

  ii) 3 – 10p
    3 – 2p
    1 – 1p

d) i) A simple algorithm is used here. (For a more elegant solution see d) iii) below.)

> START OF ALGORITHM
> Determine change needed (AMOUNT)
> REPEAT
>   If AMOUNT is bigger than or equal to 20p
>   then payout a 20p coin
>   subtract 20p from AMOUNT.
> UNTIL AMOUNT is less than 20p.
> REPEAT
>   If AMOUNT is bigger than or equal to 10p
>   then payout a 10p coin
>   subtract 10p from AMOUNT.
> UNTIL AMOUNT is less than 10p.
> REPEAT
>   If AMOUNT is bigger than or equal to 5p
>   then payout a 5p coin
>   subtract 5p from AMOUNT.
> UNTIL AMOUNT is less than 5p.
> REPEAT
>   If AMOUNT is bigger than or equal to 2p
>   then payout a 2p coin
>   subtract 2p from AMOUNT.
> UNTIL AMOUNT is less than 2p.
> REPEAT
>   If AMOUNT is bigger than or equal to 1p
>   then payout a 1p coin
>   subtract 1p from AMOUNT.
> UNTIL AMOUNT is less than 1p.
> END OF ALGORITHM.

  ii) Dry run:

Action taken	AMOUNT
Change determined	37p
payout 20p coin	17p
payout 10p coin	7p
payout 5p coin	2p
payout 2p coin	0p

  iii)

> START MAIN PART OF ALGORITHM
> Determine change needed (AMOUNT)
> COIN: = 20p
> PROCEDURE Payout
> COIN: = 10p
> PROCEDURE Payout
> COIN: = 5p
> PROCEDURE Payout
> COIN: = 2p
> PROCEDURE Payout
> COIN: = 1p
> PROCEDURE Payout
> END OF MAIN PART OF ALGORITHM

PROCEDURE Payout.
  REPEAT
     If (AMOUNT is bigger than or equal to COIN)
*   and (COINs have not run out)
       then   payout a COIN
             subtract COIN from AMOUNT.
   UNTIL AMOUNT is less than COIN.
 END OF PROCEDURE Payout.

---

*   This line takes into account that some coins have run out. It could have been used at the appropriate points in the simple solution shown in (d)(i)

A STUDENT'S ANSWER WITH EXAMINER'S COMMENTS

QUESTION

All computer systems require at least one input device and at least one output device if they are to do a useful job. The table below shows three situations. Fill in the columns headed input device and output device with the name of a suitable device.

Situation	Input device	Output device
a) A microprocessor system in a washing machine	*water pipe*	*drain*
b) An enquiry/booking system of a large airline	*screen*	*ticket*
c) An arcade video game	*joystick and fire buttons*	*screen*

(LEAG; 1988)

Examiner comment:

a) The student's answer refers to the washing machine, not the microprocessor based control system. The microprocessor will need inputs from a temperature sensor and a timer. Output devices will be activators to turn on and off the water input valve, the water heater and the washing machine motor.

b) A screen is never an input device and a ticket is not a device but an output medium. Correct answers are:
Input device: The keyboard of a terminal on-line to the main computer
Output device: A ticket printer.

c) Correct.

GETTING STARTED

The type of output generated is determined by the use to which it will be put. For instant output a **monitor** screen is best. These can be *low, medium* or *high resolution* and may vary in size. Most computers are attached to a monitor for interactive use.

For permanency, a **printer** using **continuous fan fold** stationery or single A4 sheets is satisfactory. The stationery may be pulled through the printer by a **tractor feed** or pushed through by a **friction feed**. Depending on the speed and quality of printout required a **character**, **line** or **page** printer will be used. The printer mechanism may be **impact** or **non-impact**. Because a printer is a slow peripheral a **spooling** queue may be used and also a **buffer**, so that the computer can be used for other tasks while the printer is in use.

Printed paper is bulky and in the long term will deteriorate. Computer output on **Microfilm** or **Microfiche** is more compact and lasts longer, so it is ideal for distribution, storage and reference.

Graph plotters are used for high quality drawings as the limited graphic capabilities of most printers are inadequate. Where printed output would not be understood, or to emphasize commands from the computer, **speech synthesis** may be appropriate, since the spoken word communicates more effectively.

ESSENTIAL PRINCIPLES

Output generated by computers is familiar to most people even if they have little contact with computers in other ways. A visit to a travel agency, a motor spares stockist or an estate agency may also bring us into contact with screen output. Electricity Boards, Gas Boards, Local Councils and a variety of other bodies, all send out bills which have been printed by computer. Libraries often store their indexes on microfiche; historians will use a computer to store plans and maps. This chapter contains a brief, but systematic, review of computer generated output.

1 ▷ MONITORS

When using a computer it is likely that you will receive information about the activities taking place in the computer by reading the output on a screen. This screen is known as a **monitor**. A monitor looks very much like a television set. In response to the output you may be asked to provide some input. The input prompt to attract your attention, so that you will reply to the request for data as quickly as possible, is a flashing **cursor**. The cursor is a small square that appears on the screen. The input will then be used by the computer. This cycle of input, processing and output will continue while the computer is being used. This is **interactive** processing, so called because the user interacts with the computer. Interactive processing is very similar to having a conversation with the computer, but instead of *hearing* the conversation we *see* it on the screen.

Most microcomputers must have a monitor attached before they can be used, as they are almost always used interactively. A monitor is probably the most common output peripheral in use with computers. With home computers it is very common to use a television as a monitor. Television sets do not usually give as clear a picture as a monitor, but they can receive TV programmes, which is not possible on a monitor.

❝❝ Types of monitor ❞❞

Monitors can be **high**, **medium** or **low resolution**. The level of resolution is measured in **pixels**. A pixel is the smallest area of the screen that can be changed by the computer. A pixel can be thought of as a dot that makes up a picture, similar to the dots that make up a photograph in a newspaper.

HIGH RESOLUTION

This means that it is possible to display a very detailed picture on the screen. In high resolution the screen may display, for example, 640 by 400 pixels, though higher densities are possible. High resolution monitors are used when we want very detailed and accurate screen displays. They are particularly useful for Graphic Design, Computer Aided Design and related applications. It is also possible to buy high resolution screens that are much bigger than normal screens. For example, in Desk Top Publishing there may be a need to view a whole A4 (the size of this page is A4) or A3 (twice as big as A4) page on the screen for it to be readable. Extra large, high resolution screens make this possible.

MEDIUM AND LOW RESOLUTION

These monitors provide less detailed screen displays than a high resolution monitor but they are also correspondingly cheaper. If high resolution is not required for a particular application, then a medium resolution monitor could be adequate. A typical medium resolution monitor will display 640 by 200 pixels, much less than the high resolution screen. A low resolution display may be only 320 by 200 pixels. A low resolution display is generally suitable for television sets, which can be used to good effect with computer games at home.

2 ▷ PRINTERS AND HARD COPY

Printed output from a computer is called **hard copy**. Printers use paper that is **continuous** in the sense that there are many sheets joined together. These sheets are joined by perforations that make the sheets easier to separate. The paper is folded into a box in a **fan-fold**. Down the sides of the paper are rows of **sprocket holes** which are used to pull the paper through the printer (see Fig. 10.1).

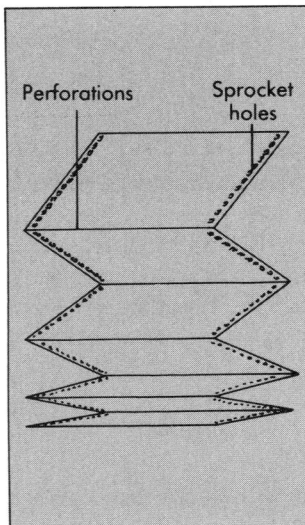

Fig. 10.1 Continuous fan-fold printer stationery

Computer stationery may be plain or can be **pre-printed** with other details beforehand. Companies sending out invoices or bills often pre-print their computer stationery with their logo and other details before the computer is used to add the details for each customer (see Fig. 10.2). This method is often used to produce individualised bills and advertising material that address the customer by name. Where several copies of the printed output are needed, perhaps for sending to the customer and filing in the office, it is possible to print on **multipart** computer paper. Multipart stationery consists of several layers of continuous fan-fold stationery with a layer of carbon paper between. Printing takes place as usual to produce a top-copy, but other copies are produced through the carbon paper. When using multipart stationery it is necessary to use an **impact** printer. This has a print head that physically hits an inked ribbon onto the printer paper. The impact transfers the ink on the ribbon to the paper. Printers that use ink jets or a thermal print head do not come into contact with the paper. These are **non-impact** printers.

Fig. 10.2 A pre-printed bill with details added by computer at a later date

CHARACTER PRINTERS

Character printers print one character at a time. They are the slowest type of printer. Their speed is measured in **cps**, i.e. characters per second. Speeds of between 80 and 200 cps are usual. Character printers are relatively cheap and can be purchased for £200 or less. They are often used with microcomputers where their slow speed is unimportant, because of the low volume of printed output, and their low cost makes them attractive.

Dot matrix printers

66 Types of Character Printer **99**

These form each character by printing part of a 7 by 5 matrix (see Fig. 10.3). Most dot matrix printers are impact printers. These have a print head consisting of a corresponding matrix of steel pins that are projected or withdrawn to form the shape of the character. The printout produced by these printers is **draft** print which is of a very low quality. Some dot matrix printers now print in two modes – draft and **Near Letter Quality** (NLQ). In NLQ mode each character is printed twice, producing a much better quality printout.

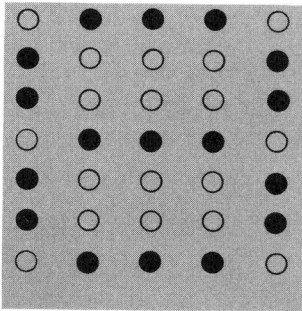

Fig. 10.3 The number 8 formed by a dot matrix print head

The flexibility of the shape formed by the print head makes these printers ideal for printing graphics, though the quality is not good enough for specialist graphics applications. This type of dot matrix printer is a good general purpose printer at an economic price (around £200) and they are used extensively in schools and offices.

Impact dot matrix printers can also be used with a coloured ribbon to produce printout in several colours. The colour cannot be blended and consequently is not sufficiently adaptable for good quality artwork, but can be used to good effect to emphasise simple graphs and bar charts.

Ink jet printers

These are non-impact dot matrix printers which have been developed recently to overcome some of the limitations of the impact dot matrix printer. These printers shoot a jet of ink at the paper to form the printed character. Ink jet printers tend to be more expensive (around £800), but produce much better quality print and graphics. The quality and range of the colour printing possible is also improved.

Daisywheel printers

These have a daisywheel print head (see Fig. 10.4). There is a character shape on the end of each spoke, or 'petal'. The daisy wheel spins in front of a hammer which strikes the required character as it passes, pressing it against an inked ribbon which prints the character shape on the paper. Daisywheel printers are very slow, and more expensive than a dot matrix printer, but give very high quality printing. They are not able to print graphics. For these reasons daisywheel printers are most often found in use with wordprocessors.

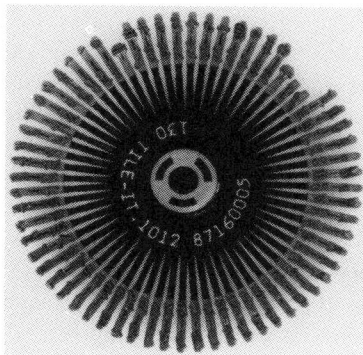

Fig. 10.4 A daisywheel print head

LINE PRINTERS

Line printers print one line at a time. Speeds of up to 2000 lines per minute are possible. Line printers are relatively expensive and may cost £1,000 or more depending on their speed and capacity. They are often used with mainframe computers where their high speed is important because of the high volume of printed output that is required. They can only print a restricted number of characters and are not capable of graphics.

> Types of *Line Printer*

Barrel printers, or *drum* printers, have a print mechanism that works on the principle shown in Figure 10.6. Each line on the barrel has one character only. The barrel contains lines for every character it can print. The barrel spins once for each line printed. There is a hammer for each print position. The hammer strikes the paper against the ribbon and the barrel, thus transferring the printed character to the paper. The line is built up as shown in Figure 10.5.

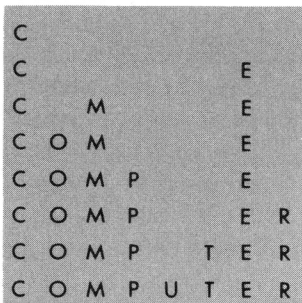

Fig. 10.5 The build up of a line containing the word 'COMPUTER' when using a barrel printer

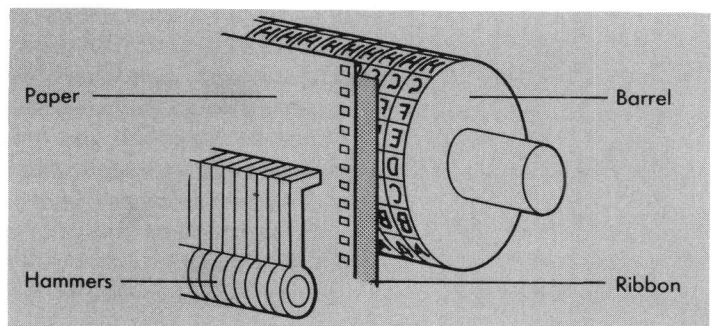

Fig. 10.6 A barrel printer mechanism

Chain printers

These also build up one line at a time. The print mechanism used is shown in Figure 10.7. The chain rotates, so that the required character will at some stage pass the print position. Commonly used characters may appear on the chain more frequently than other letters in order to speed up printing.

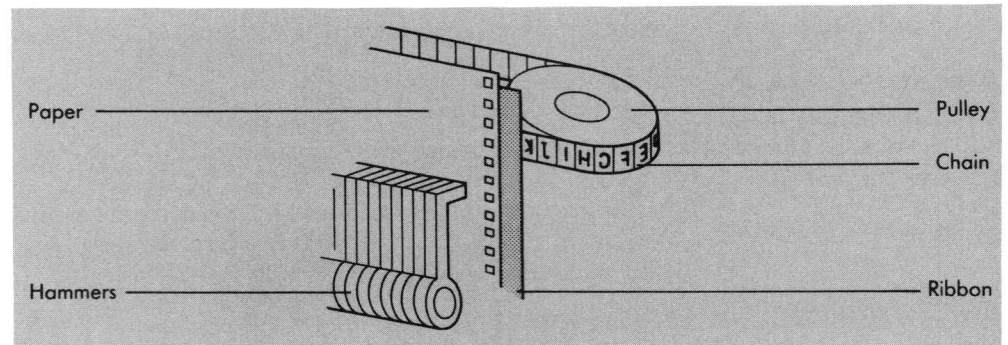

Fig. 10.7 A chain printer mechanism

PAGE PRINTERS

Laser Printers as a type of *Page Printer*

Page printers print a page at a time. The most common type of page printer is a **laser printer**. Speeds of up to 200 pages per minute are possible. Page printers are expensive in relation to other printers, though their cost depends on their speed and quality of the print. A low cost laser printer can be purchased for as little as £1500. They are found in use with many different types of computer system, as they can print a very wide range of characters and graphics.

Laser printers work by directing a laser beam at an electrostatically-charged surface. The shape of the characters is 'etched' onto the charged surface to make a template of the shapes to be printed. This is then used to transfer ink to the paper. In most cases ordinary paper can be used. Low-cost laser printers are very often found in use with Desk Top Publishing systems.

3 > BUFFERS AND SPOOLING

All printers are slow compared with the speed of the processor in a computer. If a program needs to use a printer this can prevent other programs and users from making use of the computer. It may mean a long wait while the computer is printing before other work can continue.

Buffers

Most printers make use of **buffers**. A buffer is extra memory, usually outside the IAS or RAM memory, that is used to store output while it is waiting to be printed. Many printers used with microcomputers have buffers built into them. A program that needs to use the printer will transfer any printed output to the buffer and then continue processing immediately. The printer then prints the data from the buffer while the program that produced the output, or another program, is being run.

Buffers and Spooling

Buffers are often able to hold several pages of data waiting to be printed, but even so, their capacity is limited. If there is a large volume of printout to be done then the buffer may be filled. The computer cannot continue until all the data has been printed or transferred to the buffer. This causes the processor to wait for the slower printer.

Spooling

Waiting for the printer can be avoided by **spooling** the printer output. In spooling, all printed output is first written as a data file to backing storage. Transfer to backing storage peripherals such as magnetic disc is very fast. Once the output has been stored, the program can continue processing. The data file now joins the queue for the printer. Printing takes place when the data file reaches the head of the queue. This may take some time on a computer system with high volumes of printed output. The printout may not be done until quite a long time after the program has finished processing.

Buffers are almost always found in use with printers. Even inexpensive printers used with microcomputers have integral buffers. The technique of spooling is generally confined to mainframe computers, as they are capable of multiprogramming, although with the introduction of microcomputers capable of multitasking, spooling is more likely to be used.

PRINTER PAPER FEED MECHANISMS

The **tractor feed** is the most common type of paper feed mechanism. It consists of two toothed wheels, one positioned at each edge of the paper, that engage the sprocket holes in the edge of the paper and pull it through the printer (see Fig. 10.8).

On some printers used with microcomputer systems the tractor feed is either not used, or can be removed. Instead, a **friction feed** is used. This consists of a hard rubber roller, the same width as the paper, that presses against the paper and pushes it through the printer. A friction feed mechanism is not suitable for large volumes of printout on continuous stationery but is very useful if printout on a single sheet of standard A4 is required. The sheet can be fed into the printer by hand. This is a slow and cumbersome method, so **single sheet feeders** have been developed. These supply single A4 sheets to the printer, which are then pulled through the printer by the friction feed. This method is increasingly used in small offices where there is no requirement for high volumes of printout, but letters are often printed on single sheets of paper.

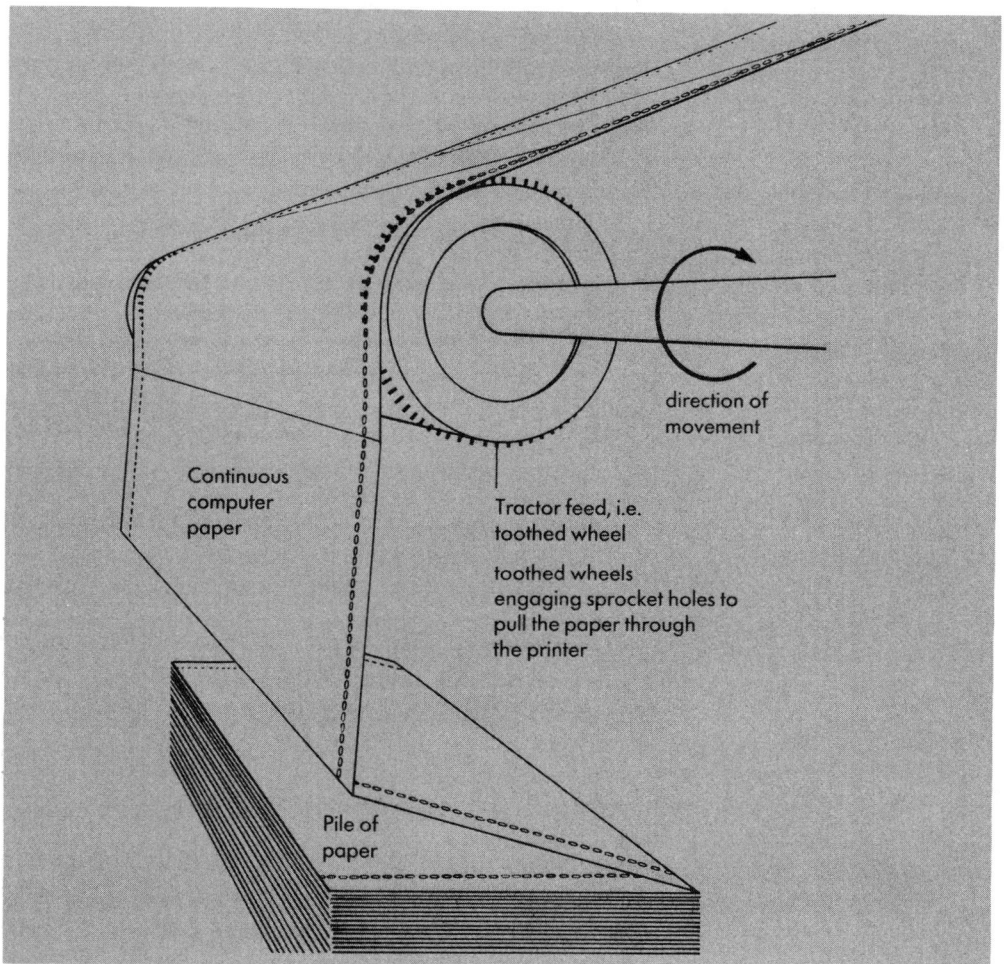

direction of movement

Continuous computer paper

Tractor feed, i.e. toothed wheel

toothed wheels engaging sprocket holes to pull the paper through the printer

Pile of paper

Fig. 10.8 A tractor feed

4 ▷ COMPUTER OUTPUT ON MICROFILM

Where it is necessary to keep a record of activities, high volumes of output may need to be kept for perhaps several years. Such records may need to be consulted infrequently, or there may be a legal requirement to keep them. Records printed on paper will take up a large amount of storage space and tend to deteriorate quickly. Instead of storing the output printed on paper it is possible to make a copy of the page on microfilm, as it would have appeared had it been printed. This is **Computer Output on Microfilm (COM)**.

66 Advantages of COM 99

Microfilm takes up much less storage space and does not deteriorate as quickly as paper. Microfilm is generally available as a roll of film 16mm or 35mm wide. The only disadvantage of microfilm is that a special reader must be used, but the expense of this is more than compensated for by lower storage costs.

COM is also useful where large volumes of information are needed at a variety of locations. A common example of this is the book index in a library. Printed output is again unsuitable because it is bulky, difficult to access and easily torn. Microfilm is not used

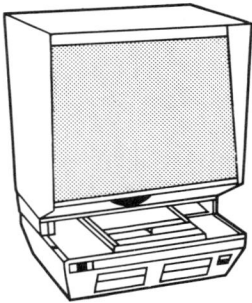
Fig. 10.9 A microfiche reader

because it is made up as a roll. Instead, the roll is converted into flat sheets of **microfiche** measuring 105 × 148mm. The microfiche index can be copied many times and be made available at any location, provided a **microfiche reader** is available (see Fig. 10.9). Microfiche is easily packed and sent through the post. For this reason it is also suitable for applications such as spare parts indexes for motor vehicles, etc. A visit to a local library, or a motor spares dealer, to see microfiche in use is highly recommended.

5 ▷ GRAPH PLOTTERS

Most printers are unable to print high quality precision graphics. Where these are necessary, a **graph plotter** is used. Graph plotters are very slow, but can draw continuous lines, often in several colours. A **flat bed graph plotter** is illustrated in Figure 10.10. The graph plotter illustrated has three interchangeable pens mounted on the rigid arm. These can be lowered for drawing, one at a time, as required. The pens can be moved from left to right, while the rigid arm can be moved backwards and forwards to allow continuous lines to be drawn on the paper.

Graph plotters are a highly specialised output device. They are especially useful for architectural drawings, building plans and Computer Aided Design applications, where a high quality precision drawing is required, but the volume of output is low.

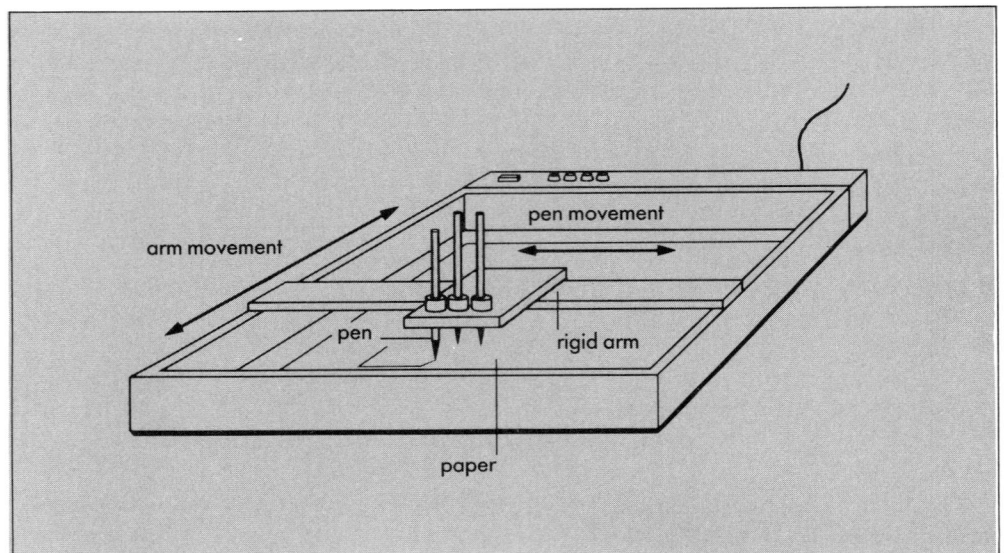
Fig. 10.10 A flat bed graph plotter

6 ▷ SPEECH SYNTHESIS

For some applications printed output, on the screen or on paper is inappropriate. It may be that only a few instructions are required in a situation where reading would be difficult. In any event, some people have difficulty reading, perhaps through disabilities of one form or another. Attempts have been made to get the computer to produce sounds similar to normal speech; this is **speech synthesis**.

Most microcomputers have available software to enable the user to program in simple speech. Educational software often uses limited speech synthesis, as do many games. However, speech as spoken by people is still not a reality. Most synthesised speech has a distinctive sound and is easily identified.

E X A M I N A T I O N   Q U E S T I O N S

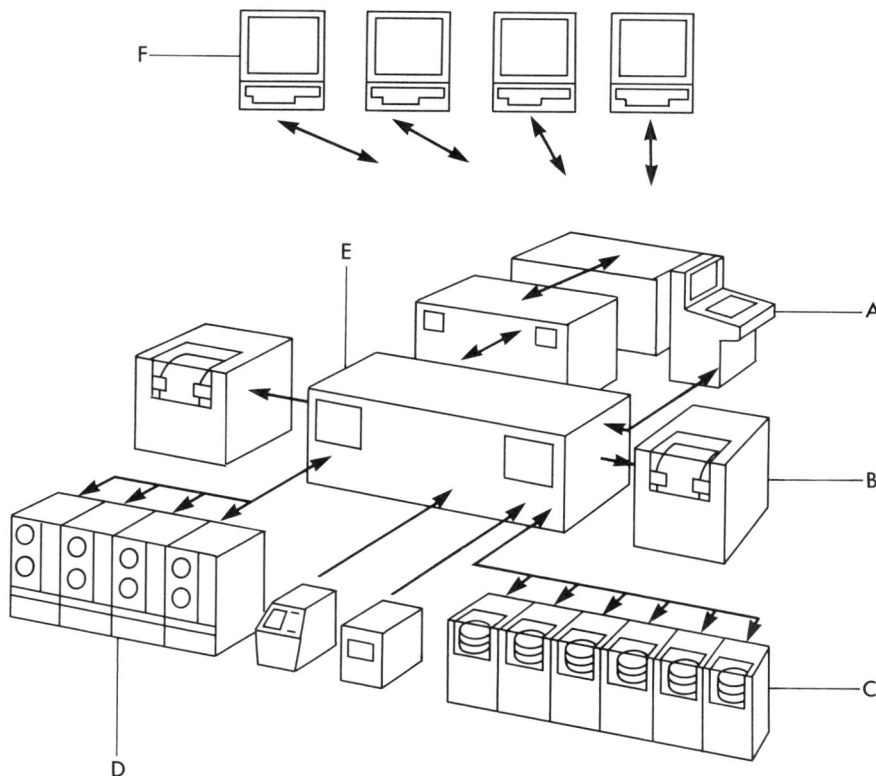

The components of a mainframe system.

1   Write down the names of the units marked **A, B, C, D, E** and **F** in the above diagram
    of a mainframe computer system using the following words: (6)
    Line Printer; Magnetic Tape Drives; Magnetic Disc Drives;
    Main Processor; Terminals; Operator's Console.
    A _____
    B _____
    C _____
    D _____
    E _____
    F _____

                                                                          (WJEC; 1988)

2   Indicate which two of these devices are computer output devices.
        graph plotter   printer   joystick   light pen   keyboard   (2)
                                                                          (MEG; 1988)

3   The following table contains a list of some computer devices. Put a tick in the column
    which best describes that device.

DEVICE	BACKING STORE	INPUT	OUTPUT
graphics tablet			
speech synthesiser			
disc drive			

                                                                                 (3)
                                                                          (MEG; 1988)

4   Answer **all** questions in the spaces provided.

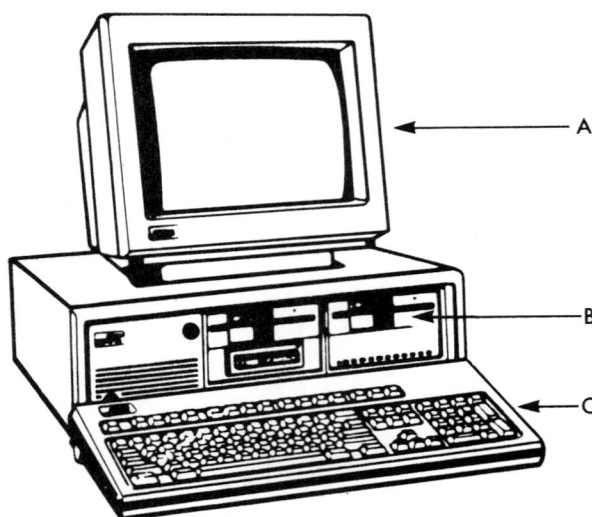

Write down the names of the units marked **A, B** and **C** on the above diagram of a microcomputer.   (3)

A   _____

B   _____

C   _____   (WJEC; 1988)

5   The following table contains a list of devices and media. Show whether each is used for input or output, by means of a tick (√) in the correct column   (4)

Device/Media	Tick (√) Input	Tick (√) Output
Mouse		
Graph Plotter		
Line Printer		
Magnetic Ink Character Reader		

(WJEC; 1988)

6   A daisywheel printer, a dot matrix printer, and a graph plotter could all be used to produce paper output from a computer.

a) A daisywheel printer and a dot matrix printer could both be used to print business letters in an office. Explain which would be better in this case.

_____

_____

b) A dot matrix printer and a graph plotter could both be used by a fitted kitchen shop to produce the plans of a kitchen on paper. Explain which would be better in this situation.

_____

_____

(LEAG; 1988)

OUTLINE ANSWERS

MULTIPLE CHOICE QUESTIONS

1 A Operator's console
   B Line printer
   C Magnetic disc drives
   D Magnetic tape drives
   E Main processor
   F Terminals

2 Output devices are: graph plotter; printer.

3 Graphics tablet – input.
   Speech synthesiser – output.
   Disc drive – backing storage.

SHORT STRUCTURED QUESTIONS

4 A Monitor (*not* VDU)
   B Floppy disc drive
   C Keyboard

5 Mouse – input
   Graph plotter – output
   Line printer – output
   Magnetic Ink Character Reader – input

6 a) A daisywheel printer would be better for business letters as it gives a higher quality printout.
   b) A graph plotter would be better for kitchen plans as it produces a continuous line drawing in several colours, giving a more attractive drawing.

A STUDENT'S ANSWER WITH EXAMINER'S COMMENTS

QUESTION

a) For each of the applications described in the table below write down the most suitable sort of output device.

Producing payslips for several thousand employees.	printer
Producing detailed drawings for a computer aided design application.	graph plotter
Producing high quality letters that can be sent to business customers.	printer
Producing listings for computer programs being developed on a microcomputer.	printer

b) The payslip below was printed using pre-printed stationery.

TAX CODE:	234H	NAME:	Mr A. N. Other
N.I. No.:	YZ12345A	DATE:	July 88
		PAY No.:	666666

PAY AND ALLOWANCES		DEDUCTIONS	
BASIC PAY	543.00	INCOME TAX	143.00
BONUS	250.00	NAT. INS.	41.00
EXPENS.	38.51	PENSION	21.00
TOTAL	831.51	TOTAL	205.00
		NETT PAY	626.51

Copy from the payslip above, **one** item that would be pre-printed on the stationery before the payslip was produced, **one** item that was copied from the master file and **one** item that was calculated by the computer.

Pre-printed item: <u>all the small printing, eg. "NET PAY"</u>

Master file item: <u>name, ie. 'Mr A. N. Other'</u>

Calculated item: <u>nett pay, ie. "626.51"</u>

c)   State **one** reason for using pre-printed stationery in this case.

<u>It is cheaper</u>

_____ (NEA; 1988)

Examiner comment:

a)   It is necessary to name the different types of printer, as follows:

payslips — line printer

high quality letters — daisywheel printer

program listings — dot matrix printer

b)   correct

c)   pre-printed stationery is used because there will be a large number of payslips printed in the same layout. Pre-printing speeds up printing and gives a more attractive wage slip.

CHAPTER 11

DATA STORAGE

GETTING STARTED

Programs and data are stored in the **Immediate Access Store** or memory while the programs are edited or run and the data is processed. The IAS is made up of both RAM, which is **volatile**, and ROM which is non-volatile. Programs and data may be stored in **files**, which are identified by their **filename**. Files are **saved** on backing storage and may be **loaded** into the IAS. Where a file contains data the file will be divided into **records**, each containing several related **fields**. The fields are in the same order in records of the same type. Fields may be **fixed length** or **variable length**. Sometimes a record will contain a **key field** which identifies the record.

If a record can only be found by accessing *all* the preceding records and if the records are in no particular order then the file is a **serial access file**. If the records are **sorted** into an order, possibly on the keyfield, then the file is a **sequential access file**. In a **random access file** it is possible to read or write a particular record without accessing other records beforehand.

A file is **created** and saved on backing storage using the filename to identify it. The file may be **merged** with other files to make one file. To bring the data on the file up-to-date, we **update** or **amend** the file. When the file is no longer needed it can be **deleted** by removing it from backing storage. A list of all the files on a particular disc or tape is called a **directory** or **catalogue**.

A **Database Management System (DBMS)** is software and data files organised to allow easy interrogation of the data by **searching** for records, having first defined a **search condition**.

Backing storage is non-volatile long-term storage, usually on **magnetic tape** or **magnetic disc**. Magnetic tape may be **reel-to-reel** for use with mainframe computers; **cartridges** for use in **tape streamers** for file backup; **cassettes** for use with microcomputers.

Magnetic discs range from **exchangeable disc packs** for use with mainframe computers; **Winchesters** or **hard discs** for use with larger business microcomputers; **floppy discs** for use with most microcomputers.

The data held on computer systems must be kept **secure**. The loss of data is prevented by taking a regular **backup** of all data files. Unauthorised users are excluded by giving each user a **user identification number** and a **password**. In addition, **physical security** is ensured by employing security guards, etc.

ESSENTIAL PRINCIPLES

1 ▷ THE MEMORY

Programs and data are stored in the **Immediate Access Store**, i.e. the main memory of the computer, while the programs are edited or run (executed) and the data is processed.

RANDOM ACCESS MEMORY (RAM)

In a microcomputer the IAS is known as **Random Access Memory** (RAM). RAM can be *written to* and *read from*. This memory is **volatile**, which means that the programs and data stored in it will be lost when the computer is switched off.

READ ONLY MEMORY (ROM)

Microcomputers frequently contain **Read Only Memory** (ROM). ROM, as its name suggests, can *only* be read. It is non-volatile and so retains its contents when the computer is switched off. ROM is usually used in microcomputers for programs which are *Uses of RAM and* convenient to have available at any time, in particular when the computer has just been *ROM* switched on. In many microcomputers the Operating System and the BASIC Interpreter are in ROM. In order to change the Operating System, or to run a language other than BASIC, the actual ROM chip must be removed and another inserted. To do this the computer must be dismantled. This is usually the case for those microcomputers with a small amount of RAM memory, say less than 512K. Where larger amounts of RAM are available it is usual to load the Operating System from disc into RAM before using other software. This allows the user to run different Operating Systems and other languages if required, provided the appropriate software is available.

Unfortunately, the contents of ROM cannot be altered, so it is unsuitable for data that *must* be changed. Depending on the volume of data to be saved, and other factors, different methods are adopted to make data available whenever it is needed.

BATTERY BACKED RAM

Some microcomputers save the date and time on **Battery Backed RAM**. This is a small amount of RAM memory powered by a battery. The contents of Battery Backed RAM can be altered, but because it is powered by a battery, these contents are not lost when the computer is switched off. Battery Backed RAM is expensive and is suitable for storing only very small volumes of data. The batteries will run out periodically and must be renewed. Backing Storage, i.e. magnetic tape or magnetic disc must be used to store larger volumes of data.

2 ▷ FILES

When data or programs are stored on backing storage, or in the IAS, they are organised so that the computer can easily find them. Data is kept on backing storage as a **file**. To store data on backing storage we **save** it. To get the data back once the file has been saved, we **load** the file into memory.

Files can contain programs or data. Each file is given a **filename**, which identifies the file and so must be different from any other filename. The filename is used when we need to save or load the file, read data from, or write data to, the file.

FILE STRUCTURE

Where a file contains data it is divided into **records**. A data file contains one or more records. A record is a collection of related data and contains several **fields**. A field is a single item of data. Fields within records of the same type will be in the same order. Each record will usually contain a **key field**. The key field is different in each record in a file; often it is an identification number that identifies the record and, in the case of personal data, also identifies the person. The key field is often used to determine the *location* of the record in the file. For example, a Sequential File may be sorted into ascending order using a *numerical key field*.

Example

A numerical key field

```
85123: SHARP: LOUISE: 740601: 109 HAVELOCH ST.: THORNTON: BRADFORD
85145: PATEL: SANDIP: 731223: 12 HOLLY DRIVE: QUEENSTOWN: BRADFORD
86234: MOORSIDE: JAMES: 740913: 3 STONES LANE: ALLERTON: BRADFORD
```

The data is taken from an entirely fictitious file of pupils attending a Bradford school.

- There are three records; one for each pupil.

- Within each record there are seven fields.

- The fields are in the same order in each record.

Using the first record as an example, we have:

```
85123              pupil number
SHARP              family name
LOUISE             first name
740601             date of birth, i.e. the 1st of June 1974
109 HAVELOCH ST    street
THORNTON           town
BRADFORD           area
```

A colon (:) has been used to separate the fields. In practice, the end of a field would be indicated by an End of Field Marker inserted by the software. How this is done need not concern us here, but an End of Field Marker is needed because there can be **variable length** fields. For example 'family name' may vary considerably in length from record to record. Without such a marker, confusion may arise as to where *exactly* the field ends. Other fields, such as 'date of birth' are described as **fixed length** because they have the same length in every record.

The pupil number is the key field. It is different for each pupil and identifies both the *record* and the *pupil*. The three records are sorted into ascending order on the key field.

Notice how the date is coded in YYMMDD format. This means that the first two digits starting at the left hand side represent the day, the next two digits represent the month and the last two digits, the year. The day, DD, always occupies two digits. For example, the 13th day would be coded as 13; the 6th day as 06. The month, MM, is coded so that January is 01, February is 02, November is 11, etc. If the year, YY, is 1989, this is coded as 89. The date is coded like this for several reasons. Firstly, it saves storage space when the file is saved on backing storage. Secondly, as the date is coded as a number in YYMMDD format, the records can be easily sorted into date of birth order. Thirdly, validation is easier. Simple range checks can be used to make sure the date is valid, i.e. DD lies between 01 and 31 inclusive, MM is between 01 and 12.

SERIAL AND SEQUENTIAL FILES

Every file contains records. The order in which records are stored, and the way the records can be accessed, varies.

In a **serial file** the records are not stored in any particular order.

In a **sequential file** the records are sorted into some order, usually on a key field.

In both serial and sequential files, it is only possible to access a record by first reading through *all* the previous records on the file.

RANDOM OR DIRECT ACCESS FILES

In a **random access file** it is possible to read the required record, or the data block containing the record, without first accessing other stored data. In other words, we can access the required record *directly*. For this reason random access files are also called **direct access files**.

Random access files, serial files and sequential files are all found on magnetic disc. On magnetic tape, only serial files and sequential files are used. Random access files cannot be used on magnetic tape, since it is always necessary to start at the beginning of a magnetic tape and read through it until the required file, and then record, is found.

FILE OPERATIONS

Files are **created** when they are first set up and given a filename. A file may originally be a serial file which is then **sorted** into some order, e.g. ascending numeric on a key field (see the example above).

If we want to find a particular record, we **interrogate** or **search** the file until we find it. The **search condition** may be very simple such as 'name is Jones', It may be more complex, for example, 'name is Jones AND age is less than 16'. Any record that satisfies the search condition will be accessed.

When we have two or more files containing records with the *same* field structure we may want to **merge** them into one file. This can be done by joining them end-to-end to give a serial file and then, if necessary, sorting the file to give a sequential file. If the files to be merged are sequential files in the same order, then it is possible to merge them *and* keep the original order by interleaving the records in the correct order.

When the data in a file are out of date because there are new data to be added, or changes are to be made to one or more of the records, we **update** or **amend** the file, making a completely up-to-date file. If we no longer need a file and wish to remove it from the disc, we **delete** the file.

To get a list of all the files on a disc we look at the **catalogue** or **directory**. This is a list of all the files on a disc.

DATABASE MANAGEMENT SYSTEM

A **DataBase Management System (DBMS)** is files of data and the software needed to access the data, using search conditions. A DBMS is always disc-based to give fast access to the data files.

3 >	BACKING STORAGE

Backing storage is long-term data storage, usually on magnetic tape or magnetic disc, that is non-volatile. Data stored in the IAS will be lost when the computer is turned off. However, if this data is first saved on backing storage, it is kept intact when the computer is turned off. When it is needed again it can be loaded into the IAS from the backing storage. Backing storage is also known as **secondary storage**.

MAGNETIC TAPE

Mainframe computers use **reel-to-reel** magnetic tape to store very large amounts of data at a low cost. It is possible to store around 100 million characters on a magnetic tape 3600 feet long, priced about £20 (a cost of 0.00002p per character).

Data is stored on magnetic tape as illustrated in Figure 11.1.

> **Uses of Magnetic tape**

The **header label** identifies the tape. The IBG or **Inter-Block Gap** separates the Data Blocks. A **Data Block** is the unit of data read from, or written to, the tape by the computer in a single read or write operation. It may contain one or more complete records. The **trailer label** is the last data on the magnetic tape and gives information such as whether the file continues on another tape and, if so, the number of the tape.

It is not possible to both *read data from* and *write data to* a file on magnetic tape at the same time.

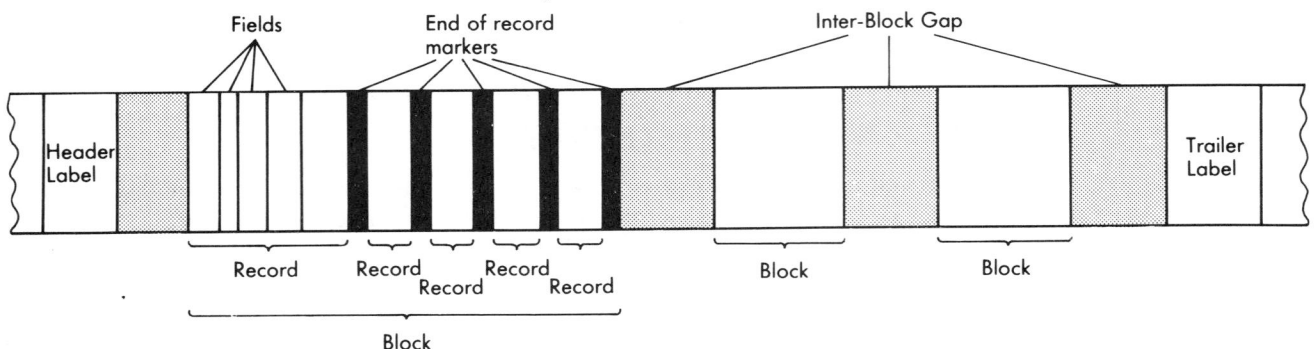

Fig. 11.1 The organisation of data on magnetic tape

Reel-to-reel tape drives

These are used with mainframe computers to read from and write to magnetic tape. A mechanism similar to that in Figure 11.2 is used. When the tape is being accessed it is pulled very rapidly from the **Supply Reel** to the **Take-up Reel** at speeds of around 120 inches per second. The computer could not read the entire tape into the IAS, as it is possible that the data on the tape file would exceed the memory available. The computer accesses the data on the tape a block at a time. When a block has been read, it is processed before another block is read.

While the data block in the computer is being processed, the tape drive stops spinning. The tape drive starts spinning again when the computer is ready for more data to process. The **vacuum tubes** take up the slack tape when necessary, by sucking in the loose tape. This means that if the supply reel stops slightly before the take-up reel, the tape is prevented from breaking. It also ensures that the tape passes the read/write heads at a *constant* speed.

Tape cartridges

Magnetic tape is also available as a **magnetic tape cartridge**. These are reel-to-reel tapes encased in a plastic case for ease of handling. They are a larger version of the popular audio cassette. Magnetic tape cartridges are used with business microcomputers.

Cassette tapes

These are also used to a limited extent with microcomputers for recording software. An ordinary tape recorder can be used with a home microcomputer. Cassettes used in this way are a cheap backing storage medium. Unfortunately, saving or loading programs or data on cassette is extremely slow and unreliable.

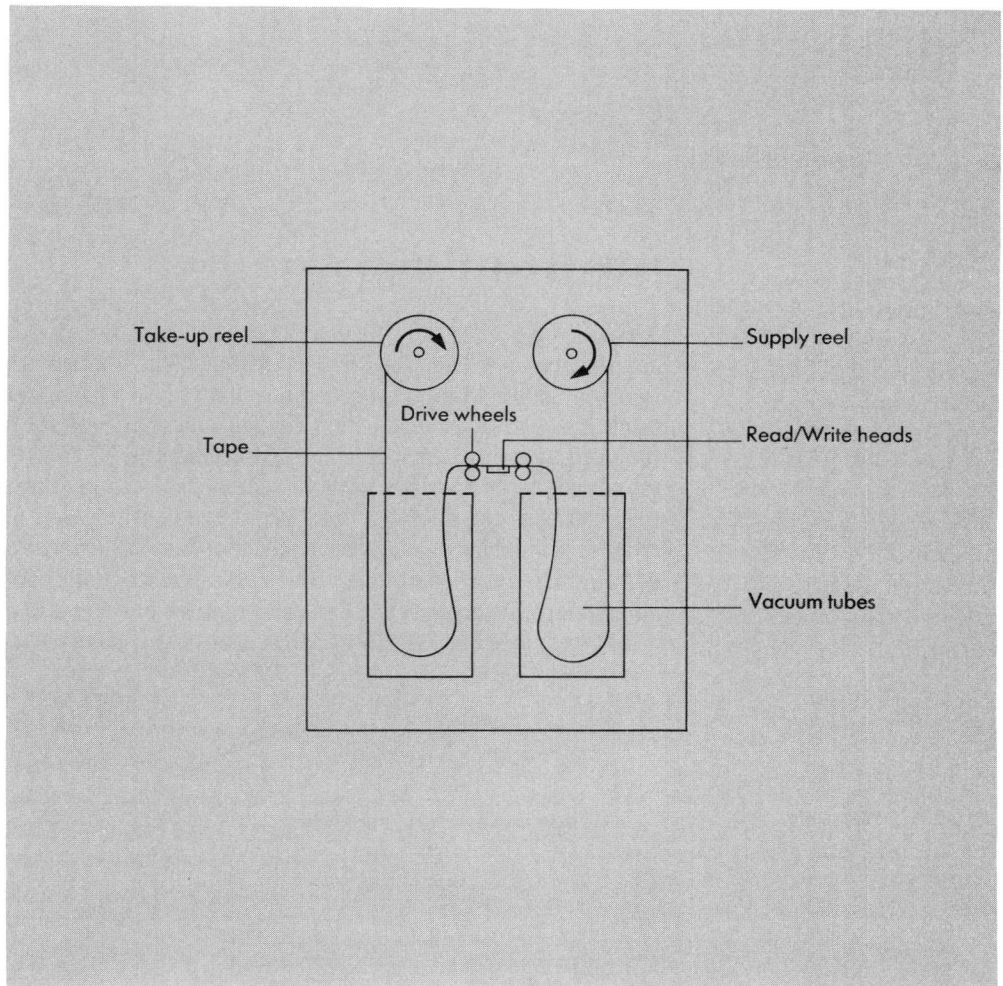

Fig. 11.2 A reel-to-reel magnetic tape drive mechanism

MAGNETIC DISCS

Magnetic discs vary considerably, depending on the size of computer they are used with. However, they all provide faster access and more on-line storage than the corresponding magnetic tape.

Data is stored on a magnetic disc on concentric **tracks** (see Fig. 11.3). Each track is divided into **sectors**, each separated by **inter-sector gaps**. A sector is the unit of data read from or written to the disc by the computer in a single read or write operation.

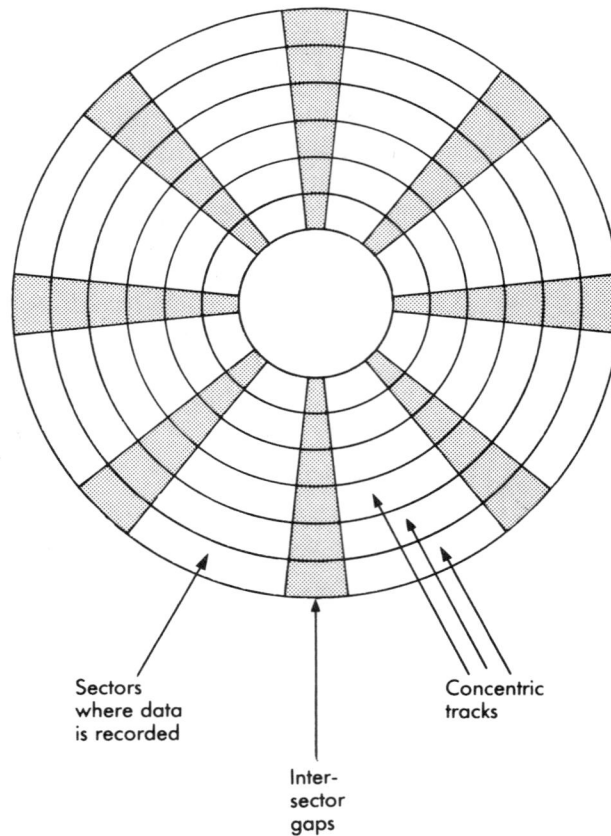

Fig. 11.3 The surface of a magnetic disc

Exchangeable disc packs

These are used with mainframe computers. They are used with **moving head disc drives** (see Fig. 11.4). The disc pack is placed in the disc drive when the read/write heads are retracted. When the drive is switched on, the disc spins at a high uniform speed, typically 3600 revolutions per minute. To access a particular sector the heads move to the track it is on. The heads then remain stationary, while the disc pack is spinning. The required sector when it is accessed is underneath the read-write heads. Data transfer rates may be up to 2,500,000 characters per second. The read-write heads do not touch the surface of the disc, but float just above it. The heads are so close to the surface, and the disc is spinning so fast, that a speck of dust is sufficient to cause a **head crash** that will destroy the disc pack. For this reason discs must be used in an absolutely clean atmosphere. Alternatively, they can be sealed into the disc drive unit.

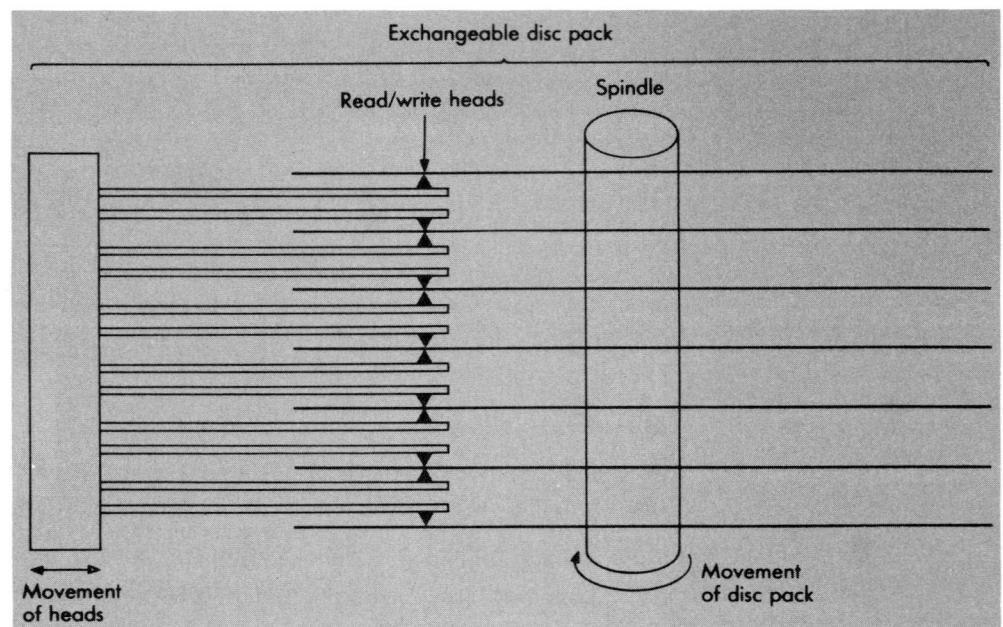

Fig. 11.4 A moving head disc drive mechanism with exchangeable disc pack. There are seven discs but only 12 usable surfaces as the outer surfaces are not used

Fixed disc packs

These provide much greater volumes of on-line storage and higher access speeds. In principle they work like an exchangeable disc pack, except that the disc always remains sealed in the disc drive and there is one head per track. This eliminates head movement, thus improving access speeds and allowing higher data densities.

The Winchester disc

This was developed by IBM. It is small, typically 5¼ inches diameter, and is contained in a sealed unit. The single disc cannot be exchanged. The read/write heads move, although there may be more than one per surface. A Winchester style disc manufactured by other computer companies is referred to as a **hard disc**. A 20 Megabyte hard disc may cost as little as £400. Hard discs are often used with large microcomputer systems and networks as they are robust and cheap. For such systems they provide a large amount of on-line storage and fast access to data at an economic price.

Floppy discs

These are flexible, circular, plastic discs coated with a magnetic material. They are contained in a protective cardboard sleeve (see Fig. 11.5). The read/write heads access the disc through the read/write hole. The heads are actually in *contact* with the surface of the disc as it spins. This reduces the life span and reliability of the floppy disc. The disc is gripped by the drive through its central hole, and spun at approximately 350 revolutions per minute. If the write protect notch is covered (usually with a sticky label), it is not possible to save data on the disc until the label is removed. This prevents valuable data from being accidentally over-written. The index hole is used by the disc drive to locate the start of each track. A typical 5¼ inch floppy disc has 80 tracks and can store 200K of data per side. Smaller 3½ inch floppy discs are also available. These store 300K or more per side.

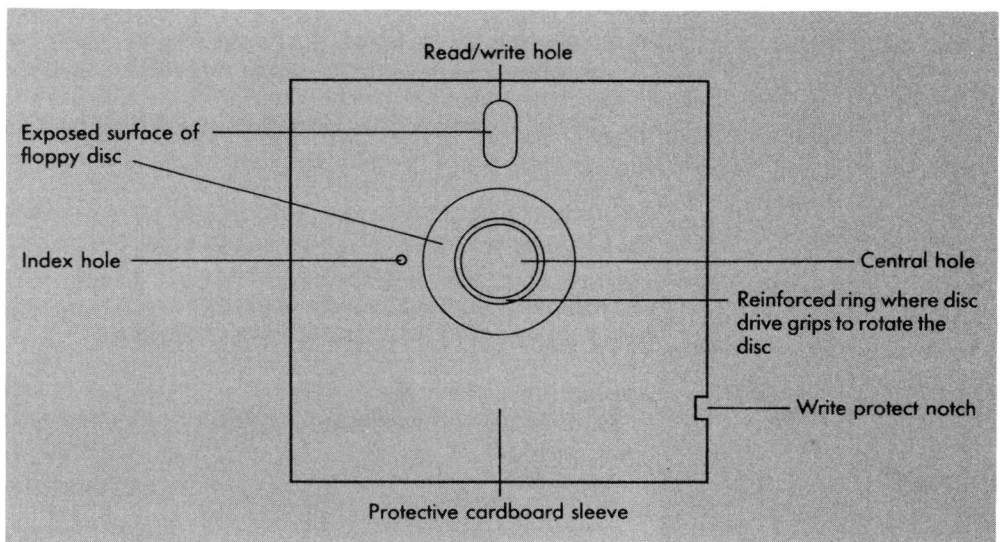

Fig. 11.5 A 5¼ inch floppy disc

LASER DISCS

❝❝Uses of laser discs❞❞

A **laser disc** can be used to store very large amounts of data, for example, 1000 Megabytes of data can be stored on a disc the size of an LP record. Laser discs are so called because data is stored on them by burning small pits on their surface, using high-powered lasers. The data is read using a low-powered laser. The presence, or absence, of a pit is used to form a binary code which represents the data. The discs are coated with a protective layer that allows them to be handled without erasing the data or damaging the disc. Data transfer times are comparable with hard discs. The advantage of laser discs is their very high on-line storage capacity and their robust qualities which make them suitable for long-term storage. The disadvantage is that they can only be written to once, when the data is initially written on them. For these reasons laser discs are unsuitable as a store for changeable data, but are very useful for storing reference data, such as parts catalogues, archive data or encyclopedias, that are not subject to frequent alteration.

4 〉   SECURITY

BACK-UPS

The most important security precaution against loss of data, files or programs through accident, malicious damage or theft is to keep extra copies of them. These extra copies are known as **back-ups**.

Magnetic tape is ideal where we need to record large amounts of data or programs and where we have no need to access the data very quickly, or very frequently. It is also a low-cost storage medium. For these reasons magnetic tape is ideal as a back-up medium for other magnetic media such as discs. Both discs and tapes are unreliable storage media and occasionally programs or data recorded on them will be **corrupted** or lost in some other way. When data is corrupted it is changed so that it is meaningless. When we back-up a disc onto magnetic tape all the data and programs on it are **dumped**, i.e. copied, from the disc to the tape. When the data on the disc becomes corrupted, the data and programs on it can be **restored** by copying them from the backup to the original disc. It is very important to make sure that all programs and data are backed-up.

In *large mainframe* computer installations reel-to-reel tapes will be used as the back-up medium. For *microcomputers* magnetic tape cartridges are used. Tape cartridges are used with a **tape streamer**, a peripheral designed to allow easy copying of all the programs and data on a disc onto the cartridge. They are particularly useful with hard discs where it is necessary to make frequent, regular back-ups of 20 Mbytes or more of programs and data.

Where it is very important to be sure that programs and data are *always* safe from corruption, the **ancestral** back-up system is used (see Fig. 11.6).

- The **son** is the copy of the programs and data currently in use. This will be backed-up on a regular basis, perhaps daily.

- The **father** is the most recent copy of the son.

- The **grandfather** is the copy of the son that was taken the day before the father.

It is usual to keep the son copies on site where they are easily accessible. The father copies are likely to be stored in a fire-proof safe nearby, probably in the same building as the computer but not in the same room. The grandfather copies should be stored elsewhere, possibly at another branch of the company using the computer, located in another town or city. This system is a very effective way of making sure it is always possible to restore corrupted programs and data (unless you are extremely careless or unlucky!).

It is also possible to use magnetic discs as a back-up medium. This is frequently done with small microcomputers that use floppy discs. The ancestral system for back-ups is still effective, but floppy discs are used instead of magnetic tape.

USER IDENTIFICATION AND PASSWORDS

Another precaution against data loss or damage is to restrict the use of the computer software by only allowing *registered users* to make use of the computer. This is done by giving each user a unique identification code, the **User Id**, and associating a particular **password** with it.

A password is a special sequence of characters, known only to a particular user, that must be presented to the computer system before it will allow access to the system. If every user keeps their User Id and password secret, it is unlikely that anyone else will gain entry to the system.

PHYSICAL SECURITY

No data file, program or computer system is safe unless it is *physically* secure. Premises must be made accessible only to registered users. Security guards should be employed and premises must be kept under lock and key. Registered users should have identification cards or similar and these should be checked regularly.

❝❝ The *ancestral* back-up system ❞❞

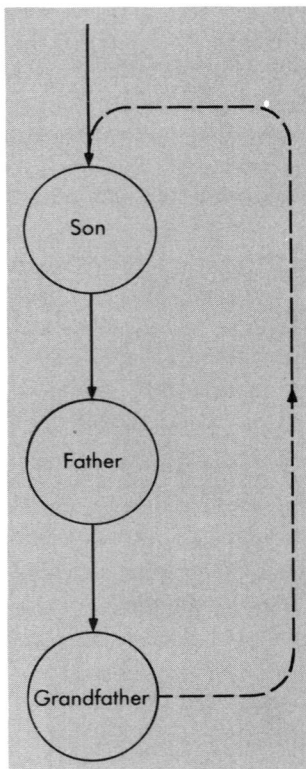

Fig. 11.6 The ancestral system for back-ups

E X A M I N A T I O N   Q U E S T I O N S

1 A form is to be created for entering pupils for examinations. This form must be designed so that the data can be easily entered onto a computer.

Each line of the form must contain space for the person's surname, initials, date of birth and four digit candidate number.

The diagram shows that 28 boxes are available for entering personal details. The rest of the boxes will be used for the subject details.

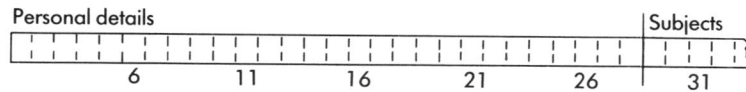

a) Draw and label columns on this diagram which will be used to divide the different fields in the records. The dividing line and label for subjects is already shown. *(3)*

b) The candidate number uniquely identifies the candidate. Give **one** reason why it is also necessary to have the candidate name on the above form.

Reason: _____

_____

(1)
(MEG; 1988)

2 Explain the following terms, giving an example in each case from a stock control system.

a) File. (4 lines available) _____ *(4)*

b) Record. (4 lines available) _____ *(4)*

c) Field. (4 lines available) _____ *(4)*
(SEG; 1988)

3 Explain the meaning of **serial access** and **direct access**. Give an example of a backing storage device which uses each of these methods of access.

Serial access: _____

_____

Example of device: _____

Direct access: _____

_____

Example of device: _____

(4)
(MEG; 1988)

4 A stock file is held on magnetic disc so that records can be read and updated in any order.

a) What is the name of this type of access?

_____

(1)

b) Could the stock file reasonably be held on magnetic tape?

_____

(1)

Explain your answer.

_____

(3)
(SEG; 1988)

5 A university has a fire in the computer room. Many magnetic tapes are totally destroyed. Some magnetic tapes were held in a different building which was not affected by the fire.

a) What would these other magnetic tapes contain?

_____

(1)

b) How could the computer staff retrieve most of the data that was held on the now destroyed files?

_____

_____

(1)
(MEG; 1988)

6 a) The diagram below shows the layout of data stored on a floppy disc. Complete the labelling on the diagram.

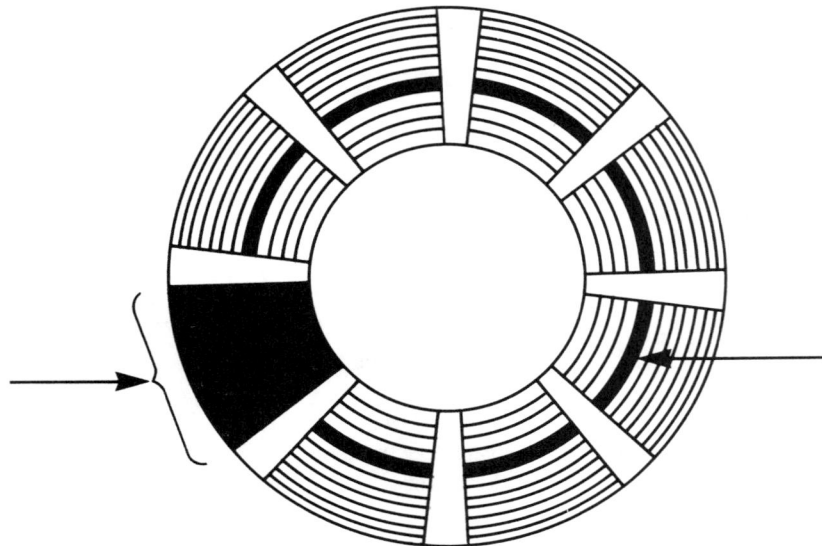

b) Complete the diagram below to show the layout of data on a magnetic tape for a mainframe computer. You should include records, fields and blocks.

(NEA; 1988)

7 a) Write down what each of the following abbreviations stands for.

i) ALU _____

(2)

ii) RAM _____

(2)

iii) ROM _____

(2)

iv) IAS _____

(2)

b) Describe the difference between ROM and RAM, and give an example of the use of each. (6 lines available)   *(6)*
(SEG; 1988)

8 A school keeps a file on its pupils. Some of the information stored on each pupil is as follows:

Pupil Number	Name	Date of Birth	Age
123	Allen, R.	21.12.76	11
073	Brown, P.R.	10.10.74	13
009	Clarke, R.V.	28.06.72	15

a) State which field is the *key field*.
b) What is *data validation?*
c) Explain how age can be validated
d) Suggest an extra field that would be useful, giving **one** reason for your choice.

(WJEC; 1988)

9 Backing storage on most commercial computer systems uses either magnetic tape or magnetic disc.

a) i) Which must use serial access? _____

ii) Which can use direct access? _____

Several computer applications are described below. Complete each sentence with either **"disk system is needed"** or **"tape system could be used"** in the space provided. Give also the reason for your choice.

b) i) In an airline for storing the flight details in an airline booking system a

_____

ii) *Reason:* _____

_____

c) i) In a factory for storing the records needed to calculate the weekly wages a

_____

ii) *Reason:* _____

d) i) At British Telecom, for storing all the frames that make up the PRESTEL database a

_____

ii) *Reason:* _____

(LEAG; 1988)

10 Tick **two** files which would need to be updated:

FILE	UPDATED Tick √
1881 census data for a town	
telephone directory	
details of vehicles registered in the UK	
results of the last general election	

(2)
(MEG; 1988)

11 A school uses a computer to store information on its pupils. One of the files holds information in coded form regarding the examination results of the pupils. Some of the fields used are as follows:

Subject   Level   Mark obtained   Date of Examination

The codes used for each field are:

Subject   *001 ≡ English*   **Level**   *02 ≡ GCSE*
          102 ≡ Maths   *03 ≡ A Level*
          304 ≡ Physics   *04 ≡ Oral*

The 'mark' is a 3 digit number in the range 000 to 100.

Date of examination is written in the following way.
$$1087 = OCTOBER\ 1987$$
$$0686 = JUNE\ 1986$$

a) Interpret the following codes:
  i) **102020560585**

  ii) **001040831187**

b) Encode the following: **a mark of 65 in an 'A' level Physics examination taken in June 1984**

c) Errors can be made on entering information. Give **one** example of an incorrect entry to
  i) the date field
  ii) the mark field

d) Suggest **one** extra field that might be useful and give a reason for your choice.

OUTLINE ANSWERS

SHORT STRUCTURED QUESTIONS

1 a)

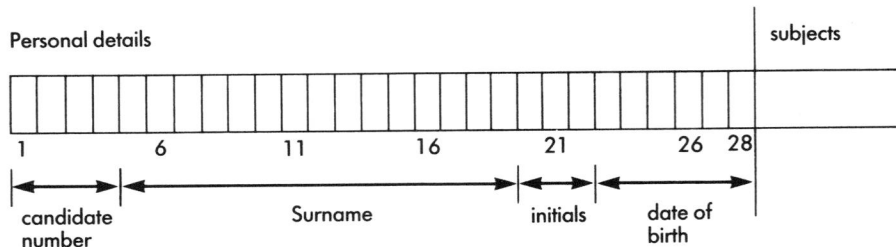

b) The surname can be used to identify the candidate in case the candidate number is wrong.

2 a) A file is a collection of related records e.g. a stock file containing records of all the goods in stock.

b) A record is an organised collection of related fields. The fields are in the same order in similar records e.g. a record for large cans of baked beans containing several fields relating to the baked beans.

c) A field is the smallest item of data in a record, e.g. for baked beans some fields might contain data as follows:
    description   : baked beans
    size   : large
    number in stock : 253

3 *Serial access:* Records are stored in such a manner that in order to access a record all the previous records in the file must be read first. The records are not in any particular order.
Example of device: Magnetic tape drive.
Direct Access: Records can be accessed without reading other records first.
Example of device: Magnetic disc drive.

4 a) Direct access or random access.
   b) No. On magnetic tape, records are accessed in the order they are stored in the file.

5 a) Backup copies of the files held on site.
   b) By restoring the data from the backup files and repeating any processing done since the backups were made.

6 a)

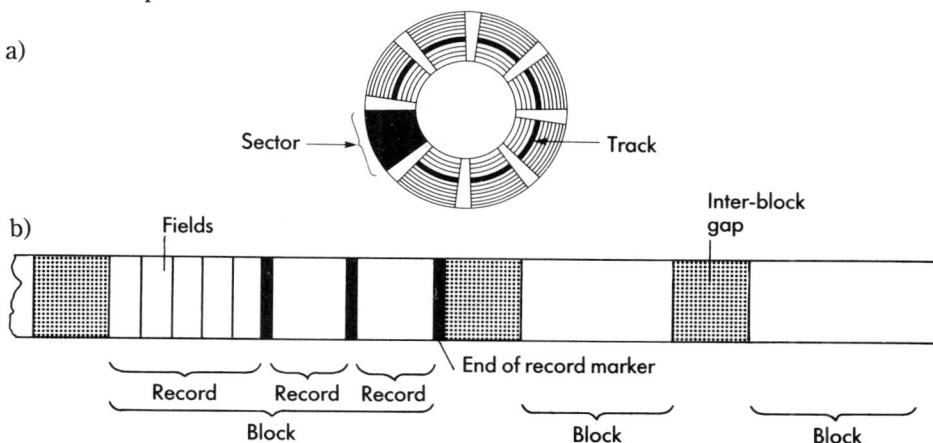

   b)

7 a) i)   ALU = Arithmetic and Logic Unit.
      ii) RAM = Random Access Memory.
      iii) ROM = Read Only Memory.
      iv) IAS = Immediate Access Store.

   b) Programs or data stored in ROM can only be read.
      ROM is non-volatile.
      Programs and data are permanently stored in ROM.
      ROM is used to store the Operating System in micros.
      Programs or data can be written to RAM or read from it.
      RAM is volatile.
      Programs and data are temporarily stored in RAM.
      RAM is used to store user programs while they are run and data while it is processed.

8 a) Pupil number is the key field.
   b) Data validation is a check to make sure that data is realistic. An example of a validation check is a range check.
   c) Age can be checked by making sure it is within a reasonable range.
      e.g. 10 < age < 19
   d) The home address of the pupil might be useful so that letters can be sent to parents.

9 a) i) magnetic tape
      ii) magnetic disc
   b) i) "disc system is needed"
      ii) *Reason:* Discs store large volumes of data giving fast access to it.
   c) i) "tape system could be used"
      ii) *Reason:* All the records to be processed are available before processing begins. They are processed in order. There is no need for rapid access or processing.
   d) i) "disk system is needed".
      ii) *Reason:* Discs store large volumes of data giving fast access to it.

10 Tick "telephone directory" and "details of vehicles registered in the UK".

11 a) i) Maths, GCSE, Mark = 56, May 1985
      ii) English, Oral, Mark = 83, November 1987
   b) 304030650684
   c) i) 1386
      ii) 101
   d) Exam board. There are several exam boards. It might be interesting to see if pupils are awarded higher grades in exams set by some boards than by others.

A STUDENT'S ANSWER WITH EXAMINER'S COMMENTS

QUESTION

A computer file on a school computer is to contain records of the pupils and will be used to produce form lists. Each record will consist of the pupil's name, home telephone number, date of birth, medical problems and comments.

Draw a diagram which shows a suitable structure for a pupil record. Use as an example Frank Dickins, telephone (0223) 61111, born on 21st June 1973, suffers from asthma. Indicate on your diagram any fields which should be of fixed length.

(MEG; 1988)

name : Frank Dickins
telephone: (0223) 61111   fixed length
date of birth: 21st June 1973
medical : asthma

Examiner's comment

'Name' should be split into two fields

surname:	Dickins	variable length
first names:	Frank	variable length

'telephone' should not contain brackets as this wastes storage space and data preparation is slower. Telephone is not a fixed length field.

telephone: 0223 61111

'date of birth' should be coded, for example, as YYMMDD.

date of birth: 730621   fixed length

'medical' is probably reasonable, though common ailments might be coded, e.g.

AS – asthma
HA – hay fever
DI – diabetes

THE COMPUTER SYSTEM'S LIFE CYCLE AND JOBS IN COMPUTING

GETTING STARTED

All computer systems go through stages of the **system's life cycle**. First, new ideas are developed in more detail in the **systems investigation**, in which the objectives of the proposed system are clearly stated. If the idea is considered useful, then a **feasibility study** is undertaken. This is a more detailed investigation; potential users of the new system are consulted to see what the system will *do* and *how* it will do it. Costs for new hardware and new software will be identified. If the feasibility study is approved, the resources to develop the system further are allocated.

Systems analysis and design shows how the system will work. All input and output data is fully detailed. A systems flowchart illustrates the processing done. The individual programs of the system are described. When the new system is complete, program specifications are used for **program design**, **coding**, **testing and documentation**.

The new system is then **implemented**. The entire system is tested for performance. Next, a parallel run checks the new system against the old. If all is well, the old system is abandoned and the new system goes live; users will be trained to use the new system.

The system design is recorded in the **system documentation**; this includes all program specifications and system testing carried out. New user manuals are prepared. System documentation is kept up-to-date as development continues. Any need for improvements is identified by constant **evaluation** of the system; design errors or useful extensions to the system may be discovered. **Maintenance** of the system is vital to sustain its usefulness, but any new system will eventually become obsolete and a replacement needed.

Jobs in computing are related to systems development and usage. The **systems analyst** is involved at all stages. They design the system and write the program specifications. Using this specification, the computer **programmer** will design programs to do the processing, written in a suitable language. The programmer tests the program, and includes the specification, the design, a listing of the program and test results in the documentation.

Data that cannot be read directly by the computer will need transferring to a computer-readable medium, such as magnetic tape or disc – this is the job of a **data preparation clerk**.

The **computer operator** looks after the computer while it is running. They change tapes, discs, printer stationery, etc. as required, and hand printed output on to the data control department.

Data control clerks regulate the flow of data through the computer system. Users send all their input data to data control, who supervise processing and return the output to the appropriate user.

Most students who are following a GCSE course in Computer Studies expect to work with computers in the future, either as users, or as computer specialists. The section on jobs in computing in this chapter is written with this in mind.

THE SYSTEM LIFE CYCLE

SYSTEMS INVESTIGATION

FEASIBILITY STUDY

SYSTEMS ANALYSIS AND DESIGN

PROGRAM DEVELOPMENT

IMPLEMENTATION

SYSTEM DOCUMENTATION

THE DATA PROCESSING DEPARTMENT

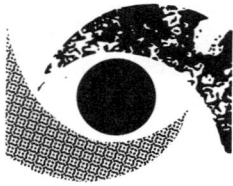

ESSENTIAL PRINCIPLES

The organisation of a Data Processing (DP) department in a large company, and the life cycle of a computer system, are inextricably linked. This is perhaps not surprising since the role of the DP department is to meet the data processing needs of the company by providing appropriate computer systems and staff with the necessary skills to run the systems. Hence the system life cycle and the needs of computer systems form the basis for specialised jobs in a DP department.

1 ▷ THE SYSTEM LIFE CYCLE

Stages in the system life cycle

Every computer system goes through a cycle of development and use until it becomes obsolete or is replaced by a better system (see Fig. 12.1). The stages in this cycle are described below in the sequence in which they occur.

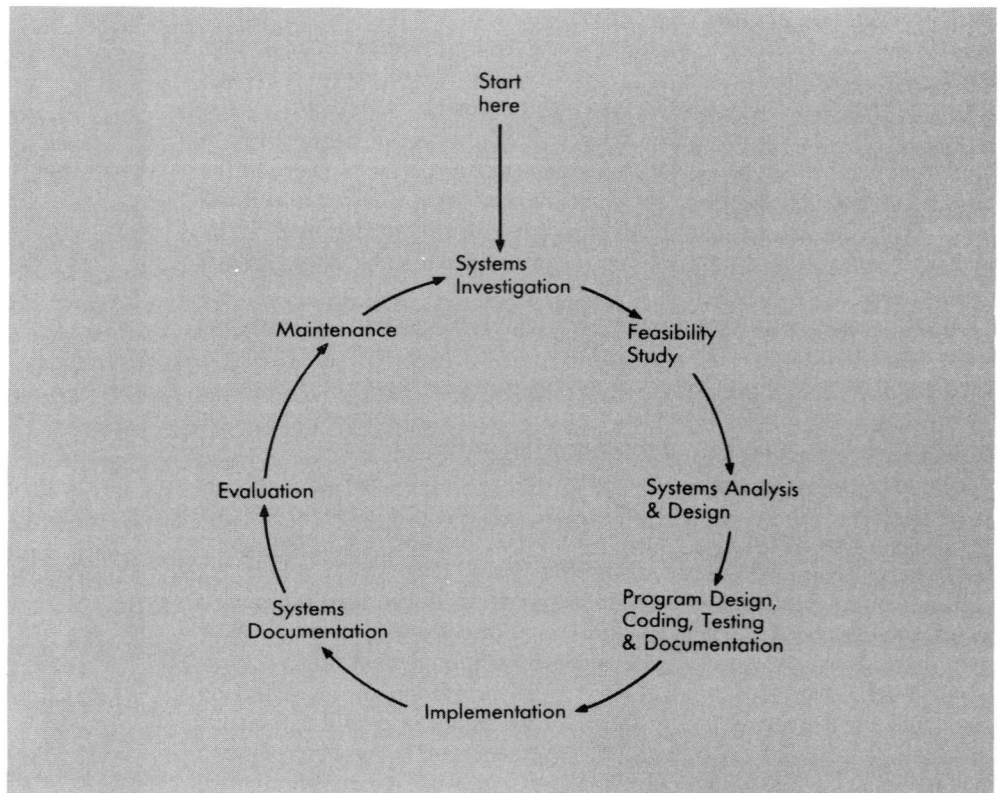

Fig. 12.1 The system life cycle

2 ▷ SYSTEMS INVESTIGATION

The realisation that it would be useful to have a computer system to do a particular task may arise due to a new and completely novel idea, or to a new technological invention. However, many new computer systems are created because the system currently in use is unable to handle increased volumes of data, or new demands on it.

A manual system for processing orders might work quite well until the rapid growth of the company and product diversification leads to many more customer orders, with a wide variety of terms and conditions of sale. Because of the increased complexity of the task, mistakes are made and there is a general confusion over what processing is required in some cases. Customers want their orders to arrive on time, to contain the items ordered and to be charged the right price! They become angry and frustrated when this does not happen. This in turn leads to a decline in orders. Having worked hard to increase production and sales, it is disappointing to find that confusion within the department dealing with order processing is responsible for lost sales. To improve this situation a computer based system to help process customers' orders is suggested.

The **systems investigation** outlines the organisational problems identified, and recognises the *need* for improvements. A brief outline of a proposed system is made. This will identify the desired objectives, in this case the processing and delivery of the correct order, within a stated period, and charging customers the right price. A system will be described in broad outline and a rough estimate of costs will be made.

<table>
<tr><td>

3 > **FEASIBILITY STUDY**

Conducting a feasibility study

</td><td>

If the systems investigation has uncovered a development that will be of use to the company, then a **feasibility study** is undertaken. This is a rather more detailed investigation of the proposed computer based system.

Firstly, the *present* system is examined in greater detail.

</td></tr>
</table>

- The order processing manager is asked what is done, and how it is done.

- The staff who do the job are asked to describe what they actually do.

- The records kept by the department, the forms they receive from customers, those filled in within department and all correspondence are looked at.

- Customers are asked to provide details of letters and forms received from the department and are encouraged to explain how the service might be improved.

The new system is now developed in greater detail in a written report. Where possible, the new system is based on existing practice, to minimise the eventual disruption and retraining of staff when it is introduced. It must be shown that the new system will achieve the original objectives of i) improved performance in the processing, ii) delivery of orders and iii) the accurate charging of customers.

Additional benefits of the new system will also be described, for example, improved working conditions for staff.

The software required to run the new system will be specified and the costs to develop it in-house calculated. The extra cost of additional hardware should be given and the extent to which this will help with other processing tasks estimated. Savings due to increased staff productivity can be taken into account and the cost of necessary re-training shown. The time taken to develop and introduce the system is also estimated.

In the case of large, complex or expensive systems, several different designs might be developed and outlined in the report. Buying in an applications package or a turnkey system could be a practical alternative and the associated benefits could be assessed.

The report on the feasibility study is passed to senior management within the company for approval. They will allocate the resources necessary if the new system is to proceed.

4 > **SYSTEMS ANALYSIS AND DESIGN**

If the feasibility study has shown that the proposed system is worthwhile, and will meet stated objectives at an economic cost, then it is likely to be approved by senior management. Further development will then proceed.

The next stage in the system life cycle is **systems analysis and design**, i.e. the in-depth analysis of the data processing and hardware requirements of the system and the preparation of a detailed design of the final system. The design outlined in the feasibility study will be further enlarged to provide a precise description of what the new system will do. At every stage in this proces the systems analyst will refer back to the eventual users of the system, i.e. the order processing department and senior management, to ensure that the detailed system design meets their needs.

OUTPUT

The **output** required from the system will be specified. In the case of the order processing system this will include:

Types of *output* from the system

- **Invoices** to be sent to the warehouse and to customers. An invoice is a printed confirmation of a customer's order. It lists what the customer has ordered, with the price of each item and the total cost. The invoice is first sent to the warehouse where it is used to select the items the customer has ordered. The invoice is then sent with the order to the customer. The customer uses the invoice to check that the order is correct and that the company has delivered everything that was ordered. The company will need to store the information shown on the invoice so that it knows what has been sold and how much is owed by the customer.

- **Internal reports and statistics**. Reports and statistical summaries of performance will be needed by senior management to help them improve the performance of the company. The total sales of every item stocked can be summarised using the stored information from each invoice, either for all items stocked, in a printed report, or for a selection of items, on a monitor screen.

The layout of all printed reports and screen displays will be shown in detail. They must be presented in a way which is clear and easy to understand. An example of what each looks like will be drawn in sufficient detail to allow a programmer to write a computer program to produce the required output exactly.

The demand for specific data displays implies a need for the corresponding output peripherals. These could be simply monitor screens and printers but may also be more specialised output devices, for example, graph plotters or COM peripherals. The way in which output is obtained from the system will also need to be examined.

- Do reports need to be obtained immediately on request?

- Are printouts to be optional or will the report *only* be printed?

These considerations may lead us to equip the order processing department with VDUs connected to local printers, so that reports can first be displayed on screen and only output if required. For reports that will always and only be printed the system line printer may be satisfactory.

INPUT

The **input** to the system is now looked at in greater detail. All the output from the system is produced from the input. It is important to be sure at an early stage that all the data needed will be *captured*. If this does not already occur in the existing system, then arrangements will have to be made to get the required data. The way in which data is input to the system should be designed in order to help data preparation staff and others to work quickly and easily.

In the case of the order processing system, it is likely that most of the input needed for the new system is already being generated by the old. It is possible that a manual system could manage without customer numbers if the orders are filed using the customer's name. However, a computer based system must have customer numbers, to be used as a key field to identify customers. If the existing order processing system does not use customer numbers, then arrangements will have to be made to generate these and persuade customers to use them.

Similarly, in a manual system the invoice containing details of the order can be identified using the date of the order. In the case of two or more orders on the same day the actual items ordered could be used to identify the invoice. This is rather cumbersome and makes reference to orders difficult. Consequently each invoice is given an invoice number which the customer and the order processing department can refer to in case of enquiries, etc. concerning the order.

The *way* in which the data is input must also be considered. Key-to-tape or key-to-disc may be satisfactory, but other methods should be considered. Customers could be sent mark sense documents, i.e. specially designed order forms that can be read directly into the computer by a mark sense reader. In some cases Kimball tags may be used to automatically re-order items that have been sold. All useful possible means of input should be looked at and the benefits of each evaluated.

FILE STRUCTURES

The **file structures** used within the system are decided on by examining the permanency of the data and whether it relates more closely to an invoice, or to a customer. Some of the data to be input could be recorded on backing storage and used several times, whereas some data will change from order to order. For example, an order from a customer will generate the following data:

```
name
address
customer number (identifies customer)
invoice number (identifies order)
date of order
for each item ordered:   item code (identifies item)
                         description
                         quantity
```

The customer number (to identify the customer) and the invoice number (to identify the order) are both generated by the order processing department.

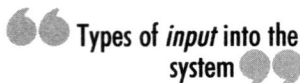

> **66** Types of *input* into the system **99**

Invoice files

The customer's name, address and customer number do not change from order to order, whereas the other data relating to the items ordered will almost certainly change. The transient data relating to the order rather than to the customer will be kept on the **invoice file**. The invoice file contains a record for each invoice as follows:

> 66 An *invoice file* 99

    customer number (identifies customer)
    invoice number (identifies order)
    date of order
    for each item ordered: item code (identifies item)
                              description
                              quantity
                              price per item

When an invoice is paid it is deleted from the invoice file. This file contains only those invoices that have not yet been completely processed.

Customer files

The name, address and customer number are kept on the **customer file**. This file has a record for each customer containing information that relates more directly to the customer rather than to an actual order. The customer file records include the following fields:

> 66 A *customer file* 99

    name
    address
    customer number (identifies customer)
    credit limit
    discount rate

Records on the invoice file can be matched with the corresponding record on the customer file, using the customer number. Invoices can be printed and sent to the warehouse. The warehouse packs the items ordered and sends them to the customer with the invoice. The total amount owed by each customer can be calculated by adding up the amounts owed on individual invoices still to be paid.

At this point it is perhaps worth noting that an order processing system is unlikely to be designed in isolation. It is likely to be integrated with, at least, a stock control system and possibly with wider financial reporting and control systems. The system described in the example is the basis of the more complex systems that are used in practice.

Following through the above discussion we can see that the output requirements of the system suggest what input is needed. The file structure is decided upon by analysing the input data and the processing needed to be done to produce the necessary output. Inevitably, the file structures, the processing to be done and the style of output chosen,

> 66 Choice of backing storage 99

influence the choice of backing storage. Sequential access files on magnetic tape will be used for economy if only printed output is needed and the slower turnaround time is acceptable. Otherwise, direct access files on magnetic disc will be used to give immediate access to up-to-date data for screen displays and printed reports. An order processing system could be designed using either batch processing or on-line interactive processing.

In the example of the order processing system, a telephone enquiry service may be offered (see Fig. 12.2). In this case, immediate access to customer and invoice files would be needed in order to answer enquiries on-the-spot. This would necessitate the use of direct access files on disc. Customer records would be accessed using either the customer number or name to find the record and the address would be used to confirm that the correct record has been located. The telephone operator would also have particular hardware needs if a large volume of enquiries is anticipated. A headset and microphone to replace the standard telephone might be useful. This would free the hands to enable the keyboard of a VDU linked to the mainframe to be used more easily.

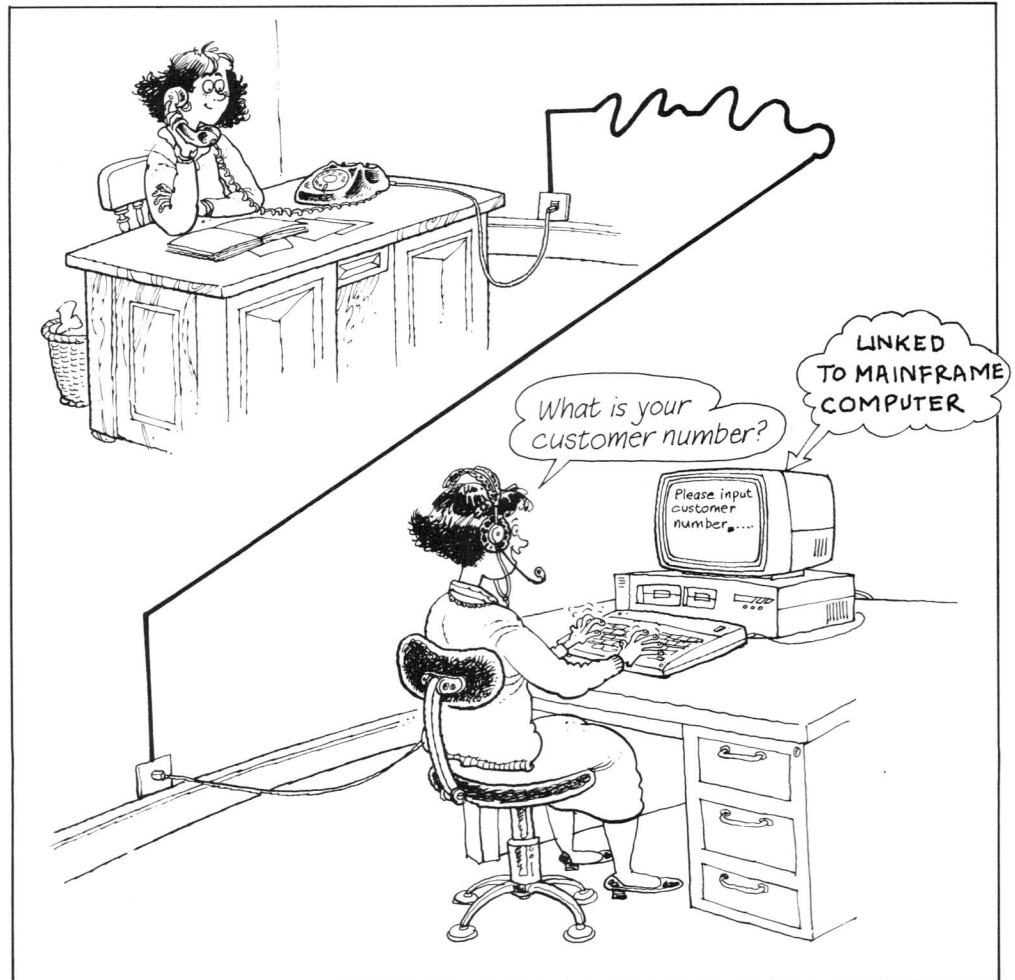

Fig. 12.2 A telephone enquiry
service

DATA SECURITY

Arrangements for data security should also be carefully thought out. The *ancestral* file system for file backup will be used and the times and frequency of backups should be stated. Arrangements for the physical security of files should be made. Each generation of backup should be kept in a different place. Fireproof safes, etc. may need to be purchased. Storage facilities at remote sites may be necessary in some cases.

> **Choice of data security arrangements**

Systems analysis and design is a searching, in-depth look at the proposed system. It results in an exact, precise statement of the input, processing and output needed and the hardware, software and data required to meet these needs. The main written report that is produced details what will be done, how it will be done, the purpose in doing it and the cost. This will be described using system flowcharts (see Fig. 12.3), tables, diagrams, screen layouts, etc. The processing will be divided into programs to do specific tasks. The system may be designed as one or more inter-related programs.

PROGRAM SPECIFICATION

A **program specification** will be written for each individual computer program. This specifies in detail the input, processing and output to be done, the file structure and type of access, and any other details needed. The program specification gives sufficient detail to allow the programmer to write the program. The computer programs are not written at this stage.

If, as a result of the feasibility study, it was decided to buy an applications package or a turnkey system, then the stage of systems analysis and design will be an in-depth evaluation of whether these alternatives are satisfactory. Again, the report will examine the alternatives in terms of the required input, processing and output, the required hardware, software and data structures and the cost of buying and maintaining the system.

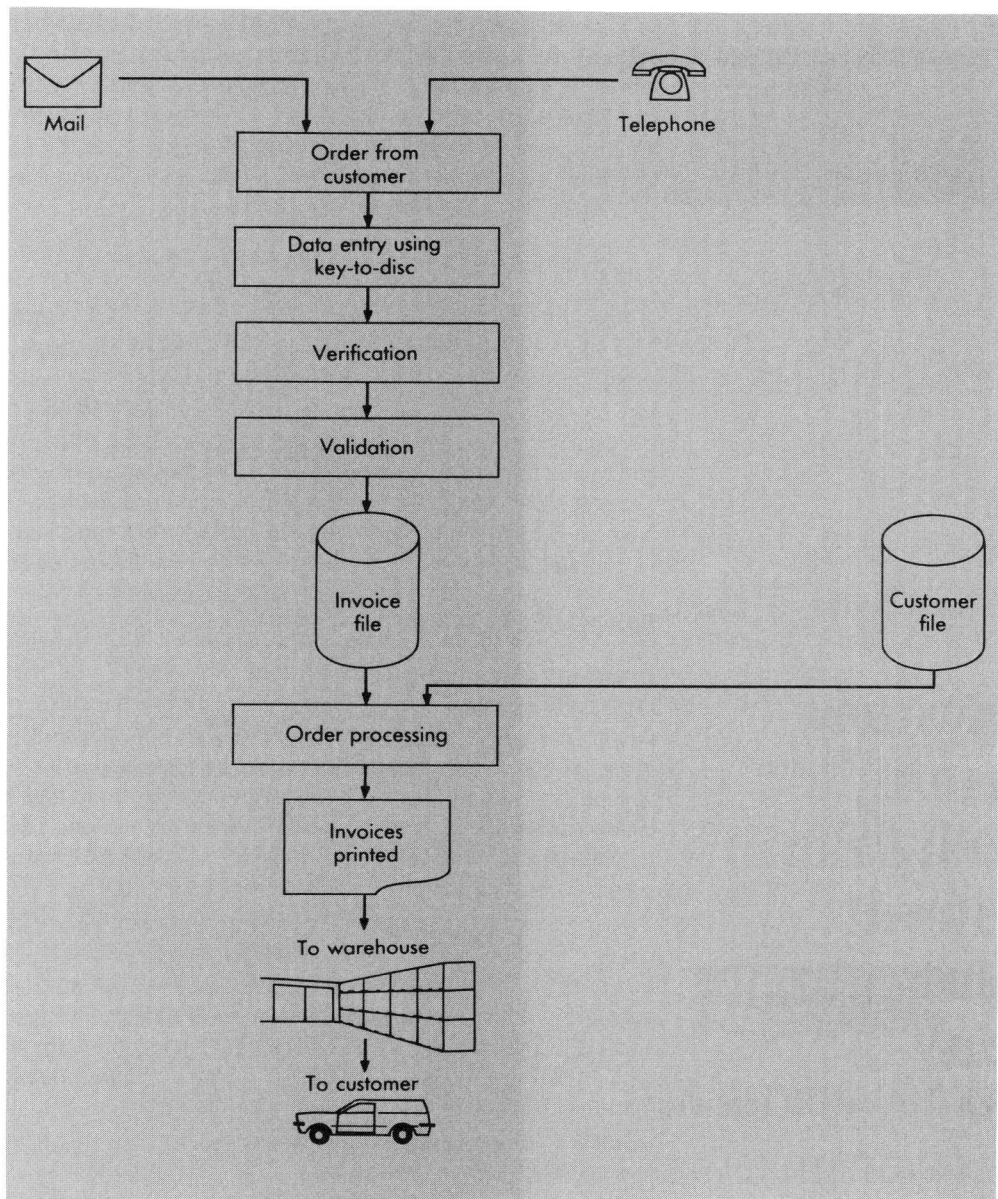

Fig. 12.3 An order processing
system

5 ▷ PROGRAM DEVELOPMENT

The program specification written during the analysis and design of the system is handed over to a *computer programmer*. It contains enough information about the program to enable the programmer to design a program to do the required processing. The structure of any data input or output will be specified and also the type of file access used. The program to be written may be part of a large system involving many programs. It should not be necessary for the programmer to know how the whole system, or any other program in the system, functions in order to design the program. The programmer will read the specification carefully, then design the program.

PROGRAM DESIGN

The **program design** can be illustrated in various ways. Often a flowchart is drawn, or alternatively a top-down design may be written in pseudo-code. There are a variety of design methodologies that can be used. The design is often **dry run** to test if it works. In a dry run the programmer uses examples of the input data and processes it according to the program design to see if the expected output results.

CODING

When the program has been designed, it is **coded**, i.e. written in a computer language. There are a variety of computer languages and the programmer may be free to choose which one to use. However, it is more likely that all programs in the system will be written in the same language. An appropriate language to use for the order processing system would be COBOL. COBOL is a very good language for file handling as it is easy to define and manipulate records and fields. Commercial applications are often dominated by file handling making COBOL particularly appropriate. In the order processing system used as an example there are no complex calculations to be done, but there will be considerable file processing.

TESTING

Next, the program is **tested** to see if it works. The programmer tests the program using test input data to see if the program produces the expected output. Test data may be typical data likely to be generated when the system is running under normal conditions, but it should also include extreme or rare data unlikely to occur in practice. The aim is to write a robust program that can deal with any input data, either processing it or reporting errors and continuing running. If the test data causes unexpected output or crashes the program, i.e. stops it running due to an inability to process the input data, then the programmer will have to amend the program and do another test run. The cycle of testing, amending and re-testing continues until the programmer is satisfied that the program works.

DOCUMENTATION

Program documentation is done throughout the design, coding and testing of a program. It is based on the original program specification and will cover the program design, including flowcharts. There will also be a listing of the source code of the final version of the program with details of test data and the resulting output. File structures for all input and output files and samples of printed output and screen displays will be included. The purpose of the documentation is to provide enough detail for a different programmer to understand what has been done in case the program unexpectedly crashes and the original programmer is not available to put it right.

**6 ▷ IMPLEMEN-
TATION**

If the extra hardware needed to run the new system has not been bought at an earlier stage, it will have to be purchased and installed before proceeding further. Consumables, such as printer stationery and discs, will need to be purchased. Extra electric wiring must be installed in the user department for powering terminals, etc. and a room with special features, such as air conditioning, may be required for a mainframe computer. Additional specialist computer staff will need to be employed to run the computer equipment and maintain the system.

When the *individual programs* that make up the system have been tested separately, then the *entire system* is tested as a whole. Test data is used and the output checked against that expected. If errors are found they must be corrected and the system re-tested.

When it appears that the system is working correctly, it is **implemented**, i.e. it is put to work. However, there will still be a possibility that the system does not work as intended. To avoid costly mistakes a **parallel run** takes place (see Fig. 12.4). Both the new system and the old system are run on real input data and the results from the manual

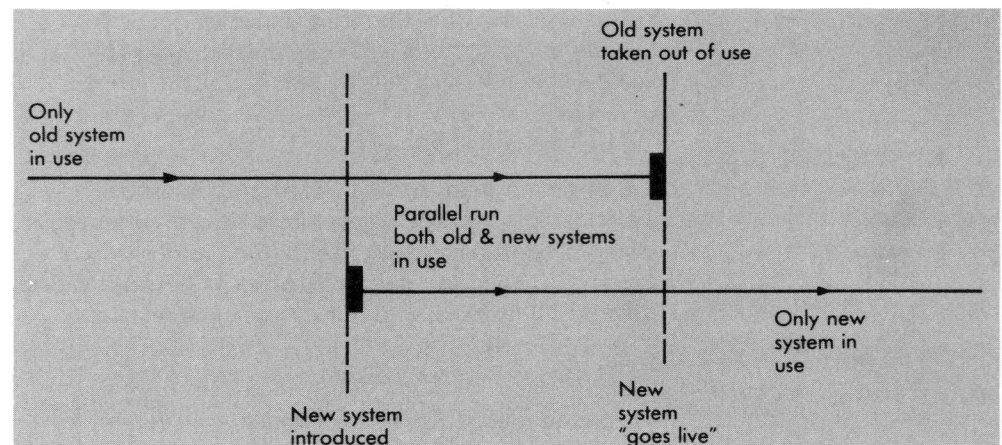

Fig. 12.4 A parallel run

and the computer based system are checked against each other. It is not unusual when looking for the reasons for differences in the output between the old and the new systems to discover that the new system is correct. Frequently, manual systems that have evolved piecemeal are found to be inferior to properly designed systems.

When the new system can be relied on to work correctly it 'goes live' and the old system is no longer used. This does not usually happen overnight. It is a gradual process, as parts of the old system are discontinued and replaced by the new system. Eventually, the only system in use is the new system.

System implementation also involves training users in the new system. There may be changes in practice which staff in the user departments, e.g. the order processing department, have to understand and follow. If the change is from an entirely manual system to a computerised system, staff will need to gain confidence in using the new technology.

System implementation involves the installation of both hardware and software and the employment and training of staff. It is extremely complex and requires adequate planning and finance if it is to be successful. Even so, mistakes *will* occur and it is important that these are seen simply as problems to be overcome rather than personal faults of particular employees. The implementation of a computer based system demands personal change and adjustment of all employees. This must be recognised in a considerate way if the new system is to be implemented smoothly.

7 ▷ SYSTEM DOCUMENTATION

System documentation is a written record of the analysis, design, testing and implementation of the system. It is written throughout the development of a system. It will include systems flowcharts for the implemented design and detailed file structures for the data files input and output, files generated within the system for use by the system and the processing done.

PROGRAM DOCUMENTATION

❝❝Documenting the system❞❞

The **program documentation**, for all the programs in the system, forms part of the system documentation. Consequently, there will be a listing of the final source code for every program used in the system in the documentation. Samples of printed output and screen displays will also be included.

The purpose of the documentation is to provide all the detail needed to understand *what* the system does, and *how* it does it. This will be useful to those unfamiliar with the system, such as new employees. If the system goes wrong, the documentation will be helpful to the maintenance programmers who will attempt to make the system work again. Similarly, if there is a need to *extend* the system, so that it can do extra tasks, the system documentation will make it easier to build on additional processing capability.

USER MANUALS

User manuals or **user documentation** that explains how to run the system are also part of the system documentation. User manuals are written to help employees use the system. They can be read separately from the rest of the system documentation and do not have the same in-depth coverage of the system. They are needed when staff are trained to use the system and so that staff can refer to them for help in the future if necessary. User documentation should include a general review of the job done by the system, instructions on how to load and run the system and a description of the input required, the processing done and the output produced.

The system documentation is written to help the computer department in running and maintaining the system. The user manuals are written for the user departments to help them make use of the system. The system documentation will be stored in a library by the computer department, so that it can be referred to when necessary. The user manuals are kept in the user departments and are likely to be referred to fairly frequently. Technical problems beyond the scope of user departments will be passed on to the computer department.

8 > EVALUATION

❝❝Evaluating the system❞❞

When the system was first thought of it was hoped that it would solve certain difficulties in running the business. In the case of the order processing department, the system was expected to ensure the processing and delivery of the correct order, within a stated period, and charging customers the right price. On implementation, the new system will achieve these objectives. However, in due course the same problems could arise again as the volume of orders increases once more.

Evaluation of the system aims to check that it is still effective in doing the job it was designed to do.

It is easier to deal with problems if they are anticipated. Instead of waiting for angry customers to draw the attention of management to the breakdown of the system as it becomes overloaded again, constant evaluation of its effectiveness will identify problems before they result in customer dissatisfaction and lost business. If problems are known to exist, they can be avoided by either increasing the effectiveness of the existing system or developing a new system.

At some point in their life cycle all systems become obsolete and are replaced by new systems. Even reliable, well designed, systems will become obsolete at some time, if only because the underlying hardware technology used is superceded.

9 > MAINTENANCE

❝❝Maintaining the system❞❞

Any system, however well designed and tested, is likely to go wrong at some time. There may be an error in the logic of one of the programs, or a condition or circumstance may arise which was not anticipated. **Maintenance** of the system involves the correction of errors in existing programs, or the extension of the system to cope with different tasks. Maintenance of the system may involve changes to any of the components of the system. It may be necessary to re-program existing software, design and write new programs to extend the capability of the system, repair existing hardware or buy new. The system documentation and user manuals will need to be updated as the system changes.

10 > THE DATA PROCESSING DEPARTMENT

❝❝Roles in the DP department❞❞

The organisation of a DP department in a large company is shown in Figure 12.5. It is not the case that *every* DP department is organised in this way, but many are organised in a very similar way.

The DP department organises the highly skilled workers who develop and use computer systems for the maximum benefit of the company that employs them. As companies vary in terms of size and organisation, so do DP departments. In some cases jobs done by individuals are broader, and in other instances narrower, than will be suggested, but the tasks to be done are the same whether they are done by one person in a small company or several in a larger company.

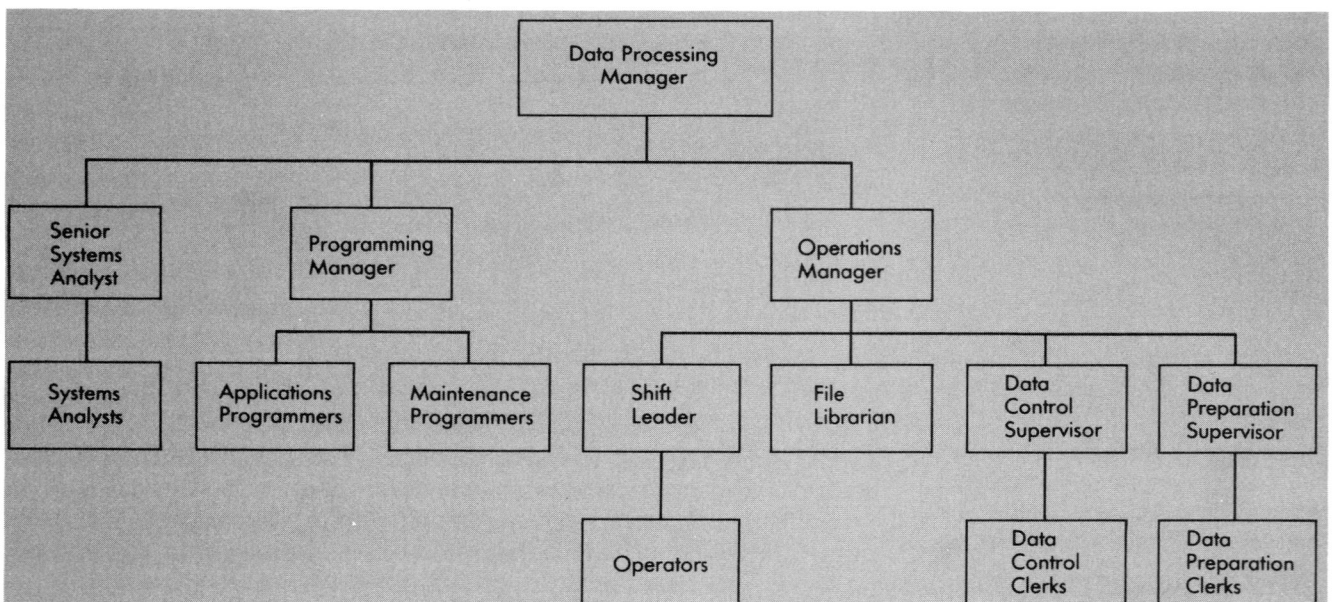

Fig. 12.5 The organisation of a data processing department in a large company

THE DATA PROCESSING MANAGER

The **Data Processing Manager** or **DP Manager** is in charge of the data processing department. Senior System Analysts, the Programming Manager and the Operations Manager all work under the supervision of the DP Manager.

THE SYSTEMS ANALYST

The **Systems Analyst** is directly responsible for the development of a system through all the stages of the system life cycle (see Fig. 12.6). An analyst is usually given responsibility for a system and will see it through from its birth to system termination. The Systems Analyst responsible for a system often works on it alone, but frequently acts as a team leader, organising others in their work on the system.

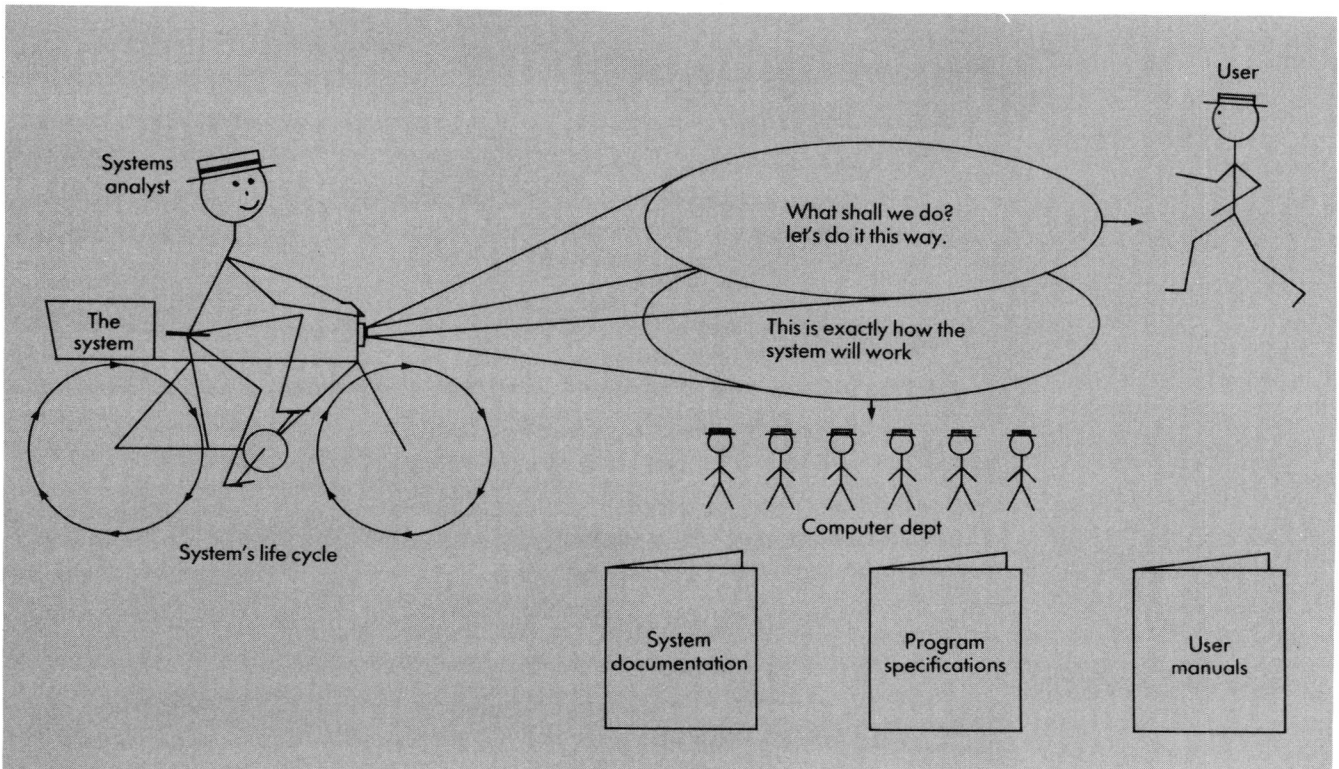

Fig. 12.6 The job of a Systems Analyst

Responsibilities of the Systems Analyst

For example, during the stage of systems analysis and design the analyst responsible will lead a team of analysts who will develop the system design as directed. Similarly, during the stage of program design, coding, testing and documentation the analyst responsible for the system will direct the team of programmers who are working on the programs that make up the system.

Computer systems are developed as a result of *teamwork* by employees with different skills and specialisms. The Systems Analyst is the person responsible for developing the computer system and leading the various teams working on the system at different times.

A good Systems Analyst must have a thorough knowledge of computers, commerce and people. Systems Analysts must be good communicators, creative, logical, persistent and work well as part of a team. This knowledge can only be acquired through hard work, training and experience. Systems analysis is intellectually demanding, but interesting and varied.

Becoming a Systems Analyst

To become a Systems Analyst you will need to find a company to employ you, since *experience* and *ability* are worth more than qualifications. To convince a company you are a good prospect to take on as a trainee, useful qualifications to acquire are one of:

- a degree in Computer Science

- an HND or HNC in Business Studies or Computer Studies

- good A-levels

- a degree in a related subject such as Accountancy or Law.

However, many Systems Analysts start as humbler employees in a DP department and through hard work and perseverence work their way up. Frequently, firms encourage study for membership of professional organisations. The British Computer Society entry exams are popular. They not only improve professional skills and knowledge, but also lead to membership of the National Society for Computer Professionals. Systems Analysts are important employees and a prudent company will pay them well and invest in their training.

Systems Analysts are employed wherever there are computer systems in development or use. They are employed by large companies, software houses, local government, the Civil Service, universities, etc. Good Systems Analysts will get to know the companies they work for very well indeed. They will probably change jobs from time to time to gain yet further experience. This overall view of business organisation can be a useful stepping stone to higher management positions or consultancy work. Salaries tend to be high for those with proven ability and experience.

COMPUTER PROGRAMMER

Computer Programmers write programs in a computer language that tell a computer to do the tasks described in the program specification provided by the Systems Analyst (see Fig. 12.7).

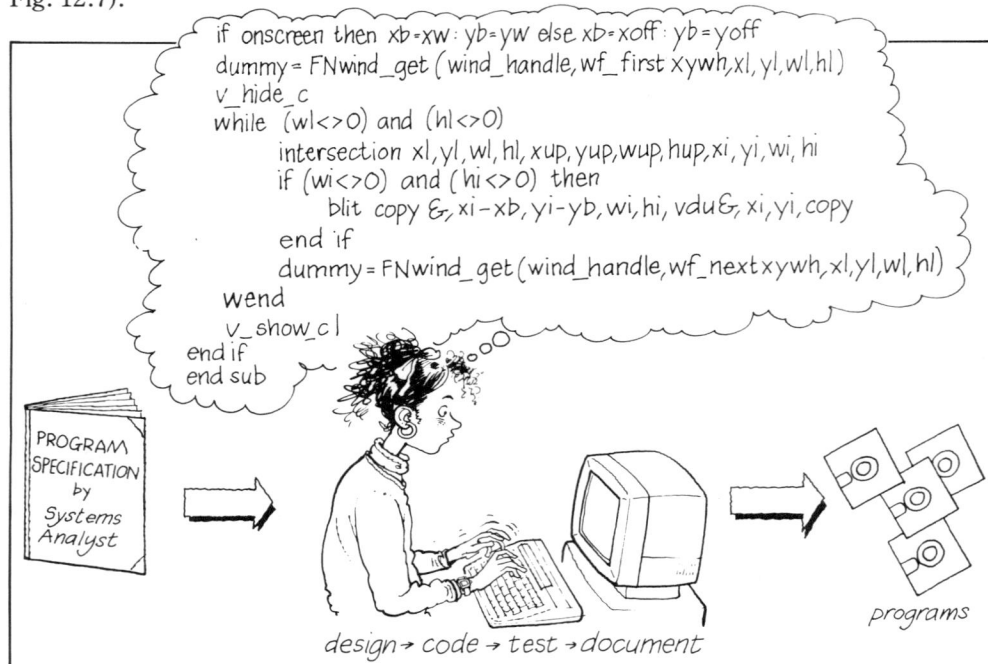

Fig. 12.7 The job of a Computer Programmer

Responsibilities of the Computer Programmer

Programmers may specialise in the development of new applications or the maintenance of existing systems. Applications Programmers design, code, test and document new programs using the program specification given to them by the systems analyst. Maintenance Programmers put right programs in systems that are already in use, but have been identified as having errors in them. They rely on the program documentation written by the Applications Programmer to help find these errors.

The program specification describes the input, output and special processing required. File structure and access type is also given. The Applications Programmer designs the logic of the program, perhaps expressed in a flowchart. The program is then written or coded, using a suitable computer language. The program is tested using both typical and unusual test data. The documentation put together by the Applications Programmer is a written record containing the specification, but extended to include flowcharts and other details of the processing done. A listing of the program is included, as well as a report on the testing carried out. This detailed documentation is used to maintain the program in working order should errors be found in the future.

Becoming a Computer Programmer

Programmers need to think logically and be good at solving problems. Programming is an interesting, high pressure job, not really suitable for those wanting a quiet life. Working hours can often be extended at short notice when an urgent job has to be done. Programmers must work well with others, as teamwork is usual. They need to be flexible and not too worried about having a routine life style. A measure of enthusiasm and an obsession with the job are also useful!

Programmers are valued for their skill and experience. However, qualifications are useful in finding a job. Most employers would expect A-levels, preferably including Maths and Computer Studies. GCSEs in Maths and English are almost essential.

Most companies would provide training in the computer language needed where a programmer was not fluent in that particular language.

As they gain experience, Programmers often specialise in an area of programming, such as Operating Systems. Another common alternative is to become a Systems Analyst.

Programmers are generally found in employment where Systems Analysts are also employed, i.e. companies, local government, etc. Skilled programmers are highly paid and there are opportunities for foreign travel. Programming skills are in short supply in most industrialised countries.

OPERATIONS MANAGER

The **Operations Manager** has overall responsibility for the organisation of the use of the computer, including the supervision of the Data Preparation department, the Data Control department, Computer Operators and the File Librarian. The Operations Manager reports directly to the DP Manager.

DATA PREPARATION CLERK

Responsibilities of the Data Preparation Clerk

When data has been captured or collected for input, it may not be in a form the computer can read. For example, an order from a customer may be written on a piece of paper. The computer cannot read the writing on the paper so the information is transferred to magnetic disc or tape. Data preparation is the entering of data at the keyboard of a VDU in use as key-to-tape or key-to-disc machine. This is the job of a **Data Preparation Clerk** (see Fig. 12.8). Data Preparation Clerks are sometimes known as **Data Preparation Operators**.

Fig. 12.8 The job of a Data Preparation Clerk

Data preparation is an essential part of any computer based system that does not use direct data capture, e.g. laser scanners, temperature sensors, etc. Data Preparation Clerks usually work in a department that deals with the data entry requirements of all the systems run by the company. All organisations that use large computer systems will have a Data Preparation department.

Becoming a Data Preparation Clerk

Good keyboard skills are important. A skilled Data Preparation Clerk can maintain speed and accuracy while doing repetitive work. Qualifications at GCSE level in English, Office Practice or Typing might be useful in getting a job, but again, it is the *ability to do the job* that is important. Touch typing skills and familiarity with wordprocessing are almost essential.

Payment is often related to the number of key depressions per hour when entering the data on the keyboard. Hours are regular, but shift work is normal. Often short shifts or limited hours can be worked. For this reason many women combine a job in data preparation with raising a family and looking after a home. A fast keyboard operator can earn high wages in comparison to similar work, perhaps typing in an office, as the wage paid relates to the volume of work done rather than the time spent.

A skilled Data Preparation Clerk can progress to a supervisory position or move into computer operations. It is possible for a determined and capable employee to be promoted from data preparation, through operations, to programming and beyond. The job is also good experience for potential secretaries and wordprocessor operators.

DATA CONTROL CLERKS

❝Responsibilities of the Data Control Clerk❞

When a system is in use, the input, processing and output are carefully controlled. **Data Control Clerks** monitor the flow of data through the system as it moves from data preparation, to verification, validation and processing on the computer (see Fig. 12.9). They collect any printed output and send it to the appropriate person. Data Control Clerks make sure that no data gets lost and that it is processed as required. The Data Preparation department receives most of its work through the Data Control department as data to be input to working systems will be sent to Data Control initially. Enquiries from other departments about the progress of their data being processed are dealt with by Data Control.

❝Becoming a Data Control Clerk❞

Data Control Clerks need to be thorough and reliable, with a good understanding of the computer systems used by the company they work for. They are an essential part of any well organised DP department.

Working hours are normal office hours. A Data Control Clerk works in a modern office environment, at times using a VDU to monitor the progress of the data being processed. Often a copy of the operators console screen display is used. This can be quite complex. Data control is a good training for operations work and a period in data control is often part of the training schedule for newly employed operators.

Fig. 12.9 The job of a Data Control Clerk

COMPUTER OPERATORS

❝Responsibilities of Computer Operators❞

Computer Operators look after the computer while it is running (see Fig. 12.10). They start up the computer and close it down. Computer Operators also monitor the status of programs running on the computer and provide tapes and discs as requested. They change the paper in the line printer and keep all other peripherals in the computer room supplied with media.

Operators are employed at all mainframe computer installations. Most such companies have purpose-built computer rooms where the operator works. Mainframe computers need a carefully controlled environment in which to run. They need air-conditioning to disperse the heat generated by the computer and air filtering to keep the air clean so that discs, tapes and machinery are not damaged. A computer room will have a false floor and a suspended ceiling so that cables and wiring can easily be concealed when laid from one part of the computer room to another. A Computer Operator works in the computer room. These are possibly the best working conditions experienced in any job!

Fig. 12.10 The job of a Computer Operator

❝❝Becoming a Computer Operator ❞❞

Operators need to be alert and react calmly in a crisis. They will need to respond in a sensible way if problems such as machine failure do arise. Attention to detail and care in doing routine tasks are very important. They must work reliably on their own, without supervision. It is not unknown for one or two Computer Operators to be left in charge of a multimillion pound computer.

Most companies train their own operators. Operators need to know *what* the computer does, *who* uses it and *for what purpose*. This is best learnt through a combination of on-the-job training and day-release courses. However, GCSEs in Maths, English and Computer Studies could well help in getting a job as an operator. Experience and ability rate more highly than qualifications once basic skills have been learnt.

Most operators will work shifts as large computers are kept running twenty-four hours a day. Operators are paid extra for working shifts and overtime is usually paid for extra hours worked. There will be a **Shift Leader** appointed for each shift to take responsibility for the team of operators working the shift.

Career opportunities within data processing are good. Operating is a skill that is transferable from one company to another. Operators may become Shift Leaders and go into Operations Management. Operating provides a good opening to higher level work with computers. A move into programming is not uncommon.

FILE LIBRARIAN

The **File Librarian** looks after all the magnetic tapes and discs used by the computer department. It is the job of the File Librarian to locate the discs or tapes required to run a particular job on the computer. The File Librarian makes sure that tapes and discs remain usable and are kept secure to prevent unauthorised use.

OTHER JOBS IN COMPUTING

Most people working in computers are employed by companies using large mainframe computers for data processing. However, these are not the only jobs.

Computer manufacturers employ sales staff to *sell* computers. They may also employ staff to provide *technical advice* to customers and *equipment maintenance* as part of their after-sales service. Research and development staff may be needed to develop new products, and there will be engineering jobs available in production and quality control.

There are also jobs available in teaching and training. These may be in training departments in large companies, or as part of customer services provided by computer manufacturers. Most schools, colleges and universities now offer courses in computing, information technology or data processing.

LOOKING FOR A JOB IN COMPUTING?

If you want to work with computers, either in a user department or as a computer specialist, and you are looking for your first job, the best thing you can do is get some experience and qualifications. There are several possibilities:

- Buy or borrow a personal desk-top computer and learn how to use it.
- Talk to someone who works in computing and if you are lucky they may show you where they work and what they do.
- Learn the basics of a programming language.
- Learn to use a wordprocessor, a spreadsheet, a database and communications software.
- Take a general course in computing and study for a specialist qualification at as high a level as possible.

You may not be able to find the time to do *all* these, but make sure you have done enough so that an employer will recognise you as a sound prospect for employment and further training. Remember, employers want *value for money*. If you can show them that you have done as much as you possibly can, short of getting a job, then you will have a much better chance in the employment market.

The next step is getting a job. Don't expect to start at the top. Do look for a job that offers *training*. However, any job is better than none and you can always use the experience gained when looking for better employment:

- Look in the local papers for jobs. Buy computer magazines. In particular, try and get hold of Computer Weekly and Computing. Most trade papers in computing are crammed with job adverts.
- Write to companies and agencies advertising for computer staff and ask if there is any possibility of being taken on as a trainee.
- Visit local agencies specialising in computer staff.

There is a national shortage of computer specialists but this varies from place to place. You would probably find a job more easily in a city such as London, Birmingham, Manchester or Leeds. Don't be put off because your first applications are unsuccessful. The next job could be yours. Good luck!

EXAMINATION QUESTIONS

SHORT STRUCTURED QUESTIONS

1   A firm wants to install a computer. They have gone to a computer company for help. The systems analyst has investigated how the firm does its stock control manually. List or describe two further jobs he would do before the computer system is fully ready to replace the manual system.

    a) Job 1. _____

    _____

    b) Job 2. _____

    _____

(LEAG; 1988)

2   Briefly describe the work of
    a) A Data Processing Manager (3 lines available)
    b) A Computer Operator (3 lines available)
    c) A Data Preparation Operator (3 lines available)   *(3)*
(WJEC; 1988)

3 Tick **three** items which would be found in the user documentation of a word processing package.

ITEM	FOUNDED IN DOCUMENTATION Tick
what commands to use to carry out functions	
how to touch type	
how to load the package	
examples of screen layout	
program listing	
how data moves round the CPU	

(3)
(MEG; 1988)

4 A flow diagram is often a part of program documentation. Give one reason why.

_____

(LEAG; 1988)

5 Here is a list of job titles to do with computers:

Computer Engineer   Computer Operator
Data Control Clerk   Data Processing Manager
File Librarian   Keyboard Operator
Programmer   Salesman
Shift Leader   Systems Analyst

For each of the tasks below, write down the most likely job title of the person doing it. You can use a job title once, more than once, or not at all.
 a) Loading a line printer with paper.

_____

(1)
 b) Coding a computer program.

_____

(1)
 c) Appointing new staff in a Data Processing Department.

_____

(1)
 d) Correcting errors in a program.

_____

(1)
 e) Finding the correct data tape.

_____

(1)
 f) Testing a new computer system.

_____

(1)
 g) Demonstrating a computer to a new customer.

_____

(1)
 h) Keying in data.

_____

(1)
 i) Repairing a faulty disc drive.

_____

(1)
(SEG; 1988)

6 A software house is planning to release a new accounts package for **small** businesses. The package is designed to do the following tasks:

1 Print out a bill for each order sent out by the business.
2 Print out a payment slip to go with all bills paid by the business.
3 Record the details of all the goods bought and sold by the business.
4 Keep a record of all stock held, and update this record when goods are sold or received.
5 Keep and update the financial records of the business, e.g. how much money is in the bank, how much is owed to the business, how much is owed by the business, profits, losses etc.

a) Give **four** essential items of hardware that would be needed to run this sort of package.   (4)
b) There are both advantages and disadvantages for small businesses in buying packages like this accounts package. State **two** advantages and **two** disadvantages, to a small business, of buying a ready made package from a software house, rather than commissioning one for its particular needs.   (4)
c) The programmers employed by the software house have written a user manual to be supplied with the package. Describe **three** sections that should be included in this user manual and say what benefit the user might get from each of these.   (6)
d) The programmers have also written the detailed program documentation which is kept by the software house. Describe **three** sections of this documentation and explain why they are included.   (6)

(LEAG; 1988)

OUTLINE ANSWERS

SHORT
STRUCTURED
QUESTIONS

1 a) *Job 1: Systems analysis and design*
       The analyst would specify in detail the input, processing and output required.

   b) *Job 2: Implementation*
       The analyst would supervise the installation of extra hardware, staff training and final systems testing, including if possible a parallel run.

2 a) A *Data Processing Manager* is in charge of the computer department. The Operations Manager, the Programming Manager and Senior Systems Analysts report directly to the Data Processing Manager.

   b) A *Computer Operator* looks after the computer while it is running. They start up and close down the computer and change discs, tapes and printer paper.

   c) A *Data Preparation Operator* transfers data from a source document to a computer readable medium, such as disc, by entering the data using key-to-disc. The data is entered using a keyboard, displayed on the monitor screen for visual checking, then recorded on disc.

3 User documentation should contain
       i)   what commands to use to carry out functions
       ii) how to load the package
       iii) examples of screen layout

4 If the program has to be changed because it has developed a bug or the program needs changing or extending, a flow-chart is useful to the programmer in understanding how the program works.

5 a) Computer Operator
   b) Programmer

    c) Data Processing Manager
    d) Programmer
    e) File Librarian
    f) Systems Analyst
    g) Salesman
    h) Keyboard Operator (Data Preparation Clerk)
    i) Computer Engineer

6 a) A microcomputer system consisting of a monitor, keyboard, CPU, disc drive and printer.

    b) *Advantage 1:*   The package is available immediately.
       Advantage 2:   The cost of the package is likely to be less than the cost of commissioning software to suit the needs of the business.
       Disadvantage 1: The business will have to change its method of working to suit the package.
       Disadvantage 2: The business cannot change the package as business requirements change, because they do not have access to the source code. Only the software house can change the package.

    c) The user manual should contain:
      i) A general description of what the program does and detailed descriptions of what functions are available and how to use them.
      ii) Instructions on how to load and run the package
      iii) Examples of typical input required and output produced.
         The user would benefit as it will be much easier to understand and use the package.

    d) The detailed program documentation should contain:
      i) a flowchart;
      ii) a listing of the program;
      iii) details of the test data used and the results obtained.

        The above will help programmers to find errors if they occur and allow them to correct the errors more easily.

A STUDENT'S ANSWER WITH EXAMINER'S COMMENTS

QUESTION

a) Describe an on-line booking system you have studied. Make specific reference to the hardware requirements as well as to the facilities provided by the system.   *(8)*

b) Name the steps involved in the development of a computer-based system.   *(6)*

c) With reference to part b) above, which tasks would be carried out by
  i) a Systems Analyst,
  ii) a Computer Programmer?   *(3)*

d) It is proposed to replace an existing manual booking system with a computer-based on-line booking system.
  i) Write down **one** advantage and **one** disadvantage expected when the new on-line system is introduced.
  ii) What are **two** likely effects of the introduction of the on-line booking system on employees?
  iii) Give **two** examples of the resulting improvements in customer service that may be expected.   *(8)*

(WJEC; 1988)

a)

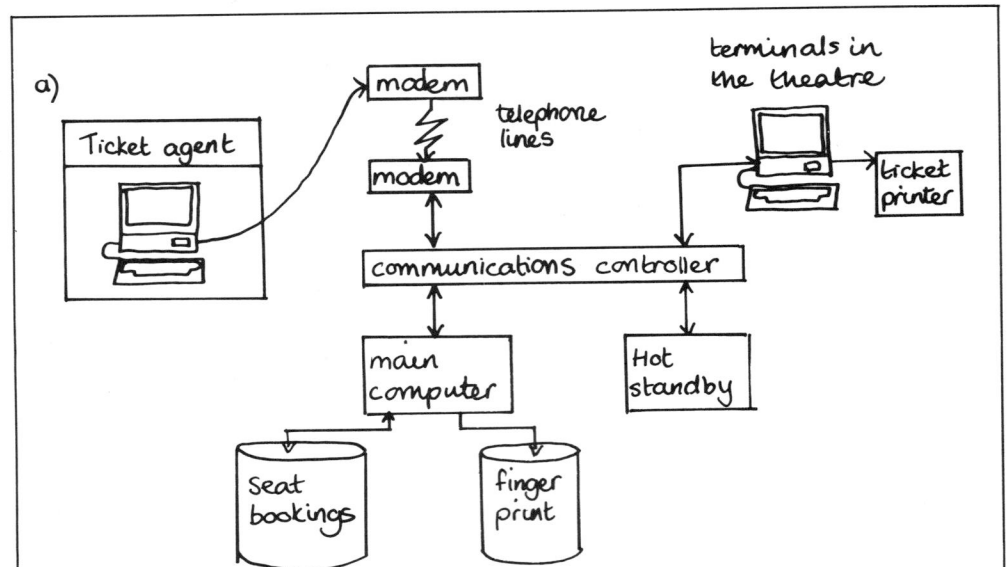

The on-line booking system I have studied is a theatre ticket booking system.

The system uses terminals connected to a mainframe computer. In the theatre the terminals are connected directly to the computer but it is possible to access the computer using a microcomputer, a modem and the telephone network from a ticket agents.

At the terminals in the theatre you can see which seats have been booked and which seats are free. You can book for shows months in advance. When you pay for your tickets, a ticket printer at the theatre terminal prints the ticket.

The ticket agents connect to the computer using the telephone lines, a microcomputer and a modem. They have to give a password to get into the system. This is to stop hackers. When connected they can do everything that a terminal in the theatre can except print tickets. These are sent to them by post if they book seats

It is very important that the system is fast, so real-time processing is used. Disc storage is needed for fast access and to store the very large amount of data processed.

For security, two computers are used; one does the processing and the other is a hot standby for use if the first computer breaks down.

Disc files are backed up by finger printing, ie. all discs have two copies which are both kept up-to-date by the real time system.

b) The system is an idea at first. If it is a good idea, a feasibility study is done.

If this is accepted the system is analysed in-depth and a detailed system design done.

All the programs are written and tested, then the whole system is tested.

When the system is working, the analyst looks at it again to see if it is still working properly.

c) i)+ii) A Systems Analyst looks after the system as described in b) except that the computer programmer designs codes and tests the computer programs.

d) i) One advantage is that it is faster, one disadvantage is that people are sacked.

ii) Two likely effects are that employees will need to retrain to use the new system and some will be sacked.

iii) Customers can expect the service to be faster and more efficient. Prevents double booking.

Examiner's comment

a) A good answer. A diagram is not asked for but is an effective illustration in this case.

b) and c) Reasonable answers but could be improved by naming the stages of the system life cycle and giving a brief comment on each. By doing this the student might have avoided several obvious omissions. For example, the candidate has not mentioned *documentation*. It is important to keep documentation up-to-date as the system evolves.

d) i) This type of question is structured to encourage candidates to look at the advantages and disadvantages of the new computer based on-line system from several points of view. You should mention six *different* points, two in each section of d).

ii) The answer given mentions the same points several times.

iii) 'Faster' and 'more efficient' are too vague.

'Faster' what? This needs explaining.

13

COMPUTERS AT WORK: INFORMATION TECHNOLOGY

GETTING STARTED

Most people use computers to make their work easier and more productive. It would be tedious to have to write a program for every task we want to do on a computer. Instead general purpose, *content free* programs are used. These provide facilities to do a range of tasks rather than being programmed for specific applications. They are described as content free because the information content processed changes from task to task, but the processing done is broadly similar.

- **Wordprocessing** software is used to prepare and print articles, reports and other documents. Letters can be personalised and address labels printed for envelopes.

- **Electronic mail** is sent from one computer to another, using the telephone network. The sending of mail by this method is faster and more convenient than using the traditional paper, envelope and stamp method.

- **Graphic design** software is used to draw pictures, produce posters, illustrate articles and design textiles and industrial products.

- **Desk Top Publishing** combines wordprocessing and graphics in a format typical of a newspaper with text in columns, varying character sizes, photographs and other illustrations.

- **Spreadsheets** are used to calculate and display financial or statistical information, where the structure of each task is similar, but the numbers used may change. They automatically re-calculate the answers to formulae when new information is entered.

- **Databases** provide fast, easy access to large files of information.

- **Expert Systems** make the accumulated knowledge of human experts available for consultation.

- **Videotext** in the form of *Teletext* and *Viewdata* systems gives quick, easy access to everyday information, such as weather reports. The information is displayed on a specially adapted TV.

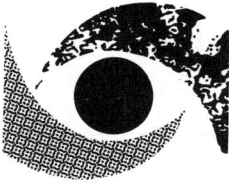

E S S E N T I A L   P R I N C I P L E S

Computers are very useful in the work place as an aid in getting tasks done and in providing up-to-date, accurate information. Computers not only do tasks that in the past were done less effectively in other ways, they also *extend* what can be done. Tasks which were too slow or too expensive without the aid of computers are now done faster and more economically.

Computers are versatile tools to be used in the work place to improve productivity and effectiveness. Their flexibility has led to their use in many different situations. They are used to perform routine office work and to provide quick and easy access to information. The software selected for use depends on the nature and scale of the task.

1 ▸ CONTENT FREE SOFTWARE

Content free software provides the user with a way of doing a general range of tasks. When purchased, the software often contains no information but has the ability to process that provided by the user. The processing possible depends entirely on the way in which the user makes use of software, the characteristics of the software and the information supplied by the user. Content free software is general purpose software; it is designed for *flexible* use rather than for a particular application.

Content free software is programs for wordprocessing, electronic mail, graphic design, desktop publishing, spreadsheets, databases, expert systems, videotext, etc. These are described in general terms in this chapter. The best way to become familiar with any computer system is to use it. This is particularly true for content free software.

2 ▸ WORD-PROCESSING

Wordprocessors, i.e. computers running wordprocessing software, have now largely replaced the traditional, mechanical or electronic typewriter. Wordprocessors can not only do any job carried out on a typewriter, they also make such tasks easier, and have additional facilities.

A wordprocessor will typically consist of a microcomputer, monitor, mouse, disc drive, printer and wordprocessing software. The quality of the printed output is determined by the type of printer used. For high quality output a daisywheel printer should be used; for high speed, and a wide variety of character styles or fonts, a laser printer is needed. For inexpensive, low quality printout, a dot matrix printer is appropriate.

❝Wordprocessing software❞

Wordprocessing software is extensive and varied. There is very often a choice of wordprocessors for a particular computer and many wordprocessors will run on several different makes of computer. It may interest the reader to know that this book was written using the 1stWord wordprocessing software running on an Atari 520 ST microcomputer (see Fig. 13.1). This software is also available for other computers, e.g. the Archimedes and the Amstrad PC. A wide variety of other wordprocessing software can be run on the Atari 520 ST, e.g. Word Perfect, Text Pro, K-Word, STwriter, etc. Wordprocessors vary in the facilities they provide. Some common facilities are as follows:

❝Common Wordprocessor facilities❞

- **Create** a document
  A *document* is a file of words or text to be processed, for example, an article or a letter to a client. When a new document is needed it is created and given a unique filename to identify it. The text is typed into the document from the keyboard and appears on the screen as it is typed.

- **Wordwrap**
  At the end of each line, when attempting to type beyond the right margin, the word that is typed in will automatically be carried over onto the next line.

- **Scrolling**
  Since it is likely that the document will be too big for all of it to be displayed on the screen at the same time, the document will scroll, that is, it will disappear at the top and reappear at the bottom when scrolling down the document. The entire document is stored in the memory of the computer but we can only see part of it on the screen.

- **Save** and **load** documents from disc
  When a document has been created it can be saved on disc. The computer can be switched off but the document will not be lost as there is a copy of it on the disc.

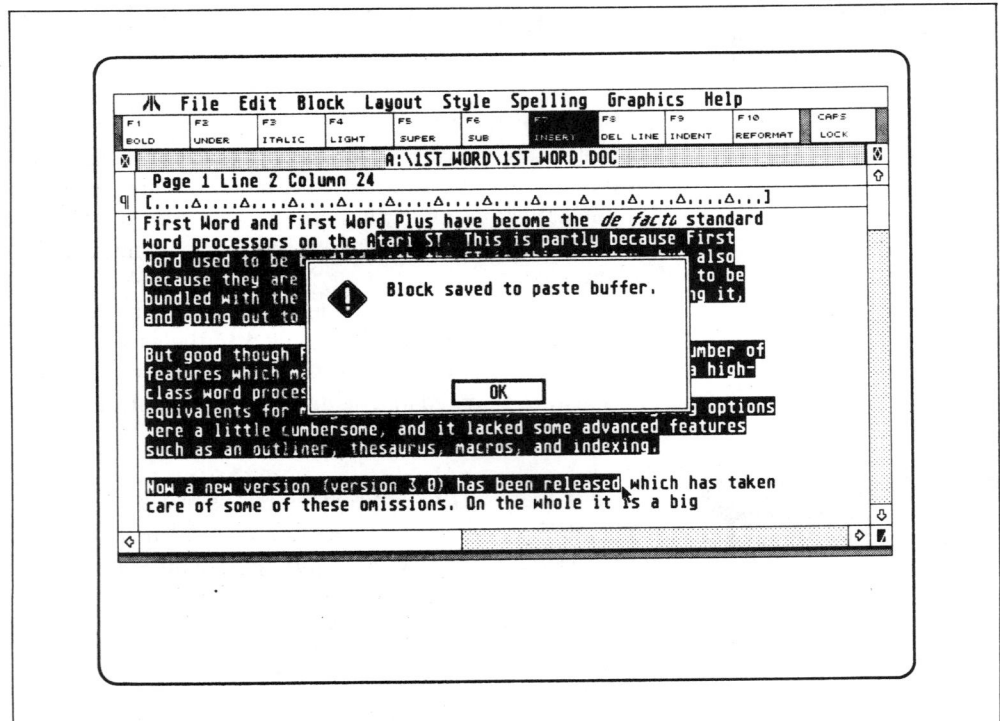

Fig. 13.1 The screen displayed by the 1st Word wordprocessor running on an Atari 520 ST

When needed, the document can be loaded from the disc into the computer.

- **Print** a document

  It must be possible to print the document on a printer connected to the word-processor.

- **Amend** a document by editing it on the screen

  When a document has been created it may be necessary to change or amend it. For example, the spelling of words may be corrected by deleting and inserting characters. To do this the cursor is moved to the position where the change is needed, using either the cursor control keys or the mouse. The existing text is now deleted and the new text inserted.

- **Search** and **replace**

  The *search* facility is used to find particular words or characters in the document. If a word has been spelt incorrectly, for example, every occurence of the word can be located and the incorrect spelling *replaced* by the correct spelling.

- **Style** facilities to enhance the appearance of the text

  Various style facilities should be available, for example, underlining, bold or emphasised text, italics, different fonts (i.e. character shapes), subscripts, super-scripts, etc.

- **Format** facilities to control the layout of the text on the page

  There should be a variety of formatting facilities. Text can be centred on a line; margins can be justified so that either the right or left margin or both are aligned; paragraphs can be indented from either margin; the width of the page can be altered; page headings and page numbers can be automatically inserted.

- **Block** move, copy and delete

  It should be possible to define a *block* of text, perhaps a paragraph or several paragraphs, and to move it or make another copy of it in a different position in the document. It should also be possible to delete blocks.

- **Spelling checker**

  The spelling of words can be checked against an extensive dictionary which can be added to or changed as the user wishes.

- **Standard letters**

  Companies regularly send letters to clients in which the content of each letter may be the same but the name, address and other limited details change. Similarly, legal documents are often almost the same for situations that are alike, only the names of clients, etc. change. In these cases a standard letter can be saved on disc. This is the part of the document that does not change from client to client. The position in the standard letter that does change can be indicated using a marker.

- **Mail shots**
  A file of clients names and addresses can be merged with a standard letter to print an individualised letter for each client. The name and address of each client can also be printed on address labels that can be stuck on the envelopes before they are posted.

The job of an office typist has changed greatly due to the introduction of wordprocessors. There is much less need to retype letters and less routine copy typing. More attention can be given to the presentation of work and more style and format facilities are available to encourage this. Correspondence does not have to be stored printed on paper in filing cabinets but can be saved on disc until needed. Consequently, much less manual filing of correspondence in filing cabinets is necessary and it is easier to locate the documents saved on disc.

Wordprocessors increase the productivity of typists, allowing them to complete *more* work of a *higher* standard. This may lead to fewer typists being employed. The operating of a wordprocessor demands different skills to those necessary to use a typewriter so that typists have had to retrain, learning new skills. Not all have easily adapted to the new technology. However, those that have learned wordprocessing skills benefit from higher pay and status. The client has also benefited due to the use of wordprocessors. Replies to letters can be quicker and more personalised. Correspondence will be more likely to be clearly printed and error-free. The cost of the service is also likely to be held or reduced, allowing savings to be passed on to the customer.

3 > ELECTRONIC MAIL

Advantages of Electronic Mail

Using a modem and a telephone line, data can be transferred from one computer to another. Using this method of communication, computers can send documents, possibly prepared on a wordprocessor, to each other. These documents are then available to the user of the receiving computer. This is **electronic mail**.

Companies can prepare their mail on a wordprocessor during the day. Each letter to be mailed is stored along with the telephone number of the receiving computer to which the document must be sent. At night, the computer automatically dials up the receiving computers and transfers their mail to them. For example, this method of communication is used by some household appliance service departments to send details of the next day's work to service engineers who work in widely dispersed areas. Each service engineer has a microcomputer which must be ready to receive data at a predetermined time during the night. At this time, documents prepared at the central computer location during the day are transferred.

Electronic mail is also possible by transferring the document to an intermediate computer. This avoids the need for the sending and receiving computers to be in direct contact. Mail can be sent to an intermediate computer which is always available. At a later date this mail can be accessed by the receiving computer, whenever it is convenient to do so. This is the basis of most public electronic mail systems e.g. Telecom Gold.

4 > GRAPHIC DESIGN

Graphic design software provides a means of drawing pictures on the computer screen. It varies in complexity and capability and must be carefully selected depending on the use to be made of it.

Most graphics software is 2-dimensional, i.e. there is no attempt to represent solid objects. For convenient use of graphics software a mouse is essential as a WIMP environment will almost certainly be used to some extent. The facilities available are likely to be represented by icons or to be listed in pull-down menus. They can usually be activated by pointing at the appropriate icon or menu entry with the mouse-controlled pointer and clicking the button on the mouse to select them. A wide range of facilities may be available which will differ, depending on the software used. Some common facilities are as follows:

- **Draw** on the screen
  A line can be drawn on the screen by moving the mouse. The line corresponds to the movement of the mouse. Various types of standard line can be selected, e.g. straight or dotted, in a variety of patterns, perhaps rays, circles, boxes, etc.

❝❝ Common facilities of
Graphic Design
software ❞❞

■ **Colours**

A variety of colours will be available on a colour monitor. There will be a range of standard colours to choose from and perhaps the facility to mix colours to produce a unique blend. These colours can be used in combination with other features of the software to draw coloured lines, for example.

■ **Fill**

Closed shapes can be filled with patterns. These patterns may be standard, or designed by the user, perhaps in several colours.

■ **Airbrush**

Fill patterns or colours can be applied in a texture that mimics the effect of an airbrush or spray gun. Different brush patterns can be selected or designed by the user.

■ **Text**

Words and characters can be typed in a variety of styles or fonts. It may be possible for the user to customise an existing font or design a new one.

■ **Blocks**

An area of the screen can be defined as a *block*. This block can then be moved or copied to another part of the screen. Blocks can be transformed by stretching, reflecting or rotating them. Blocks can be transferred between pictures and can be saved on disc for later use.

■ **Zoom**

Areas of the screen can be magnified, or zoomed in on, to allow very fine detail to be added or changed.

■ **Pictures**

Pictures can be saved on disc and loaded back into memory when needed. Pictures can often be imported from, or exported to, other graphics software. Standard pictures can be saved. This could be helpful in, for example, designing micro-electronic circuits, where a limited range of symbols is used.

■ **Printing**

Colour printing is still expensive, although ink-jet printers using 4 or 5 colours are available at a reasonable price. It is difficult to get an accurate printout on paper of the colour seen on the screen. The printout provided by a dot matrix printer is adequate if a black and white tone print is acceptable.

The above facilities should be available in most basic graphic design software. Using such facilities it is possible to do textile design, wallpaper design and produce high quality business cards and tickets for dances, etc. Typical systems are the RM Nimbus running PCpaint software, IBM PC compatibles running PixelPaint, Atari ST systems using DegasElite or Neochrome and the BBC Master running Image.

❝❝ More specialised
facilities of Graphic Design
software ❞❞

More specialised facilities are sometimes available for specific tasks. For example, some graphics software will accept images captured by a video camera when input via a video digitiser. These images can be changed or enhanced using the facilities of the graphics software. This technique can be used to add text to video film or to create a mixed sequence of video and graphic designs such as cartoons.

Three-dimensional objects can be designed with some specialised graphics software. These objects can be displayed on the screen as wire frame images, or as solid objects which can be rotated or viewed in plan and elevation.

In manufacturing, graphics software can be used to design products. A library of standard components can be provided so that the new design can be made up from existing manufactured parts as far as is possible. It becomes relatively easy to redesign products as their designs are easily changed using graphics software without the need to redraw the entire design.

5 ⟩ DESK TOP PUBLISHING (DTP)

Desk top publishing software allows the user to produce printout in the style of a newspaper (see Fig. 13.2). That is, in columns with pictures and other graphics. DTP software is run on a microcomputer system with a laser printer for high quality, fast printout. A mouse is essential, as DTP is inevitably run in a WIMP environment. A scanner will be needed to import photographs and possibly a video digitiser to capture video images.

DTP software can be thought of as integrated wordprocessing and graphics, with additional features to enable pages to be laid out in columns and illustrations to be inserted where necessary. Different character styles or fonts will be needed on the same page. Some facility to import photographs and video images will be required.

Often, DTP software will have only primitive wordprocessing and graphics facilities, providing the structure to manipulate documents into columns, etc. and to cut and position graphics as required. In this case the DTP software is relying on the user to use the specialised facilities of wordprocessor and graphics software to prepare documents and illustrations before importing these into the DTP software for placing in the desired page format.

Typical systems are Fleet St Publisher software on Atari ST microcomputers and NewsSpa on RM Nimbus.

Fig. 13.2 Desk Top Publishing

6 > SPREADSHEETS

Spreadsheets provide numerical reporting facilities. They can be used with a microcomputer system and a dot matrix printer. A wide carriage printer might be useful, though not essential.

A wordprocessor could be used to prepare and printout reports involving numerical calculations such as financial reports, stock records etc. However, spreadsheets offer facilities which are not usually available in wordprocessing software. Using spreadsheet facilities the structure of calculations can be programmed. The actual numbers may change from time to time but the effect of these changes on any pre-programmed calculations is automatic.

For example, the following could be programmed into a spreadsheet:

	1	2	3	4
1	Computer Shop Plc			
2				
3	description	cash	quantity	value of
4		price	sold	sales
5				
6	Atari 520 ST	389.95	35	13 648.25
7	Archimedes A310	899.00	10	8 990.00
8	Amstrad PCW 8256	399.00	52	20 748.00
9	Amstrad PC 1640	559.00	41	22 919.00
10	BBC Master	439.95	20	8 799.00
11	Commodore Amiga A500	469.95	23	10 808.85
		Total Sales =		85 913.10

Converting to a *Spreadsheet*

In the above table we have text, numbers and calculations. Each entry in the table is called a **cell** and each cell has a unique location. For example, the text 'BBC Master' is located in the cell at row 10, column 1; the number '41' is located at row 9, column 3.

Calculations are described using formulae. In the above example, the value of sales for each row can be calculated by multiplying the cost price and quantity sold from the same row. For row 11, the cost price in column 4 is found by multiplying the contents of row 11, column 2, i.e. 469.95, and the contents of row 11, column 3, i.e. 23. In each entry in the value of sales column a formula is programmed in, not a value. The value is calculated using the formula. If different values are entered in the cost price or quantity columns, the *new* value of sales will automatically be calculated.

Spreadsheets may be printed directly or can be transferred to a wordprocessor or DTP software for improved presentation. They are especially useful where the same calculations are done on a regular basis and for record keeping. A spreadsheet can be set up by an expert, e.g. an accountant, to do complex calculations and the actual details can be entered by someone who needs the information that is produced, but whose expertise is different, e.g. a tradesman. A spreadsheet could be used in a small business for stock control, the entries in the spreadsheet being changed as the levels of stock change.

Typical spreadsheets are Multiplan software for RM Nimbus computers and IBM compatible PCs, Viewsheet for the BBC Master and K-spread for the Atari ST.

7 ▷ DATABASES

A **database** is a collection of structured data. The data will usually be structured in the form of files, records and fields.

A **Database Management System (DBMS)** consists of the database and the necessary software needed to access the database. Often, this distinction between a database and a DBMS is not made, both being loosely referred to as a database. This practice will be continued here!

Databases enable the user to search through large volumes of data, selecting certain information and displaying it on the screen or printing it in whatever format or order is required. Database software is often supplied to the user without files of data. The user is expected to create and maintain any data files required.

Some basic facilities provided by database software are:

■ Create

Common facilities of database software

The user must set up a data file before data can be stored. This involves, at least, giving the file a filename and defining the structure of each record. For each field in the record it is necessary to specify a unique fieldname, what type of data will be entered in the field, i.e. numbers or characters, and the length of the field. For example, a record containing four fields could be defined as follows:

field name	type of data	maximum length
name	characters	20 characters
address	characters	100 characters
age	number	2 digits
income	number	5 digits

■ Insert

Having created a record structure and defined fields it should be possible to enter data and create a data file containing the desired information, inserting new records into the file as required.

Records inserted into the structure above would contain data similar to the following:

```
1 Shoard, M : 12 Heaton Road, Mayfield MY9 2A7    : 36 : 15 000
2 Daniels, M : 24 Ashtree Drive, Burnley BD3 7D5  : 31 :  9 000
3 Lewis, P : 9 Oaks Lane, Mayfield MY2 8H3        : 18 : 18 000
```

■ Amend and delete

It should be possible to change the structure of the data, e.g. to add an extra field to all records, and change the contents of any field without disturbing existing data. It should also be possible to remove fields from a record and records from a file.

■ Search

By defining a *search condition*, data can be selected from the file. Examples of search conditions are:

a) Name contains 'Daniels'. This selects record 2.
b) Address contains 'Mayfield'. This selects records 1 and 3.
c) Age is greater than 30 and income is less than £10000. This selects record 2.
Using a search condition the file would be looked at and all the records that satisfied the search condition would be identified.

■ Sort

In practice, a file would contain more than the three records shown in the example above and a search of the file would be likely to yield many records that satisfy the search condition. It may be helpful to sort the data selected from the file into some order, e.g. alphabetic order of the name, before reporting on the results of the search.

■ Report

Having searched the file, perhaps sorting any records selected, a report to the user on the results of the search is required. This report could be on the monitor screen, or a printout. In either case a report can be constructed that contains either all, or some, of the contents of each record selected. The report might be in columns containing the reported fields. Each row might contain the details extracted from one record. Other formats may be defined by the user.

Uses of databases

Databases are useful when it is necessary to extract information very quickly from large volumes of data. For example, an Electricity Board has a very large number of customers. A record containing the details for each customer will be stored in a file. The details stored for each customer will include the name, address, customer identification number, details of previous electricity meter readings, method of payment and credit status. This customer file will be stored on a mainframe computer with several terminals. These terminals can be used to access the customer database.

The customer file will be used when calculating bills and mailing them to customers. Some of the bills will be calculated from new meter readings and some will be estimates based on previous meter readings. For various reasons, customers may wish to query their bills. They may also contact the Electricity Board to arrange for the supply to be connected or disconnected. Many customers will use the telephone to make their enquiries. Telephone enquiries demand the fast response times provided by a database.

A customer who telephones the Electricity Board will speak to a telephone operator wearing a headset that allows the hands to be free to use the keyboard of one of the terminals connected to the mainframe computer that is running the database. Ideally, the customer will tell the operator their customer identification number, so that this can be used as a search condition to locate their record. Unfortunately, many customers will not know this identification number. In these cases the operator will ask the customer their name and make a search of the database, extracting all those customers with that name. Next, the customer will be asked their address to confirm that the correct record has been found. Customer enquiries over the telephone are only practical because of the search facilities and fast response available using a database.

Examples of some of the large number of databases available for microcomputers are Quest on the RM Nimbus and the BBC Master, DBase2 on the IBM PC computer (and compatibles) and Superbase on the Atari ST.

Some large databases are only available via the telephone network using a microcomputer and modem as a terminal to a mainframe computer running the database. These databases are usually maintained by the provider. The user has access to the information, but may not change it. An example is the National Educational Resource Information Service (NERIS).

8 EXPERT SYSTEMS

An **expert system** or Intelligent Knowledge-Based System (IKBS) allows users to benefit from the accumulated knowledge of human experts. It consists of software that enables users to recognise particular situations and advise on the appropriate action to take.

For example, an expert system used in medicine for diagnosis of diseases will ask the doctors who use it a variety of questions concerning the symptoms of the patient. Using the answers given, the expert system will identify the specific disease or provide a list of possible illnesses. It will then suggest appropriate action to be taken to cure the disease.

The knowledge built into an IKBS is only as good as the knowledge of the experts who set up the system. As experience grows, or new knowledge is discovered, the IKBS will need to be changed to include this. Some IKBSs do not incorporate any knowledge when first used, but have been acquired by experts to help them build their own methods and ways of working into a coherent system.

The full potential of expert systems has not yet been exploited. They have the potential to give everyone access to the most advanced human thinking, but due to the difficulties in setting up such systems this is still only a possibility. They tend to be used only where their usefulness outweighs the problems and expense involved.

9 > VIDEOTEXT

Videotext is a page-based information retrieval system (see Fig. 13.3). When displayed on the screen, one page occupies the whole screen. Each page has a number and can be accessed using it. There is usually some form of index that directs the user to the page containing the information required. For example, a page may contain a weather report; other pages may contain stock market reports, etc.

Fig. 13.3 A page of videotext

TELETEXT

Teletext is a form of videotext broadcast by television and received on a modified domestic TV or using a teletext receiver connected to a microcomputer. Ceefax (broadcast by the BBC) and Oracle (from ITV) are teletext systems. Teletext pages are broadcast interleaved with the television signal in a repeated cycle of page numbers. Pages are broadcast constantly whether they have been selected or not. When a page number has been selected, the user must wait until that page is broadcast in the cycle before it will be displayed. Once displayed, the page is updated every time it is rebroadcast. The advantages in receiving teletext using a computer rather than a TV are that the computer can store pages on disc for later use and can print pages if requested. Often, computer software can be downloaded from teletext, saved on disc and run when needed.

VIEWDATA

Viewdata is another form of videotext. It is like teletext in that it is also a page-based system and its appearance on the screen is similar. However, viewdata is a two-way system; data can be both received and transmitted. Teletext is one way, pages can only be received. To access a viewdata system, a microcomputer and modem are preferable, although very basic hardware involving a simple numeric keypad can be used. The viewdata software is run on a mainframe computer and is accessed by using the microcomputer as an on-line terminal. Pages are only transmitted when requested. Access to some pages may be charged for by the information provider and access may be restricted in some cases by requiring a password. The information stored on viewdata systems and the services provided are more extensive than those transmitted by a teletext system. For example, goods can be bought by mail order by providing a credit card number and money can be transferred between bank accounts. Prestel, run by British Telecom, is a typical viewdata system.

VIEWDATA OR TELETEXT EMULATORS

These are available for some microcomputers and allow users to set up their own videotext system. Typically, they provide indexes and can be made to display a repeated cycle of pages. It is sometimes possible to download pages from Ceefax, Oracle or Prestel into the emulator. Emulators are useful for providing local information in libraries and other information centres.

10 > INTEGRATION

Much of the data used in a database could be useful with wordprocessing software, e.g. addresses extracted from a database might be useful in a mail shot. Bar charts and other graphics could be used to illustrate some of the output from a spreadsheet. This in turn could usefully be included in reports produced on a wordprocessor or DTP software. There is frequently a need to transfer data between different types of specialised software. Often this is not possible because of the different ways in which the data is represented in memory. The authors of software packages are free to structure files as they wish!

This general incompatibility has led to the writing of **integrated software**, e.g. software for wordprocessing, graphics, databases and spreadsheets, etc. that can *share* data or *transfer* data between each other.

EXAMINATION QUESTIONS

SHORT STRUCTURED QUESTIONS

1 Write down **two** computer applications which affect the work people do in an office.

Application 1: ___Word processing___

Application 2: ___Spreadsheets.___

(2)

(MEG; 1988)

2 a) Name a teletext service that is available through an ordinary television signal.

_____ *(1)*

b) Name a widely used public Viewdata service that uses the telephone network.

_____ *(1)*

c) Apart from costs and equipment, describe **two** main differences between these two forms of videotext. (6 lines available)

(6)

(SEG; 1988)

3

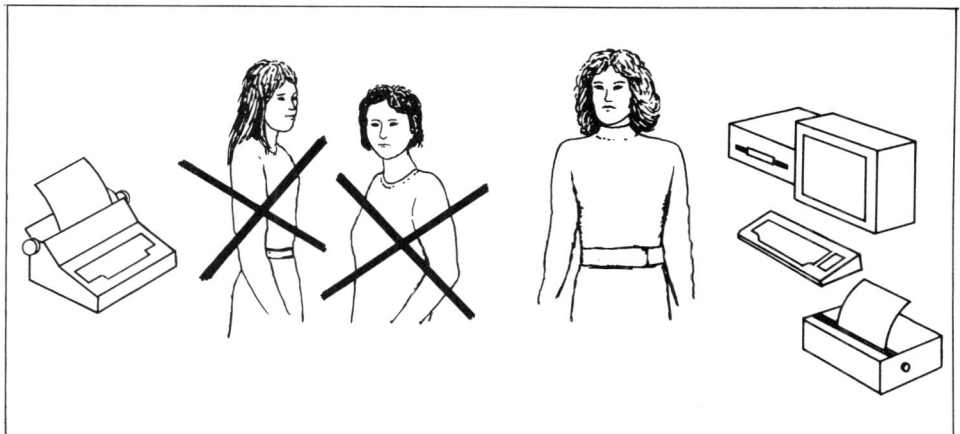

a) Although some people may lose their jobs due to word processors, there are advantages to be gained by using them in an office.

Give **two** advantages gained by using word processors.

i) _____

ii) _____

b) As yet few workers have lost their jobs to computers. Name **two** kinds of jobs where people have had to retrain because of computers.

i) _____

ii) _____ *(8)*

(WJEC; 1988)

4   A disc jockey has a collection of about two thousand albums, and wishes to index them using a computer. He needs to be able to find albums with a particular title, performed by a particular artiste or written by a particular composer.

a) He may either buy an existing software package, or write software specially.

   i) Give **two** advantages of buying an existing package.

   First advantage: _____

   _____

   Second advantage: _____

   _____ *(3)*

   ii) Give **two** advantages of using specially written software.

   First advantage: _____

   _____

   Second advantage: _____

   _____ *(3)*

b) If he were to buy a package, what type of computer software package should he buy?

   _____ *(2)*

c) What would be the most suitable type of backing store for this application?

   _____ *(1)*

d) When planning the record structure, he will need to complete a table like that below. Add four more items that might be needed.

Information	Type	Size
Title	String	50 Characters
Price	Numeric	5 Characters

(3)
(3)
(3)
(3)

e) For the problem outlined above, he would probably need to use some key fields.

   i) Explain what is meant by a *key field*. (3 lines available)

   (3)

   ii) Name the key field required for this application. (3 lines available)

   (3)

f) Describe a suitable non-computer system for this application (5 lines available)

(4)

g) A friend of yours has a hundred albums to index similarly, and does not own a computer. Would your advice be to buy and use a computer, or to use the method you have described in part f)? Give reasons for your answer.

(3)
(SEG; 1988)

5 Many businesses make use of electronic mail and electronic funds transfer to improve efficiency, reduce costs and speed up communication.

a) State **one** advantage of using electronic mail instead of having a telephone conversation.

_____

_____

b) State **one** difference between electronic mail and electronic funds transfer.

_____

_____

c) Name **two** applications that might use electronic funds transfer.

1 _____

2 _____

d) Describe how electronic mail and electronic funds transfer might change the work patterns and lifestyles of people using them.

_____ (NEA; 1988)

6 a) Viewdata systems such as Prestel provide users with a wide range of information. The diagram below shows the stages necessary for a user to access a particular page of information. Complete the flowchart by choosing suitable statements from the list provided.

Statements
enter page number
enter password
dial computer
load communications software
download software
does the page exist?
exit code selected?
copy page
enter a key word

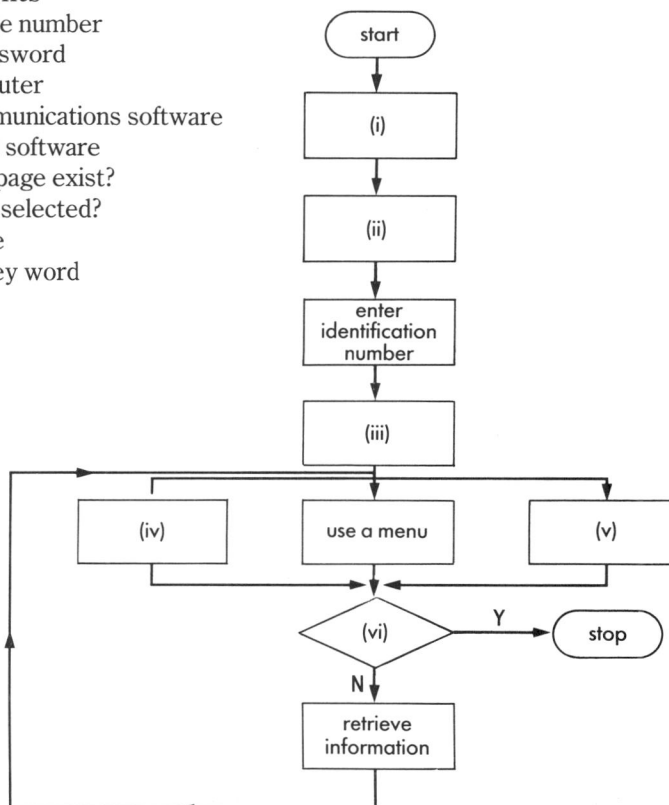

b) State the main charges that would be made for accessing information from Prestel. Your answer should **not** include the cost of any equipment or software.

_____ (NEA; 1988)

O U T L I N E   A N S W E R S

1 *Application 1:* Wordprocessing
   Application 2: Spreadsheets

2 a) Ceefax or Oracle
   b) Prestel

   c)

CEEFAX OR ORACLE	PRESTEL
i) All the pages are broadcast in a cycle that repeats itself. This happens all the time whether the user requests a page or not. When a page is selected, the user has to wait until it is broadcast again in the cycle.	When a page is selected it is displayed immediately. Pages are not broadcast unless they are selected.
ii) The user can only read the information. The system is one way only.	Prestel is a two-way, interactive system.

3 a) i) Letters can be typed in, checked and corrected before printing out.
      ii) It is not necessary to keep a printed copy of letters to customers, etc. These can be filed on disc. This uses less space and when they are wanted again it is easier to find them.

   b) i) Journalists have had to learn to use wordprocessors and communications software.
      ii) Travel agents; on-line booking systems have meant that travel agents have had to retrain to use them.

4 a) i) *First advantage:* It is available immediately.
         Second advantage: It is likely to cost less than the time taken to write software specially.
      ii) *First advantage:* The software will be designed to suit the disc jockey rather than having to adapt methods of working to suit an existing software package.
         Second advantage: If the software needs to be changed at a later date this will be possible, as the source code is available.

   b) A database
   c) Hard disc
   d)

Information	Type	Size
Title	string	50
Price	numeric	5
Artist(e)	string	30
Composer	string	20
Manufacturer's Record number	string	10
Date of issue	numeric	6
Number sold	numeric	8

   e) i) A key field uniquely identifies a record.
      ii) Manufacturer's record number.
   f) This could be done using a card file index. There should be three copies of the same file. One in title order, one in artist(e) order and one in composer order.
   g) Use the method in part f).
      Because only a few records are involved, these could easily be located in a card filing system. The cost of a computer system is only justified when finding a record takes a long time and costs too much money using other methods.

5 a) The sender and the receiver do not have to be available at the same time.
   b) Electronic mail transfers text documents, i.e. letters. No processing is done on the
       data transmitted. The documents sent are stored on a central computer so that the
       receiver can read them in due course.
       Electronic Funds Transfer is the transmission of data that causes money to be
       transferred from one bank account to another. The transmitted data is not available
       to the owner of either account. The transfer of funds is immediate.
   c) i) Retailing: paying for goods at POS terminals.
       ii) Payroll: paying workers directly into their bank accounts.
   d) It will no longer be necessary to visit the Post Office to post mail or the bank to pay
       in and withdraw money.

6 a) i)   load communications software
       ii) dial computer
       iii) enter password
       iv) enter page number
       v)   enter a key word
       vi) exit code selected?
   b) Prestel membership subscription.
       Phone charges.
       Charges to access restricted pages.

A STUDENT'S ANSWER WITH EXAMINER'S COMMENTS

QUESTION

A large company intends to buy a network of microcomputers for use in general office
work.

a) Draw a diagram showing the links between the various devices you would expect to be
   attached to the network.   (4)

b) i) Describe **three** facilities you would expect to be available in wordprocessing
       software.
   ii) How would the use of wordprocessing software change the work carried out by
       typists?
   iii) Give **two** advantages to the general public of introducing wordprocessing in
       commercial organisations.   (5,4,4)

c) Identify two other types of software that would be useful in an office. Give **one** example
   of the use of each.   (4)

d) What new security problems would you expect to encounter due to the introduction of
   this network? Explain how you would deal with them.   (4)
                                                                            (WJEC; 1988)

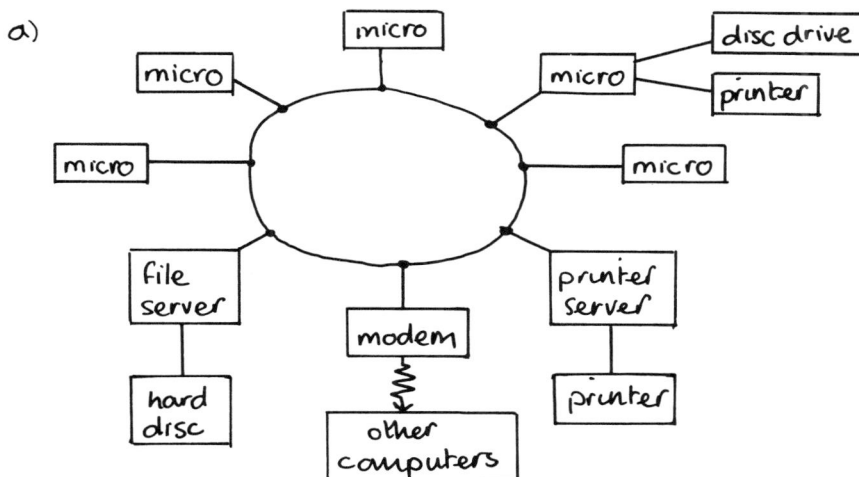

b) i) load, save and delete documents

     ii) less routine copy typing. less manual filing.
Some typists will lose their jobs, others will
re-train to use word processors.

     iii) Faster and better quality.

c) Database, for keeping records, e.g. a file of
customer names and addresses.

     Spreadsheet, for doing financial calculations,
e.g. book-keeping.

d)

security problem	how to deal with it
many people have access to the network	user ids and passwords security guards locks opened by plastic cards
Network could be got into by hackers or people tapping into the network cable	Install cable in inaccessible trunking. Use data encryption. Change passwords every month.
Data on cable could be corrupted by magnetic field from high voltage cables, etc.	Shield cable with a Faraday cage.
Virus, hard disc failure etc.	Backup hard disc regularly using grandfather, father, son method.

Examiner's comment

a) A good answer.

b) You are asked to name three facilities. Are "load, save and delete documents" three
facilities or one, i.e. "disc commands"? Give the examiner plenty of opportunity to give
you marks. If you know more facilities, briefly list them. You will not lose marks for
giving more than 3 facilities.

For example:

     i) load, save, delete documents, text underline, bold, italics, margin justification,
character insert, delete, block move, copy, delete, dictionary & spelling checker,
printout.

     ii) The comments on job losses and retraining do not describe how the work carried
out by typists has changed. Though true, they are irrelevant.

     iii) Too vague. "Faster and better quality" what? Answers of this kind are too
common and receive few, if any, marks. A better answer would be:- Turn around of
correspondence may be faster. The ability to do corrections before printout should
give a better quality of expression and appearance.

c) A good answer.

d) An answer in table form and/or in note form can often be clearer than an essay. You may
do this if you wish. A good answer.

COMPUTERS AT WORK: DATA PROCESSING

APPLICATIONS SOFTWARE

PAYROLL

AIRLINE BOOKING SYSTEM

PROCESS CONTROL

SUPERMARKET STOCK CONTROL

GETTING STARTED

The data processing needs of large companies are many and varied, and very high volumes of data are captured and processed. Specialised computer software and hardware are often required for particular **applications**, i.e. tasks, to meet such data processing requirements.

Batch processing is suitable when the data to be processed is all available at the start of the task and there is plenty of time to get the job done. Batches of data are sent to the computer for processing and in due course the output is returned. The user is not connected to the computer since there is unlikely to be any input while the system is being run. An example is a system for **payroll** data processing.

Real time processing is used when a fast response is needed. Here, data input is processed immediately before any further data input is processed. Data can be input at any time and must be processed instantaneously. Real time systems are extremely fast, reliable and, consequently, very expensive. An international **airline booking system** is an example, but real time systems are also used to control industrial and manufacturing processes and to control robots, etc. Real time systems are designed for a specific purpose.

On-line interactive systems are the most frequently used. They are multiaccess systems with many terminals of different types and supporting multiprogramming. They have fast response times but are slower than real time systems. Many data processing needs can be met using a terminal connected to a mainframe computer. Terminals can be VDUs or, in the case of a **supermarket**, Point of Sale (POS) terminals, where data is collected using laser scanners to read bar codes printed on products. On-line interactive computers are flexible, general purpose systems that may be used to run a variety of different applications at the same time.

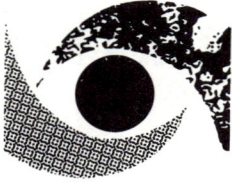

ESSENTIAL PRINCIPLES

Large companies and businesses have to process high volumes of data every day. They need to be able to do this quickly, accurately and inexpensively. Because of the large scale of their data processing needs they invest in software and computer systems that are designed to meet their requirements. They are likely to employ their own computing staff to design and implement data processing systems that will provide solutions to their own information needs. To do these tasks, large companies are most likely to use mainframe computers that they have purchased or leased.

1 ▷ APPLICATIONS SOFTWARE

> **Role of the *Software house***

Applications software is designed to do a *specific* data processing task. It is not general purpose software and can only do the task it is designed to do in the way in which it is designed to do it. Applications may be designed and written by a team of analysts and programmers employed by the company, i.e. **in-house**, or a **software house** may be hired to do the job.

A software house is a company specialising in designing and implementing software for computers. In anticipation of a demand for software to do a routine job, such as payroll, a software house may write an **applications package**. They will later sell the applications package to several companies. Applications packages are designed to be as flexible as possible, but cannot usually be re-written to suit the purchaser.

For large tasks demanding specialised computer hardware and software a **turnkey** system may be bought. This is so called because on receiving the computer system the user simply turns the key to start the computer and the system runs as required!

The applications described in this chapter have been chosen to illustrate the different types of processing possible and the variety of demands placed on computer systems. The systems have been characterised as **batch processing**, **real time processing** and **on-line interactive processing**. These types of data processing are commonly found in commercial and industrial data processing.

2 ▷ PAYROLL

> **An example of a payroll system**

Every company or business has to pay its employees. Although this is a fairly straightforward task, it has to be done frequently and accurately. Employees will be annoyed if they are not paid the correct amount at the appropriate time. However, it is not a task which needs to be done instantaneously. The data to be input is readily available when required and it might be possible to do the data processing needed over a few days or longer. Provided the system is well organised and the payroll applications software works to our satisfaction, all should be well! In following through the description of the payroll system given below, it would be useful to refer to the systems flowchart (see Fig. 14.1).

Data capture

In a warehouse, workers each have their own 'clock-card'. When they arrive at work they 'clock-in', that is they put the clock-card in a slot in a machine which prints the time onto the clock-card. When they leave work, they 'clock-out' by putting the clock-card in the slot again, so that the time they finished work is printed on the clock-card. Workers find their own clock-card by using their name which is printed on the card but there is also an 'employee number' printed on the clock-card that uniquely identifies each worker. The clock-card is used to *capture* the data needed for processing so that a wages slip can be printed for each employee.

> **Capturing data**

The information about an employee on each clock-card is:

    name
    employee number
    clock-in time and clock-out time for every day worked

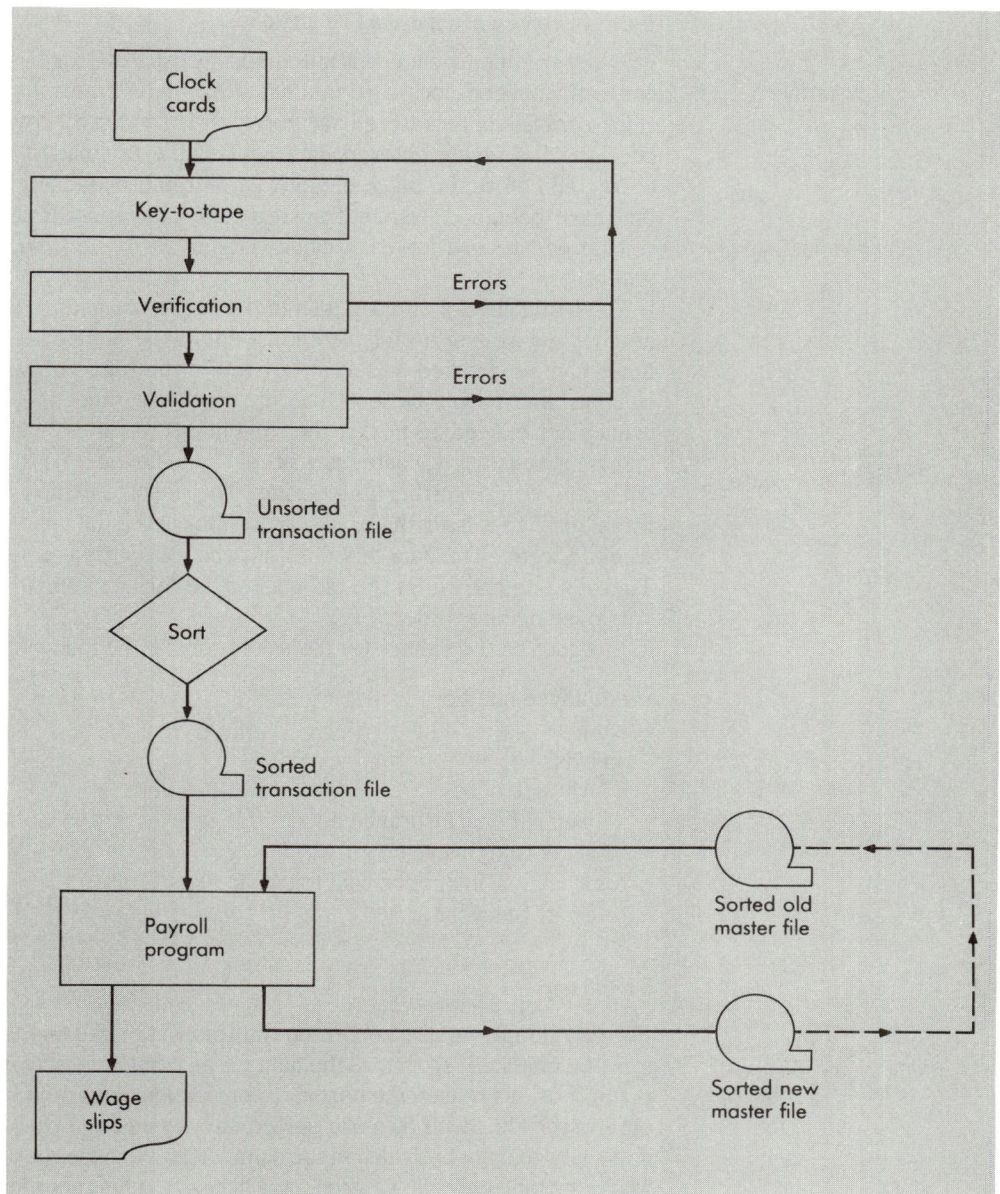

Fig. 14.1 A data processing system for Payroll

Workers are paid a week in arrears, that is they are paid for the week *before* the one they have just worked. If the clock-cards are collected at the end of the week there is one week to process the payroll data.

When the clock-cards have been *collected*, as there are a very large number of them, they are divided into *batches*, i.e. bundles, of 50. A hash total is calculated for each batch by adding up the employee numbers. This total is a meaningless number, but each time it is calculated it should be the same. To check that all the cards are in the correct batch and that none have been lost or misplaced, all we have to do is re-calculate the hash total. If it is unaltered, the batch is complete; if it is different, there is something wrong and we will have to carefully check the batch. This will be done by data control staff after each step in the processing.

❝Collecting and batching❞

❝recording❞

Now that the data has been collected and batched, it must be *recorded* on a computer readable medium. The computer cannot read the printing on the clock-cards, so this data must be prepared in a form the computer *can* use. This is done using a key-to-tape machine. The data is *entered* at the keyboard and recorded on magnetic tape. During data preparation, the data entered from each clock-card is:

❝entering❞

> employee number
> clock-in time and clock-out time, for every day worked

Note that names of employees are not entered. This is not necessary, as each employee is identified by their unique employee number.

Verification and validation

Verifying

The key-to-tape machine will automatically calculate the hash total of employee numbers to check that every clock-card in a batch has been entered. To check that the data on each clock-card has been entered accurately, it is *verified* by keying in the entire batch again and checking the newly entered data against the original. If any errors arise they must be corrected before the batch of clock-cards can proceed any further. Batches of clock-cards that have been successfully transferred to tape and verified can now be *validated*. There will be one record for each clock-card in the file on magnetic tape containing the data entered.

Validating

Validation checks on each field in the record can be performed. Employee numbers can be checked against a table of known employee numbers; the clock-in time and clock-out times can be checked to see if they are in the range between 0.00 Hours and 23.59; the clock-in time should be less than the clock-out time; the hours worked each day should usually not exceed 16 hours; the total hours worked should usually be less than 60. Data that is successfully validated is written to the unsorted transaction file; invalid data must be corrected before further processing. The unsorted transaction file contains only the data transferred to it from the clock-cards. This is the data about employees that changes from week to week. The data that does not change so frequently is saved on the old master file. There is one record on the old master file for each employee. The records are stored in employee number order.

A record on the old master file would contain the following:

employee number
name
address
hourly rate of pay
tax and national insurance details
total tax paid this year
total national insurance paid this year
total pay this year

Sorting

Sorting

For each employee the record on the transaction file and the record on the old master file must be matched, so that all the data for an employee is available when the payroll program is run. For this reason the unsorted transaction file is next *sorted* into the same order as the old master file. Both files are sorted into ascending order on the employee number. It is important to have both files in the same order because they are recorded on magnetic tape. Magnetic tape only allows sequential access to files recorded on it, that is, records are read in order from the beginning of the file to the end. If the sorted transaction file and the old master file were not in the same order, matching the corresponding records for an employee would be very slow.

Data processing

Now that the data to be processed has been captured, entered, verified, validated and sorted, it can be *input* to the payroll program. In the payroll program each sorted transaction file record will be matched with the corresponding old master file record. The *hours worked* will be calculated from the clock-in and clock-out times on the sorted transaction file. The *hourly rate of pay* is found on the old master file so that *gross pay* can be calculated. Gross pay is the amount earned before deductions. Tax and national insurance details on the old master file are used to calculate deductions from the gross pay to arrive at *net pay*. Net pay is the actual amount paid to employees after deductions from the amount earned.

The *tax paid* will be added to the total tax paid this year and the *National Insurance contribution paid* will be added to the total National Insurance paid this year. These totals are changed each week, so a new master file record is created containing the updated totals.

Wage slips

A *wage slip* is printed for each employee, giving all the pay details necessary (see Fig. 14.2) and including the name of the employee, taken from the old master file. The wage slips will be printed on continuous computer stationery with perforations between each one. The stationery must be trimmed to remove the sprocket holes and separated at the perforations before distributing the wage slips to employees.

It will also be necessary to *add* records for new employees to the new master file and *remove* the records of those who have left the company. This is done by adding extra records to the transaction file containing the necessary data to indicate which records are to be inserted and deleted. When the payroll program is run, an extra record is created on the new master file for each new employee. The records of those employees that have left are not copied across from the old master file to the new master file.

File backup

Backups of files for security purposes are generated as a consequence of the need to create a new master file each time the payroll program is run. Using the ancestral backup system, the new master file is the son, while the old master file (which was the previous son) becomes the father. The previous old master file (which was the father) now becomes the grandfather. Copies of the sorted transaction file must also be kept. Such a system allows recovery from the loss of current files by regenerating them from the historical data contained in the backup files.

This payroll processing system would run effectively using either magnetic tape or magnetic disc files on a mainframe computer. Provided the files are sorted into the same order before input to the payroll program, magnetic tape is unlikely to be significantly slower than magnetic disc relative to the time available to do the job. Consequently, magnetic tape should be used in preference to disc, as it is a cheaper medium for storage of high volumes of data.

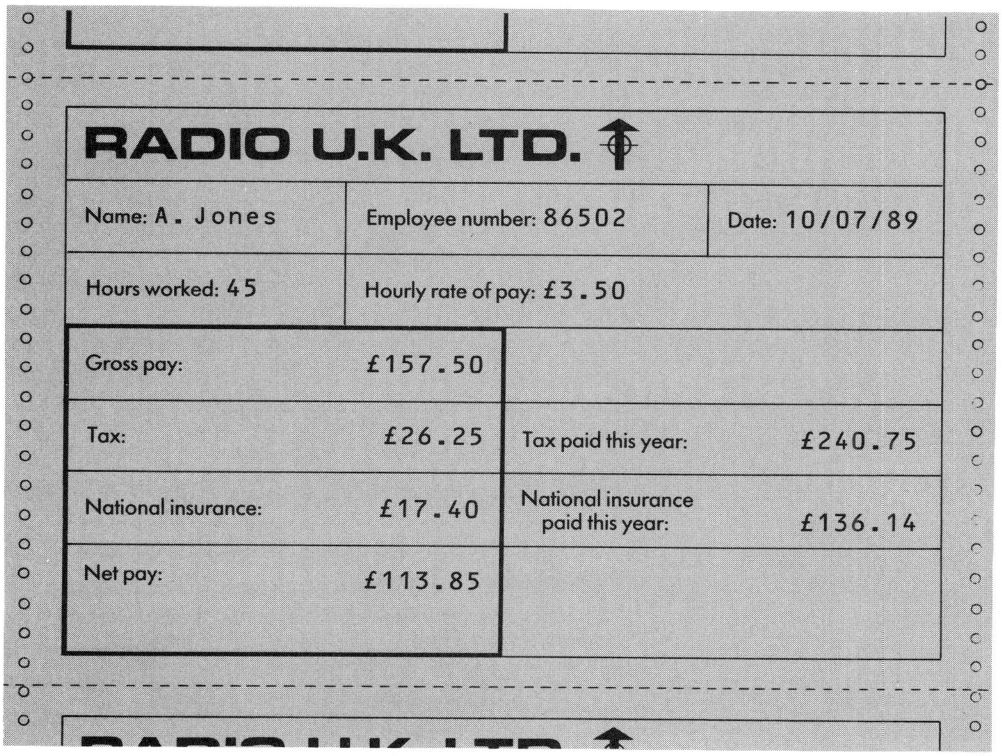
RADIO U.K. LTD.

Name: A. Jones | Employee number: 86502 | Date: 10/07/89

Hours worked: 45 | Hourly rate of pay: £3.50

Gross pay: £157.50

Tax: £26.25 | Tax paid this year: £240.75

National insurance: £17.40 | National insurance paid this year: £136.14

Net pay: £113.85

Fig. 14.2 A wage slip printed by the Payroll data processing system

BATCH PROCESSING

The system described above is known as a **batch processing** system because the data captured is divided into batches before processing. It is characteristic of batch processing that *all* the data to be processed is available *before* processing begins and that there is no need to process the data immediately. The system is not interactive. The user sends the batches of data to be processed to data control who pass it on to data preparation for input, computer operators supervise the processing and then the final output is returned to the user. There is no need for additional input from users of the system while the payroll program is running.

Users may run batch processing systems on their own computer or they may send the data away for processing to an independent **computer bureau**. A computer bureau is a company which rents out computer services. Sometimes they own and run their own large computer system on which they rent time to companies without their own computer. They may also act as agents for companies who rent out the spare capacity on their computers. The user sends data to be processed to the computer bureau. The bureau arranges for the processing to be done and returns the output to the user.

3 ▷ AIRLINE BOOKING SYSTEM

A large airline keeps details of flight schedules and passenger bookings on a mainframe computer (see Fig. 14.3).

Finding a seat

Passengers may make enquiries at travel agents anywhere in the world to find if a seat is free on any of the flights operated by the airline. Passengers require immediate up-to-date information. The travel agent can make on-line contact with the mainframe computer using a microcomputer and a modem as a terminal connected via the telephone network. This gives the agent and the customer access to the flight information and booking file held on magnetic disc on the mainframe computer run by the airline.

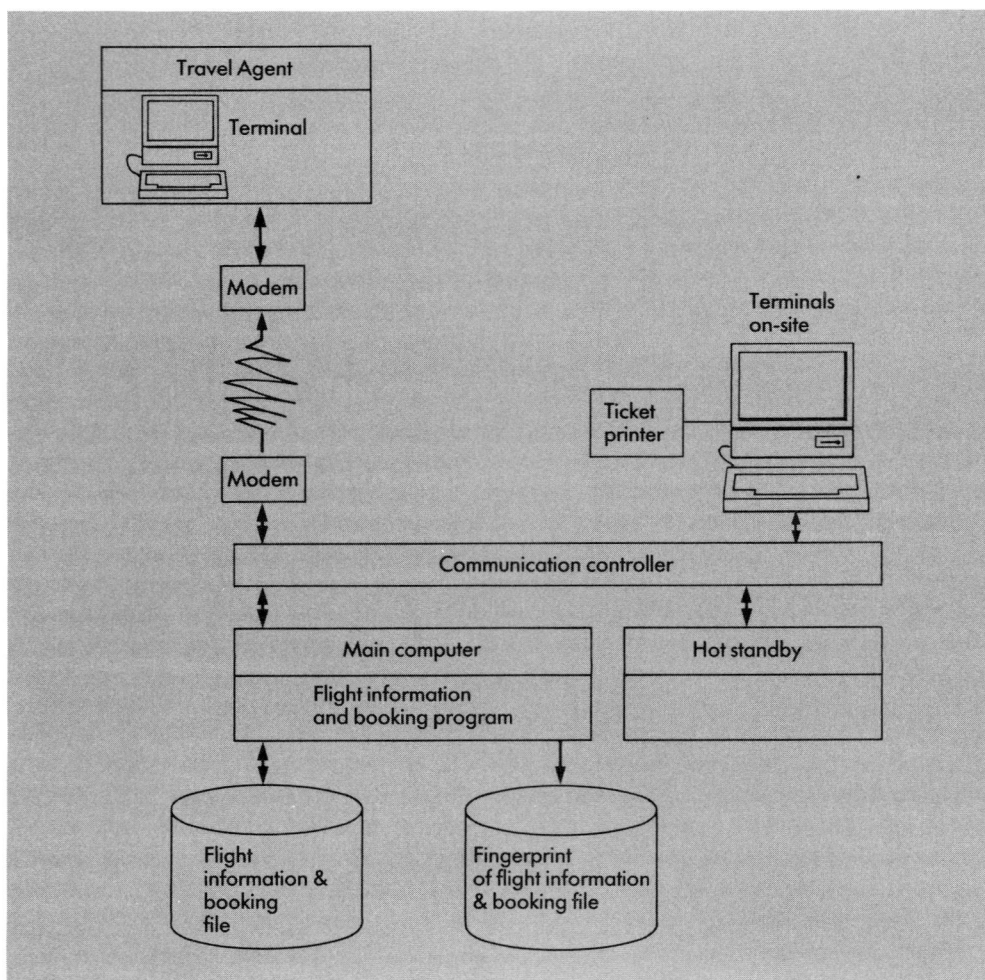

Fig. 14.3 An airline booking system

The mainframe computer should support multiaccess from many terminals, as there may be a large number of travel agents wanting to make enquiries at the same time. The flight information and booking file must be held on magnetic disc as data held on disc can be read by direct or random access. This means that any record on the file can be read without having to read previous records. Access to the flight information and booking file must be made using direct access for high speed data retrieval. The information requested can be displayed instantaneously and will be kept up-to-date while displayed on the screen.

Booking a seat

The customer may decide to book a seat on a flight. The travel agent books the seat using the terminal. Once a seat has been booked the flight information and booking file must be updated immediately so that further enquiries, perhaps by other agents, show the seat as already booked. When the flight information and booking file is being accessed to book a

❝❝Example of an airline booking system❞❞

flight, to avoid double booking, all other attempts to book the seat must be locked out. Tickets for booked seats may be printed out on-the-spot or may be sent to customers at a later date. Payment may also be made via the on-line link using a credit card, or customers may be sent the bill by mail some days later. If a customer pays the travel agent in cash this will be charged to the travel agent in due course. There should also be a facility for cancellation and refund of payments using the on-line link.

Security

Security of access to the system is maintained by giving travel agents a unique user identification and password. Since the system may be on-line twenty four hours a day, it is very important that the computer is not out of action for any time due to mechanical breakdown. This is avoided by having two identical computers, the main one in use and an additional computer available as a **hot standby** to be used if the main computer breaks down.

File backup

As the system is in constant use, file backups cannot be done in the usual way by dumping all the files on disc to tape. This would mean halting the flight information and booking program while the backups are done. Instead, two discs are used, both having copies of the flight information and booking file on them. Any changes that are made to the file are made on both discs at the same time. This technique is known as **finger printing**. It ensures that if one disc becomes faulty there is an exact copy of the file immediately available on the other disc.

The computer hardware and software involved are only used for running the airline booking system. This is a highly specialised system and any other data processing required must be on other computers.

REAL TIME PROCESSING

An on-line booking system such as the one described above is an example of a **real time processing** system. It is so called because processing is in real time, i.e. as data is input it is processed, before any further input can be processed. A real time computer system must be fast enough to ensure that input data is processed immediately because the results can influence any further input. Typically, data can be input to a real time system at any time, from a variety of sources. Even so, processing must be instantaneous and immediate.

4 ▷ PROCESS CONTROL

Example of process control

Real time systems are also commonly used in industry for **process control**. A manufacturer of a chemical product may use electronic sensors at various points in the production process to monitor the progress of dangerous reactions. For example, a heat sensor may be used to record the temperature. If the reaction becomes too hot, an explosion may occur. To avoid this the process must be cooled or shut down immediately if it overheats. If the heat sensor is connected to a computer control system, via an Analogue to Digital converter, the computer can be used to monitor the heat of the reaction. When the reaction overheats, the computer will take immediate action to lower the temperature or shut down the reaction if necessary. A computer control system must be a real time system as a slow or delayed response could lead to an explosion or some other disaster.

The need for the immediate response of a real time computer system is also important when computers are used to control the movements of robots and other machines. A slow reaction to a touch sensor indicating an obstruction could mean loss of life to workers or damage to the robot.

5 ▷ SUPERMARKET STOCK CONTROL

Example of supermarket stock control

A large modern supermarket will have a computer system situated within the store. At the checkout, the Point of Sale (POS) terminal has attached to it a laser scanner. This is used to read the bar code printed on most items sold in the supermarket (see Fig. 14.4). The POS terminal also has a keyboard for entering the product details of items that do not have bar codes printed on them. A small screen is used to display messages sent from the central computer to the POS terminal and a small dot matrix printer built into the terminal is used to print receipts. There will be several checkouts in the supermarket, each with a POS terminal. All of these are connected to the mainframe computer located in the store. This mainframe computer also has VDU terminals located in the warehouse and elsewhere. There are disc drives, a printer and a modem link to other computers via the telephone network.

Fig. 14.4 Supermarket checkout

The computer system is a general purpose system and is used for all the data processing done by the supermarket, including payroll, etc. However, we are only going to look at its use for stock control.

Using bar codes

Most products sold by the supermarket have on them a bar code. The data held on a bar code identifies the product and includes a *product code* and a *check digit*. When an item is sold, the bar code is read by the laser scanner and the data on it is transmitted to the central mainframe computer. Here the check digit is re-calculated from the product code and checked against the check digit received from the POS terminal. If these are not the same, the bar code must be re-entered. If both check digits are the same, the product code is checked against the product information file. A record on this file contains the following fields for each product:

> product code, e.g. 152907
> name of product, e.g. baked beans 570 g
> price

If the bar code received from the POS terminal is *not* on the product information file, the bar code may have been entered incorrectly. In this case the bar code must be re-entered. When it is necessary to re-enter a bar code an error message is displayed on the screen of the POS terminal. The entry of valid bar codes is indicated by a loud beep.

The product code is used to find the corresponding record in the production information file. The name of the product and the price contained in this record are sent to the POS terminal from the central mainframe computer. These are printed on the customer's receipt by the small dot matrix printer built into the POS terminal.

It is a very common belief that the bar code contains the name of the product and its price. This is not so. These are only kept in the product information file stored on the central computer. They are transferred to the POS terminal when required. For every item sold, the price is added to the total for the customer and printed on the receipt when the bar codes on all the items purchased by the customer have been read by the laser scanner. Access to the product information file must be fast enough so that customers are not kept waiting and, in consequence, it is a direct or random access file on disc.

Stock control

The sales made at each checkout are recorded in the daily sales file as the goods are sold. It is sufficient to record the product code of each item sold. At the end of every day the individual product codes are read from this file. The quantity of each item sold is calculated and a *report printed* showing the product code, name of product and the total number of each product sold. An extract from this report follows:

Wed 23rd March		
product code	name of product	total number sold
152907	baked beans 570g	500
923673	pea soup 300g	258
025993	peaches 420g	367
300609	pasta 500g	124
007085	tomato puree 50g	356

The information printed out is also used to update the stock control file. The stock control file contains a record for each product with fields as follows:

> product code, e.g. 152907
> number in stock, e.g. 1200
> re-order level, e.g. 1000

For each product, the total number sold that day is *subtracted* from the number in stock, which is updated. In the above example the total number of baked beans 570g sold on Wed 23rd March is 500. The number in stock is 1200 so the updated number in stock is 1200 *less* 500, i.e. 700.

❝❝Occasional stock report❞❞

The supermarket has to be careful that it does not run out of stock as this will annoy customers, and sales and profits will be lost. Periodically a *stock report* will be printed showing existing stock levels as recorded on the stock control file. Those products that have a lower number in stock than their re-order level will be emphasised in the report. The supermarket manager will go through the report and re-order those products that are needed, using the information contained in the report.

Automatic ordering

If the manager wishes, items can be ordered automatically when the stock control file is updated. For these products, if they have a lower number in stock than their re-order level, the manufacturer is contacted and asked to send more of the product. This is done automatically using electronic mail sent by the supermarket's computer to the manufacturer's computer using a modem and the telephone system.

When items that have been ordered arrive at the supermarket they are sent to the warehouse. At the warehouse the goods are checked as they arrive and stored until they are moved into the supermarket to be sold. As they arrive, the warehouse manager enters the quantity of each product that is delivered at the terminal in the warehouse. This data is used to update the stock control file, e.g. if 800 cans of baked beans 570 g are delivered then the number in stock is updated to 700 plus 800, i.e. 1500, bringing the number in stock above the re-order level. Using this system the manager can control the flow of stock into the supermarket in response to sales of stock to customers.

Extra information

The above description focuses on one basic aspect of a stock control system. In practice, the same system would be used to do a range of *additional* tasks:

■ the *number of items sold* and the *takings at each till* could be recorded and used to monitor the performance of checkout operators;

- the *rate of sales of each product* could be calculated and used to increase the choice of popular goods or to reduce stocks of unpopular items;

- the *pattern of sales* of every product could be recorded so that the stocks are not held at times of the year when goods are unlikely to sell;

- the *effectiveness of sales promotions* can be monitored;

- goods that have *high profit margins* can be stocked in preference to those with lower profit margins.

Low stock = low costs

To keep business expenses to a minimum, stocks of goods should be kept as low as possible. If a *maximum stock level* is recorded for each product on the stock control file, then the quantity re-ordered can be adjusted so that this level is *not exceeded* when new supplies arrive at the warehouse. This maximum stock level can be adjusted so that the extra costs involved in frequent re-ordering are balanced against the expense of storing larger quantities of a product in the warehouse.

Security

Reducing the loss of stock

The system can be also be used to determine the extent of theft from the supermarket and improve security. If the actual number of each product in stock is counted and found to be less than the number in stock on the stock control file, then this difference is due to loss of stock. Loss of stock can be due to damage or theft. If damages are recorded as they occur, then loss due to theft can be calculated. This information can be used to improve the security of high risk products.

Advantages of a computer based stock control system

Computer based stock control systems allow managers to monitor stock levels very closely and to exercise greater control over the business. This allows the manager to increase the profitability of the business and improve customer service. Prices can be kept lower and customer service is quicker due to the speed of the POS terminals. The customer's receipt is itemised and fewer mistakes occur at the checkout. However, the purchase cost of the system is high and it will be necessary to train employees to use it. Because the productivity of checkout employees is increased there will be a reduced number of employees at the supermarket.

ON-LINE INTERACTIVE PROCESSING

The stock control system described above is an **on-line interactive processing** system. On-line systems use terminals connected to a computer. These terminals interact with the computer system, sending data to it and receiving data from it. A real time system is an on-line interactive system but not all such systems are real time. The stock control system described here is not real time.

Sales data is captured using the POS terminals, which must be permanently connected on-line to the computer. In order to print an itemised receipt showing the description and price of every item sold, this data must be found in the product information file, using the product code contained in the bar code input by laser scanner, i.e. interactive processing is necessary as an interchange of data takes place. However, there is no need to immediately update the stock control file as goods are sold. Stock control data does not need to be updated immediately. It is quite acceptable for recorded stock levels to be a day or two out of date, as this is unlikely to significantly affect the business. The expense of a specialised real time system cannot be justified in these circumstances.

Only simple outlines of the payroll, airline booking and supermarket stock control systems have been given. In reality, these computer based systems are much more complex than described. The data structures will be more extensive and detailed and the volumes of data processed much greater than can reasonably be described in a GCSE revision text.

It is also most likely that, in practice, a computer system will be a *hybrid*, involving some batch and on-line interactive processing with links to a real time system where one is in use. For example, both payroll and stock control could be run by the supermarket on the same mainframe computer.

EXAMINATION QUESTIONS

MULTIPLE CHOICE QUESTIONS

1 Ring **two** of these applications which need to use on-line processing.
producing club membership lists
airline booking systems
printing electricity bills
producing pay slips
traffic control

(2)
(MEG; 1988)

2 Tick the **three** applications in the following list which would be carried out using batch processing.

APPLICATION	USES BATCH PROCESSING Tick √
printing gas bills	
producing payslips	
airline bookings	
word processing	
controlling a chemical plant	
producing invoices	

(3)
(MEG; 1988)

3 Ring **two** of these applications which a person working in a travel agency would expect to use.
air traffic control
information retrieval
computer aided design
flight simulation
airline booking systems

(2)
(MEG; 1988)

SHORT STRUCTURED QUESTIONS

4 Choose an application which uses on-line processing. Give **one** reason why on-line processing is used in this application.
Application chosen: _____
Reason: _____

(2)
(MEG; 1988)

5 Part of an employee's weekly payslip is shown below:

employee number *employee name* *gross pay* *deductions* *net pay*
023145   C. Newbury   £400.00   £140.00   £260.00

To produce this payslip the employee number, employee name, deductions and rate of pay per hour are required. What **one** other piece of data is required?

_____

(1)
(MEG; 1988)

6 A master file and a sorted transaction file are stored on magnetic tapes. The transaction file has been checked and is known to contain only new records to be inserted into the master file. Describe how a new master file can be generated using the existing master file and the transaction file.

(MEG; 1988)

7 A travel agent uses an on-line booking system to book seats on aircraft flights. The telephone system is used to communicate between the travel agency and the airline's computer.

a) Give **one** advantage of having travel agencies connected on-line to the airline's computer in this way.

_____

_____

(1)

b) Choose **one** of the following secondary storage devices which you consider to be most appropriate for the airline's computer. Give **one** reason for your choice.

     a magnetic tape unit   a cassette tape machine
     a floppy disc drive   a fixed disc store

Secondary storage device: _____

Reason: _____

_____

(2)

c) Whilst booking a seat for a customer there is a power failure at the travel agency. The power does not come back for an hour. Give **one** possible effect of this delay in communication.

_____

(1)
(MEG; 1988)

8 a) Number the following steps in the order they will be carried out at the terminal when an item is being purchased.

STEP	STEP NUMBER
Look up price	
Input item code	
Work out change	
Input money given	

(4)

b) Write down **two** methods by which the item code could be input at the terminal.
Method 1: _____
Method 2: _____

(2)

c) The record for each item on the computer file contains its price and the number left in stock. What change is made to this record when an item is sold?

_____

(1)
(MEG; 1988)

9 Give **four** advantages and **two** disadvantages of using electronic point-of-sale terminals rather than older types of tills.

First advantage: _____

_____

(1)

Second advantage: _____

_____

(1)

Third advantage: _____

_____

(1)

Fourth advantage: _____

_____

(1)

First disadvantage: _____

_____

(1)

Second disadvantage: _____

_____

(1)

(SEG; 1988)

10 An electricity board uses a computer-based system to charge customers for the electricity they use. Each customer has a meter which records the amount of electricity used (see diagram below). Every three months a meter reader visits the customer's house to read their meter. The new meter reading is written on a data collection form next to the customer's account number. Using the new meter reading and the previous meter reading the actual electricity used can be calculated. The customer is then sent the bill for the electricity used.

A typical electricity meter

| 10 000 | 1 000 | 100 | 10 | 1 |

This would be recorded on the data collection form as

| 5 | 7 | 8 | 2 | 1 |

a) Design a suitable data collection form to allow the meter reader to visit each customer and record the new meter reading. Show clearly which information is printed by the computer and which is written by the meter reader. *(6)*

b) The electricity board keeps a record of each customer's details. Describe the different fields you would expect to find in each customer's record that enable the system described above to function. *(3)*

c) A customer receives an incorrect bill for about £1,000,000
   i) Explain how this could happen.
   ii) What steps could be taken to prevent this? *(8)*

d) Customers often telephone the electricity board to enquire about bills, etc. The telephone operator must be able to access each customer's details immediately in order to answer the enquiries. Describe a suitable computer-based system to achieve this. Make specific reference to the required Hardware, Operating System features and Method of Access to the data files *(8)*

(WJEC; 1988)

O U T L I N E   A N S W E R S

MULTIPLE CHOICE QUESTIONS

1 Ring 'airline booking systems' and 'traffic control'.

2 Tick 'printing gas bills', 'producing payslips' and 'producing invoices'.

3 Ring 'information retrieval' and 'airline booking systems'.

SHORT STRUCTURED QUESTIONS

4 *Application:* theatre booking system
   Reason: the details of which seats have been booked and which seats are free must be kept up-to-date to prevent double booking.

5 Number of hours worked.

6   Assuming the master file and transaction file are both sorted into the same order, then:
REPEAT
Read transaction file record.
Copy old master file to new master file until the point at which the transaction file record to be inserted is found.
Write transaction file record to new master file.
UNTIL   the end of the transaction file.

7   a) Seats can be booked on-the-spot in the travel agents and double booking is prevented.

b) *Secondary storage device*: a fixed disc store
Reason: high volumes of data can be stored and accessed very quickly.

c) The customer may lose the seat as it may be booked by someone else from another travel agents.

8   a)

STEP NUMBER	STEP
1	Input item code
2	Look up price
3	Input money given
4	Work out change

b) *Method 1:* By entering the item code at a numeric key pad.
Method 2: Using a bar code and a laser scanner.

c) One is subtracted from the number left in stock.

9   *First advantage:*   Faster customer service at POS.
Second advantage: Fewer mistakes in entering item code and item pricing.
Third advantage: More detailed receipts describing the items purchased, etc.
Fourth advantage: Up-to-date on-line stock control.
First disadvantage: Items on the shelf may not be priced or prices may be out of date.
Second disadvantage: Some items may not be coded and a different way of pricing these will be needed.

10 a)

Printed by computer

Preprinted

NORTHERN ELECTRICITY BOARD

NAME	J. Bloggs
ADDRESS	5 Higher Fold Row, Springfield SP3 2SY
ACCOUNT NUMBER	02/53719

OLD METER READING	5 7 8 2 1

NEW METER READING	5 8 9 4 3

Handwritten

b) Name, address, account number, previous meter readings, new meter reading, date of next reading, credit rating, current debt, etc.

c)

How it could happen	Steps to prevent it
Incorrect meter reading	1. Helpful method of recording new meter reading. 2. Old meter reading on data collection form
Data entry incorrect	Verify all data entered
Data input is unrealistic e.g. new meter reading is too high	Validate all data input
Program logic error	1. Debug and re-test the program 2. Validate all data prior to output and retain unusual data for checking
Faulty hardware	Regularly check and maintain all hardware, including gas meters.
Overall	Train staff to follow procedures carefully.

d) *Hardware:*

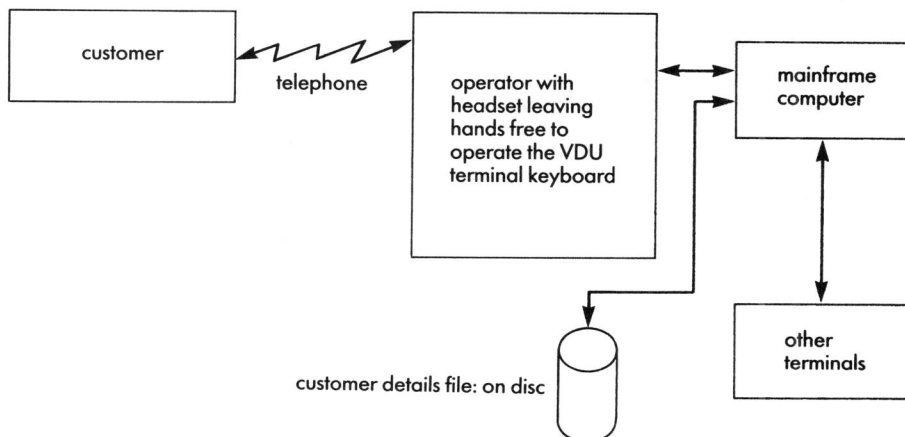

Operating System: On-line, interactive, multi-access.

Method of access to data files: Files will be random or direct access. Discs will be used to store customer details. When a customer rings the electricity board the telephone operator will ask for the customer's account number. If this is available it is entered at the terminal and the customer's record is displayed on the screen. If it is not available the customer is asked for his or her name and address. This can also be used to find the customer's record. The telephone operator is using a database system.

Other: The system may also allow the operator to make notes for later reference using a notepad facility, send messages over the network to other users and do other work such as wordprocessing letters in reply to customer enquiries.

A STUDENT'S ANSWER WITH EXAMINER'S COMMENTS

|||||||||||| barcode ||||||||||||

5 000175 915975

The diagram above shows coded data that could be input into a computer.

a) Which one of the following is the name given to this method of input?
   A   Magnetic ink character recognition
   B   Optical character recognition
   Ⓒ   Bar code reading
   D   Cash card reading
   E   Mark sensing

b) State **two** applications that would use this method of data input.
   1 _Supermarkets_
   2 _Libraries_

c) For **one** of the applications you have given, state **two** items of information that might be represented by the coded data.
   1 _description of item_
   2 _price_

d) State what hardware is needed to enter the coded data into a computer and describe how this hardware is used.
   Laser scanner

(NEA; 1988)

The bar code is passed over the laser scanner.
There is a beep when the bar code has been read.

Examiner's comment

a) Correct
b) Too vague. Better answers would have been:
   1 stock keeping in supermarkets;
   2 recording books on issue from libraries.
c) A bar code *never* holds a description of the item or its price. Better answers would be:
   1 an item code that identifies the product;
   2 a code that identifies the manufacturer.
d) Correct.

15

SOCIAL IMPLICATIONS

COMPUTERS AT WORK

THE INFORMATION EXPLOSION

INDIVIDUAL PRIVACY

LIFESTYLE AND LEISURE

THE PACE OF CHANGE

GETTING STARTED

Computer and microprocessor technology has had, and is still having, a great impact on our lives. As the technology is introduced into the work place, old skills are no longer needed, existing jobs are done in new ways and entirely new jobs are created. Workers must re-train in order to adapt to the new technology or be made redundant. Young people starting work will need some knowledge of how computer and micro-processor technology works, and know how, and when, to use it.

Computers can store very large volumes of information and give fast access to it. Information about an individual can be stored on computer files, which is useful to doctors, hospitals, the DHSS, local authorities, schools, the police, the security services and others. Computers help keep down administration costs and improve services.

However, individual **privacy** – the right to control information about oneself – may suffer. Some organisations which keep information about individuals are more concerned with profit than individual welfare. The **1984 Data Protection Act** gives individuals some rights to know what information is kept on them and to control its use.

Lifestyle and **leisure** have been affected by new technology. Domestic work has been made easier. *Automatic* washing machines have replaced manual washers. TV, microcomputer and video technology has greatly affected leisure in the home. Remote control units, satellite TV, videotext and computer games have altered the way we spend our time at home. Home micros can be linked to other computers via the telephone network, using a modem, giving access to home banking, information services, electronic shopping, teleworking, etc.

Computers are used for **financial control** by the banks and other institutions. The use of cash cards may lead to the *cashless society* where cash in notes and coins is no longer used.

The pace of change is rapid and will continue. It is important to keep up-to-date with new developments in order to ensure that we use technology effectively.

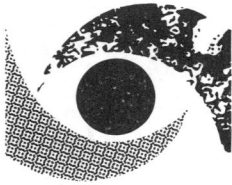

ESSENTIAL PRINCIPLES

New technology has an effect on the lives of individuals and changes the way society is organised. These changes affect us at home, at school and at work. The way we do domestic chores and spend our leisure is affected. Technology has an immediate and lasting impact. It is important to understand what changes have taken place and to ensure that these changes are used to make the world a better place to live in. This chapter looks at some of the most important changes that have taken place as computer technology has been introduced throughout society.

1 ▶ COMPUTERS AT WORK

❝ New technology brings new skills ❞

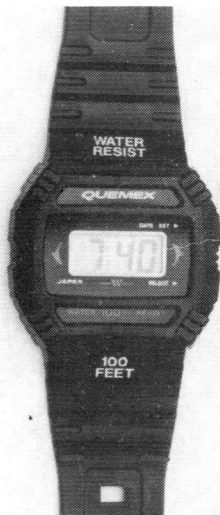

Many people have lost their jobs because of the introduction of microprocessor and computer technology into the workplace. The development of new technology often results in older skills and occupations dying out as they are no longer needed. These changes cause unemployment, but also create employment. Different skills and knowledge are needed to use new technology. Older workers must re-train or face redundancy and young people must be prepared to use modern technology when they start work.

THE NEW TECHNOLOGIES

There are many examples of this process of change from old technologies to the use of microprocessor and computer technology. Mechanical Swiss watches were once highly prized for their accuracy and were consequently very expensive. In 1979, a cheap mechanical watch costing around £10 might be accurate to within five minutes per day. Modern digital watches (see Fig. 15.1) based on microprocessor technology cost less and are accurate to within one hundredth of a second per month. As a result, digital watches dominate the market. The skills of the mechanical watchmaker are much less in demand. Digital watches are manufactured and assembled in highly automated factories.

Fig. 15.1 A modern digital watch

Robots

Cars were once completely assembled by a team of mechanics. As production techniques changed, cars were built on assembly lines where each worker repeatedly performed one highly specialised task, such as welding. Now, microprocessor controlled robot welders (see Fig. 15.2) have taken over from these workers. The robot welder is programmed to do the required task by an expert human welder. This human expert does not do the repetitive welding but programs the robot to do the task. Once programmed, the robot can do the required task indefinitely.

❝ Microprocessor-based technologies in car production ❞

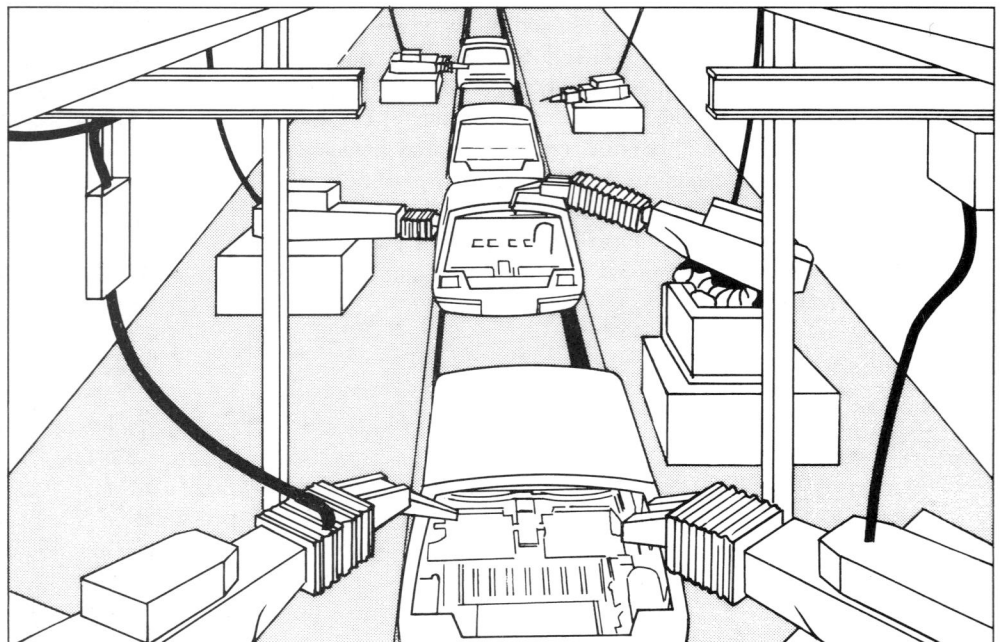

Fig. 15.2 Robots used on a car assembly line

Petrol pumps

Self service petrol pumps are now almost universally used at garages. These are controlled by one employee, who also collects the payment from the customer. Before the introduction of computer and microprocessor technology, several petrol pump attendants were needed to supervise the sale of petrol from mechanical pumps and collect the money. These attendants worked outside in all weathers. Their job is now done from the comfort of the garage reception area.

Telephones

Telephone exchanges were once staffed by large numbers of operators who connected callers to the line they required. Now, computer controlled exchanges (see Fig. 15.3) automatically switch callers, giving access to the national and international telephone systems.

Fig. 15.3 A modern automatic telephone exchange

Offices

In commerce, large numbers of clerks were once employed to do payroll, stock keeping, sales records, etc. These tasks involved careful written recording of all transactions. These tasks are now done on computers. The clerk's job has changed and now involves control of the data as it passes through the computer system.

Companies once employed large numbers of typists. It was not uncommon for fifty or more typists to work in the typing 'pool'. Much of the work was routine copy typing and standard business letters. This work is now done by a few wordprocessor operators. The skills required to operate a wordprocessor are quite different from those needed to use a mechanical typewriter.

In the above examples, fewer workers were required, if any, when the new technology was introduced. Where there was a continuing need for workers, the skills involved were quite different from those used previously. However, the examples are all of changes to *established* industrial products and commercial practices. Microprocessor and computer technology has significantly extended the way some jobs are done and created *entirely new* products and employment opportunities that did not exist previously.

JOBS IN THE COMPUTER INDUSTRY

Computers obviously create jobs in the industrial and commercial sectors concerned with their own design, manufacture, sales, maintenance and use. Many people now work in jobs in these areas. There are designers, assembly line workers, sales staff, installation and maintenance engineers, data control clerks, data preparation staff, operators, programmers, systems analysts, etc. There are journalists who write about computers and technical authors who write manuals for software and hardware.

New jobs

The jobs created are not only replacements for old jobs, in the sense that exactly the same job is done in a different way using a computer. Computers may be originally purchased to do the same job more efficiently, but, once their potential is understood, they are then used to dramatically extend the scope of the job or for entirely new tasks that were impossible or impractical before. For example, stock control has always been an essential routine task for a shopkeeper, but many supermarkets have taken advantage of computer technology to install POS terminals with laser scanners for on-line stock control. Most people now use some form of computer technology at work.

New products

Many new products have been designed and manufactured that are based on microprocessor technology and improvements have been made to old machines. Electronic calculators (see Fig. 15.4) are an entirely new product made possible only through the use of microprocessor technology. Washing machines have changed from mechanical, manual washers to single program machines to multiple program machines. These programs are stored in a microprocessor which controls the washer. The heating and lighting in buildings may now be monitored by a microprocessor programmed to maintain different temperatures in different rooms and to switch lights on and off at certain times. The work involved in the manufacture, installation and maintenance of such devices has created jobs.

New technologies

There have been radical changes in telecommunications technology. Metal core lines are being replaced by optic fibre cables; long distance cables laid under the ocean or overland are replaced by satellites; automatic exchanges have been installed in place of manually operated ones. The control and operation of these systems is computer based. These changes have improved local, national and international communications. This process of improvement and innovation has created entirely new jobs.

Fig. 15.4 An electronic calculator

2 > THE INFORMATION EXPLOSION

The use of computers has created *demand*. **Information** is more readily available, which has created the demand for more information. This is known as the information **explosion**. Cheaper, more reliable microprocessor based products have broadened the market, making these products available to more people. This has increased consumer demand. Increased demand for more information and more goods has led to new jobs in factories and offices.

Computers are increasingly used for creative work. Artists, cartoonists, graphic designers, authors, journalists, etc. are now making use of computers in their work. Computers can be used to control synthesisers playing music and for musical design. On television, computer graphics are now common. Computers have opened up many possibilities for the expression of human creativity.

It is not clear whether the introduction of computer and microprocessor technology has led to overall job losses or gains. Jobs have been lost, but jobs have also been created. There have been other effects of the increased use of computers at work which are also important.

" Jobs have been lost . . . and gained "

Job skills

The skills required in many jobs, where computers are now used, have changed. For example, a wordprocessor operator uses different skills than a typist. Many repetitive tasks have been automated so that fewer people now have boring, routine factory jobs. Some complex tasks have been made easier, for example, the use of CAD/CAM has speeded up the design to manufacturing cycle, allowing more flexibility in changing the design, so that better products are made sooner. Improved production control has also contributed towards a better quality product. Productivity per employee is high and the product is better designed and manufactured.

Working conditions in computer related jobs tend to be pleasant, perhaps because most computers require a clean, dust-free environment at about the same temperature that people find comfortable. Air conditioning and central heating is the norm. Salaries tend to be above average, perhaps because of the general lack of understanding of computers and the high demand for staff with computer skills

Working from home

It is increasingly common for employees in computer related jobs to work at home, using a microcomputer to communicate with the workplace via a modem and the telephone network. This is called **teleworking**. There has been a small number of disabled workers in computing for many years, particularly blind people. Teleworking has allowed more housebound or disabled workers to find jobs in computing. Other employees often prefer teleworking, because there is no commuting and working hours are flexible. From the employer's perspective, teleworking reduces the need to provide expensive office accommodation. Teleworking is expected to increase. Some estimates have suggested that over half the working population will work from home within a few years.

Computers are now essential to most businesses and are widely used in most jobs. The introduction of computer and microprocessor technology has taken place at the same time as many other remarkable changes, such as the development of new synthetic materials for use in manufacture. These changes have not taken place in isolation, so their direct consequences are impossible to determine. It is certain that computers have had a dramatic effect on employment and that they are here to stay.

Information about individuals is kept on computers (see Fig. 15.5). Because computers can store large volumes of data and access it very quickly, they are a more useful way of storing data than in a filing cabinet. The information can be accessed from a large number of widely spread out locations so that it is available immed..tely where it is needed. Usually there will be a large, central mainframe computer system which is accessed using terminals. Access will often be via the telephone network using a modem and may be possible from a moving car c~ van. The DHSS, the police, the DVLC, the Inland Revenue, credit card companies, n   order firms and many other organisations keep information about individuals in this w..y.

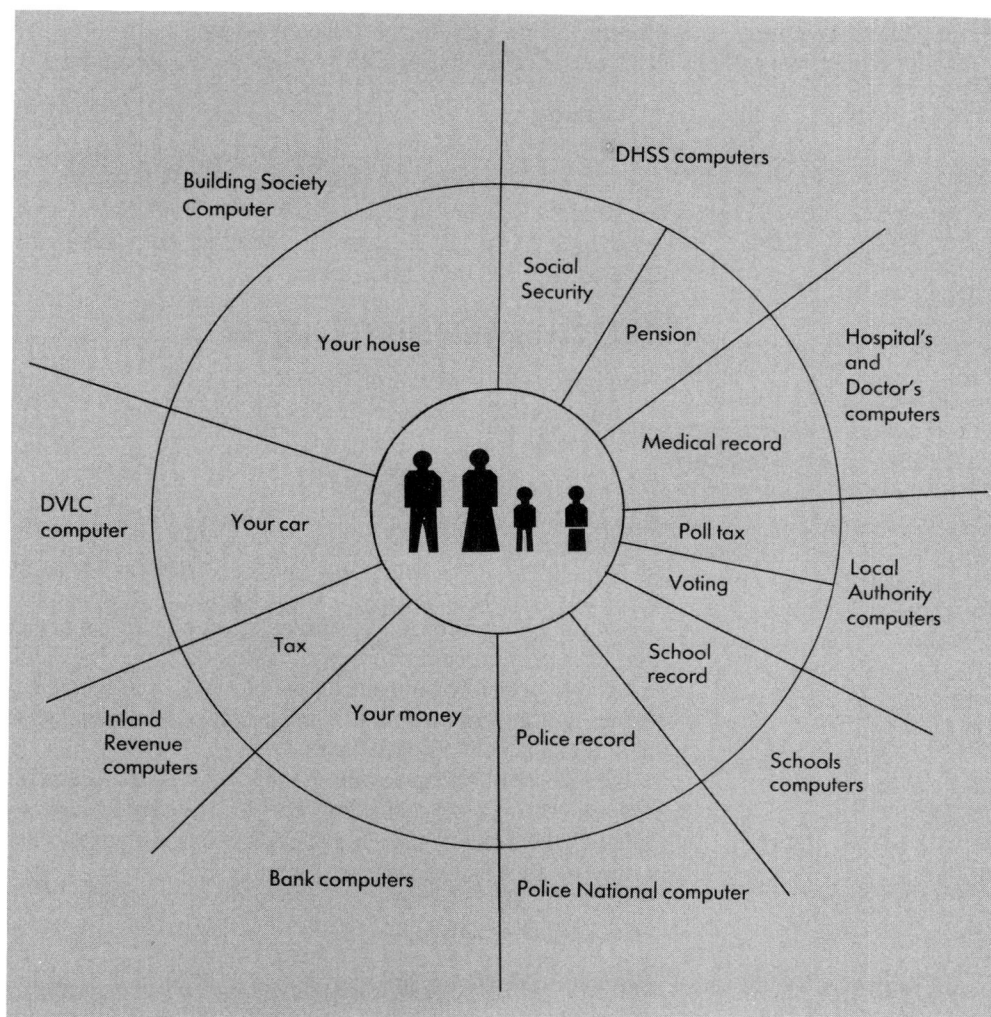

Fig. 15.5 The information about individuals kept on computers

PERSONAL DATA

⁶⁶Uses of personal data⁹⁹

Keeping **personal** data about individuals on computer systems has advantages and disadvantages. For example, it is important that the police have access to information to help them arrest criminals and to enforce the law. If my car was stolen I would be very pleased if this information was available to police forces throughout the country, so that the car could be returned to me as soon as possible. I would be less enthusiastic if other organisations had access to the files linking my name, address and the type of car I own. This personal data could be useful to companies selling car insurance, new cars or specialising in spare parts for my car. These organisations might use this personal data to send me unwanted advertising literature by mail. The same information could be used for individual surveillance. This may or may not be acceptable, depending on the situation. It is reasonable to track a criminal or terrorist in a free society, but the same computer system could be used by dictators to enforce unreasonable levels of social control.

In any society there is conflict between the rights and freedoms of individual citizens and the need of national organisations to control and limit individual freedom in the interests of society as a whole. Similarly, businesses acting in their own interests may be in conflict with the needs of individuals. How these conflicts of interest are resolved is particularly important to you, because it will soon be possible to hold all the data about you on computers. Your medical, school, employment and criminal records will all be fully integrated and any information about you will be available instantaneously. You should have no need to worry if this information is used reasonably. However, events in Europe during the second world war, for example, may suggest the need for some concern. Might not Hitler have eliminated the Jews much more efficiently with the use of computers? The major problems for individuals are concerned with privacy, accuracy, how the data is used and security.

Privacy

Privacy is the right to control information about yourself. To do this you will need to know if anyone is keeping data about you and have some control over how they intend to use it.

> Need for privacy . . . and for accurate data

Accuracy

Accurate data is realistic, objective and up-to-date. Data is realistic if it describes a real situation. For example, your actual date of birth should be recorded. This could be important if you are applying for a car driver's licence, which is restricted depending on your age. You would be upset if you were not issued with a licence because the date of birth on your record was incorrect.

OBJECTIVE AND SUBJECTIVE DATA

Data can be subjective or objective.

Objective data is measureable. If the measurement is repeated by someone else, the same result would be obtained. Your height in metres is *objective* data. However, an assessment of your potential as a pop singer is *subjective*. One person may enjoy listening to you and rate you very highly, another may not like you at all.

Subjective data is a personal assessment. If your rating as a pop singer was recorded on a computer file it would be coded, perhaps on a scale from A to G. This code has the appearance of objective data, even though it is subjective. Anyone accessing your data would treat this code as a true assessment of your singing potential. People tend to believe that data kept on computers is accurate. This may be satisfactory if you were coded as A but would probably be unacceptable if your code was G! For this reason subjective data should not be recorded. If it is important to record subjective data, it must be made very clear that it is not objective data.

If data is not kept up-to-date it may cease to be accurate. Your address will change when you move. You may change schools or leave school to get a job or go to college, polytechnic or university. Old data is not accurate data. Data files must be kept up-to-date if they are to remain accurate.

THE USE OF DATA

> Privacy and the uses made of data

The **use of data** is an important aspect of privacy. This is where the needs of individuals, organisations and society may come into conflict. For example, suppose you have invested some money in a bank. The bank will pay you interest on the money. The bank will also tell the Inland Revenue, which collects taxes, that they have paid you interest. This may lead to a demand from the Inland Revenue for payment of extra taxes. As an individual, you may not want to pay extra tax and feel it is unfair for the bank to give information about your income to the Inland Revenue. This might lead to you withdrawing your money from the bank and investing it elsewhere. The bank does not want to lose your investment, but is legally obliged to tell the Inland Revenue about interest paid to you. The Inland Revenue wants to collect all the tax that is due. This tax is used to benefit the whole of society. In this case, individuals cannot be allowed complete control of their own personal data, as this would lead to social injustice. However, it is important that you know what is being done with this information. How personal data is used by the organisation that holds it could influence what you do.

DATA SECURITY

If personal information is to remain private and accurate, and is to be used only in ways agreed by the individual or controlled by the law, then the data must be kept secure. **Security** is the protection of data from corruption and misuse. Data is normally recorded on a backing storage medium such as disc. Data recorded on disc may be corrupted due to faulty hardware, faulty software, accidental or deliberate interference. If data is corrupted, it is important to be able to restore it to its original state as soon as possible. This is done by keeping backup copies of data files, using the ancestral method. If the current copy of the data file is corrupted, it is restored from the backup.

Deliberate interference with data is always a possibility, especially where networks are in use. To prevent unauthorised access to data files several precautions should be taken. To prevent unauthorised copying of data files saved on backing storage, discs and tapes should be kept in a safe when not in use. Physical access to terminals on the network should be restricted using security guards or electronic locks that only open when identity cards are inserted. The network cable should be inaccessible and shielded to prevent intruders connecting themselves to it. If unauthorised users do connect to the network there should be a system of user identification with passwords at all levels to prevent access to the system and to data files.

THE DATA PROTECTION ACT

The **1984 Data Protection Act** establishes the principles of data protection and gives individuals some right to control personal data. Anyone who holds personal data on computer files must register with the *Data Protection Registrar*. You have a right to know if personal data is kept on you and what that data is. Personal information must be obtained fairly and lawfully. You have a right of access to information kept about you and a right to have incorrect data changed. The data can only be used for specified purposes. Personal data must be accurate and up-to-date. It can only be kept as long as it is in use. Security measures against unauthorised access, corruption of data files, copying of files, and loss or destruction must be taken.

Although the Act protects individual privacy to a greater extent than was the case prior to 1984, it has been criticised for not dealing with some important issues. Manual files, that is, files kept on paper in filing cabinets, are not covered. Besides being a dis-incentive to computerise, this allows any infringement of privacy in this area to continue. The police and security forces are exempted from all the provisions of the act. While this is understandable, it is unfortunate. For example, there are occasions when doctors may need to cooperate with the police. Doctors are covered by the Act but the police are not. This could affect liaison between doctors and the police for the good of individuals and the community. It is unfortunate that these issues are not covered in what is otherwise a comprehensive Act.

Another criticism of the Act is that misuse is an offence under civil law, rather than criminal law. This means that individuals must seek damages for misuse of personal data through the civil courts. Individuals are unlikely to do this because of the cost of taking court action.

4 ▷ LIFESTYLE AND LEISURE

Earlier in this chapter, the effects of the use of computers at work was discussed. It was noted that computers encourage better working conditions and higher productivity. This leads to higher wages and lower prices. Many people spend a large part of their life at work and depend on their wages to buy the goods and services they need. Better working conditions and greater purchasing power are important improvements in lifestyle. They are welcome in themselves and also because they open up other possibilities. A wider range of lifestyle and leisure options becomes available.

COMPUTERS AT HOME

In the *home*, domestic work has been made much easier. Programmable automatic washing machines and tumble driers allow clothes to be washed and dried with a minimum of effort. It is no longer necessary to spend a lot of time and effort on this necessary task. In the days of manual washing machines and clothes lines only, the family washing could take a day or even longer in bad weather! It is a pity the ironing has not been similarly automated!

Computers are used in the manufacture of most domestic appliances, keeping prices down and quality up. Television viewing is more convenient because of remote control pads to alter the volume and contrast, change channels and switch the set on or off. Video recorders have similar facilities. TVs with a built-in teletext receiver can display pages from Ceefax or Oracle. The pages contain general information, including the times of TV programmes. These features make viewing more convenient, particularly for housebound or disabled viewers. Computer and microprocessor technology is an essential factor in providing these services.

Microcomputers at home

Microcomputers in the home are often used for leisure pursuits. Many people play computer games or use the computer for personal amusement. Programs are available for Wordprocessing, databases, etc. that can be run on a home micro. Software packages are available for home and financial management.

Home finances

Many people have plastic cash cards or credit cards (see Fig. 15.6). These cards can be used to access a wide range of financial services:

- Money can be withdrawn from automatic teller machines throughout Europe;

- cheques can be guaranteed;

- goods can be paid for in shops or by telephone;

- wages can be paid directly into the account by an employer;

- bills can be automatically paid at regular intervals from the account by standing order.

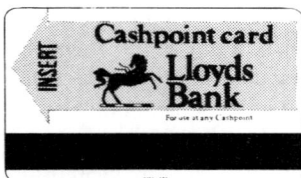

Fig. 15.6 A cash card

It is easy to get a statement of payments made or received and find out how much money is left. This can be done in the bank or at an automatic teller machine. Some banks allow customers to access their accounts from home using a microcomputer and a modem to connect to the bank's central computer. They can transfer money between different accounts, pay bills or do any other transaction while on-line. The banks and credit companies themselves rely heavily on computers to operate these systems and keep accurate records of all financial dealings.

Electronic shopping

Electronic shopping using Prestel or local systems is possible. The customer connects to the host computer via the telephone network using a microcomputer and a modem. A selection of goods is offered for sale. These can be ordered and paid for by credit card. Companies operating national schemes often sell goods at a lower price than in the shops. The goods ordered are delivered by mail. Some local schemes allow groceries and other consumables to be ordered. This type of service is particularly useful to the housebound or disabled. The use of cash cards, credit cards and electronic shopping are features of the **cashless society**. Some people believe that these and other developments will eventually lead to money in notes and coins becoming obsolete. Money will then only exist as numbers recorded on the bank's computer system.

> The cashless society

Improved transport and communications have helped families that live apart to keep in touch. They have also led to families becoming more widely dispersed. Cars are designed using computers and are built to much higher standards using microprocessor controlled robots. The production process is computer regulated. Motorways are planned and designed using Computer Aided Design. The telephone network is also designed, built and controlled using microprocessor and computer technology.

The institutions of society, that is, Local Authorities, Hospitals and doctors, schools, the police, libraries, the DHSS, the DVLC, etc. all use computers to keep administrative records and to help improve operating efficiency. This is also true in a European and International context.

5 ▶ THE PACE OF CHANGE

Most of the changes that are described in this chapter have taken place during the last thirty years and are mainly due to the widespread use of computer and microprocessor technology.

- The range of *consumer products* has greatly increased. Their quality has improved and their price has dropped.

- Old skills have become redundant and knowledge of computers and information technology is now essential for all workers.

- Employment patterns have changed; jobs have been created and lost.

- Concern for individual privacy is not new, but before computers were in common use it was not a widespread problem.

- The standard of living has improved greatly for those in employment.

Author's comment

My experience of technology as a teenager was very different from that of teenagers today. The pace of change has obviously been extremely fast. I believe this will continue. What you are learning about computers for GCSE will be a sound basis for the future. However, I am sure that some new event will soon occur in the rapidly changing world of computers. It is important to learn about these new developments. Try and constantly update your knowledge by reading computer magazines, visiting exhibitions and local shops that stock computers. Don't be afraid to admit things are new to you too. It is important to learn to deal with rapid, unexpected change. Try and anticipate the effect of new technology on yourself and others. This will help you to use technology effectively for your benefit and for the benefit of society as a whole.

EXAMINATION QUESTIONS

SHORT STRUCTURED QUESTIONS

1   The picture shows robot welders on the Mini Metro line.

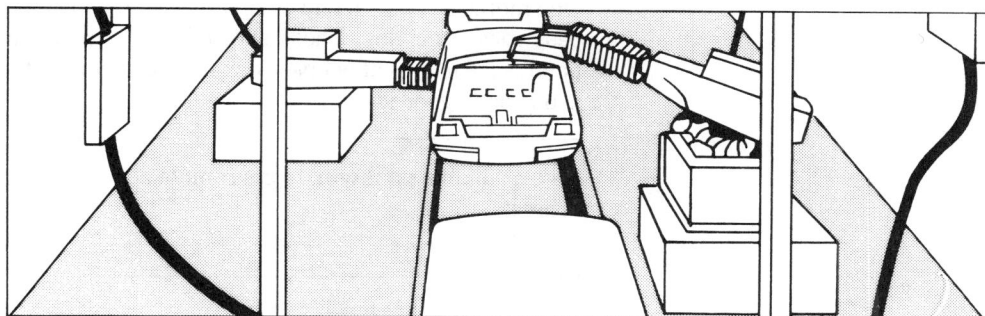

a) Give **two** ways in which it is better to use robot welders rather than human welders.

i) _____

ii) _____

b) Give **one** way in which human welders are better than robot welders.

_____

_____

(6)

2   When computers are used to automate work, some human jobs disappear, some change, and some are new. If a car production line is automated, suggest, with a reason for each:

a) **One** type of human job which will disappear. (3 lines available).   *(3)*

b) **One** type of human job which will change. (3 lines available).   *(3)*

c) **One** type of human job which will appear. (3 lines available).   *(3)*

(SEG; 1988)

3 Many goods and services can now be paid for using plastic cards. All the card companies use computers to work out the bills each month. This means that the card company computers store a lot of personal details about their customers and their purchases. If another organisation got hold of the information it could be used against the card holder.

a) Give **two** different organisations that might want to have access to this personal information.
   Organisation 1: _____
   Organisation 2: _____

b) Explain why the card holder might suffer if these organisations did get access.
   _____

                                                                           (LEAG; 1988)

4 The use of the computer system has changed the jobs of many police officers. For each police officer below, explain how the use of the computer has changed their job.
   Police constable on foot patrol: _____
   _____
   Police sergeant in the station: _____
   _____
   A detective: _____
   _____

                                                                           (LEAG; 1988)

5 "Hacking" is where someone tries to gain illegal access to a computer system. This is usually done using a remote terminal or microcomputer.

a) Give **one** example of harm that a "hacker" might do if successful in breaking into a computer system.
   _____

b) One method of protecting computer systems from "hackers" is to have a system of passwords or codes. These should be secret and known only to legal users. Some people use names of people close to them because they are easy to remember. Why is this not a good idea?
   _____

c) Give a suitable **password** for a remote access computer system. Say why you have given it.
   Password: _____
   Reason: _____
   _____

d) Give **one** further simple method of protecting a computer system from "hackers" trying to use remote terminals.

                                                                           (LEAG; 1988)

6 A manufacturer now makes electronic digital watches whereas previously mechanical analogue watches were made. How did the change from making mechanical watches to electronic watches affect watch makers?

7 Computer-controlled self service petrol pumps are introduced at a garage to replace manual pumps operated by attendants. How does this affect:

a) The owner.
b) Employees.
c) Customers.

8 Many organisations have databases that store personal data. The diagram opposite shows some of these and how they can be linked together.

Write down the names of **three** other databases that contain personal information.

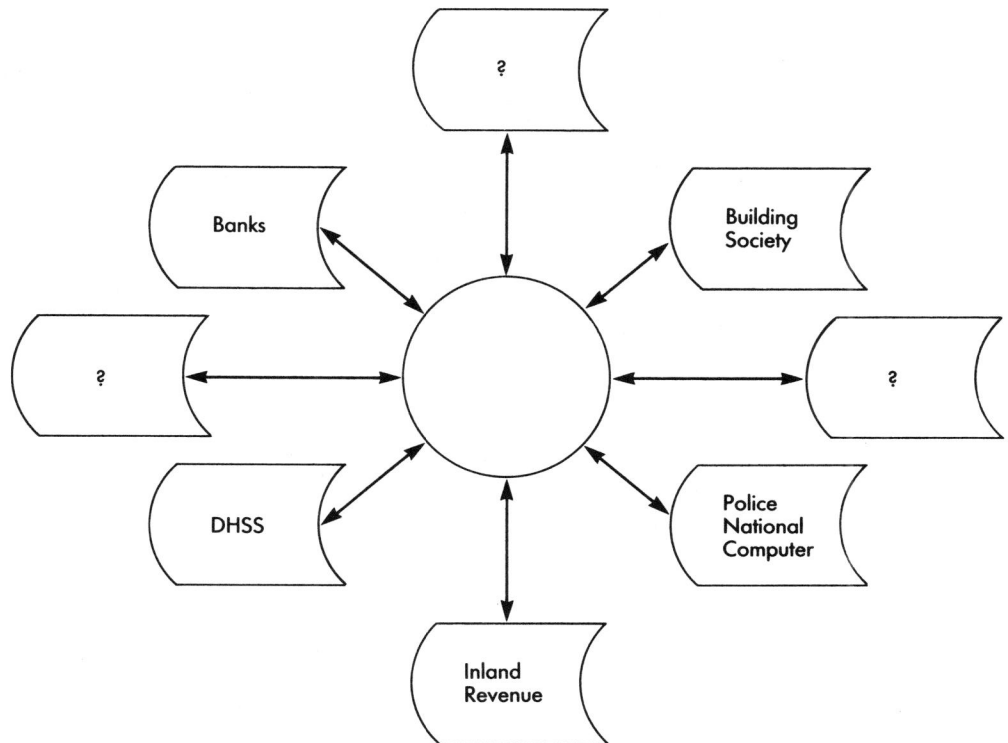

O U T L I N E   A N S W E R S

1 a) i) Robot welders can do repetitive tasks to the same high standard every time.
      ii) Robots can work without stopping.

   b) People are more flexible. They can quickly move from one task to another and deal
      with unusual events.

2 a) Human welders will not be needed as robots can do the job to a higher standard,
      consistently, at a lower cost.

   b) The job of a maintenance engineer will change as the machinery used will have more
      electronic components.

   c) People will be needed to program the robots to do their jobs.

3 a) *Organisation 1:* Inland Revenue.
      Organisation 2: Mail Order Company.

   b) Inland Revenue could find that the card holder was spending more than the income
      being taxed and ask for more tax to be paid. A mail order company might send
      unwanted advertising to the card holder, encouraging the purchase of more
      products on credit, leading to high levels of debt.

4 *Police constable on foot:* They are now constantly in touch with the police station so that
   they don't have to go to the station for instructions or to get information from police
   files.
   Police sergeant in the station: The sergeant can direct constables to deal with offences
   reported by telephone as soon as they are reported, broadcasting any relevant
   information obtained from the police files at the same time. The sergeant spends much
   more time in the police station.
   A detective: He can easily inspect all police files for relevant information using database
   software. More information is available faster.

5 a) Corrupt important files or copy confidential information.

   b) Because a potential hacker could easily get this information and try the names as passwords.

   c) *Password:* B61X7
   Reason: It is short enough to remember and is meaningless. This will make it much harder for a hacker to guess.

   d) All data on the network should be scrambled using data encryption equipment. The hacker may not have this equipment or know how it is set up to scramble the data.

6 Fewer workers were needed as digital watches have fewer components and can be assembled by machines.
   The skills of mechanical watchmakers became obsolete. They had to retrain or be made redundant.
   For those remaining in employment higher productivity leads to higher wages.

7 a) The owner employs fewer workers. The wage bill is reduced. The owner must choose between higher profits or lower prices to customers.

   b) Most of the attendants are made redundant. A few attendants may learn to operate the centralised pump information system inside the garage. Their job is now more comfortable as they work inside, collecting payments.

   c) Customers must now fill their cars with petrol themselves. They may miss the contact with the pump attendants and feel that the garage has become more impersonal. However, petrol may cost less.

8 Doctors and Hospitals.
   Schools.
   Local Authorities.

A STUDENT'S ANSWER WITH EXAMINER'S COMMENTS

QUESTION

a) Explain why the introduction of a computer system may result in unemployment.

Because computers never sleep and do not need breaks or cups of coffee. They do not go on strike and will work day and night.

b) Explain why incorrect use of a computer system may result in loss of privacy.

Computers can be used to look into peoples files and find out all about them.

c) Describe **two** methods which are used to ensure that data held on a computer is secure.

Method 1: *User identification numbers and passwords.*

Method 2: *Security guards.*

(WJEC; 1988)

Examiner's comment

a)   This is true, but misses the point slightly. Computers complete tasks faster, are more accurate and more reliable than people. They can perform tasks automatically for an indefinite time. Consequently, they are likely to do a better job than human workers, at a lower cost. As a result, computers may be used to replace human workers.

b)   Again, this is true but slightly off the mark. Computers hold information about people. This can be accessed quickly, perhaps by unauthorised people, from many different places. Because it is almost impossible to be sure that only authorised people access the data, there is a resulting loss of privacy.

c)   Correct.

INDEX